MOTHER KIRK

ESSAYS AND FORAYS IN PRACTICAL ECCLESIOLOGY

DOUGLAS WILSON

CANON
PRESS
MOSCOW, IDAHO

Douglas Wilson, *Mother Kirk: Essays and Forays in Practical Ecclesiology*

© 2001 by Canon Press. Published by Canon Press, P.O. Box 8741, Moscow, ID 83843. 800–488–2034 / www.canonpress.org

06 05 04 03   9 8 7 6 5 4 3

Cover design by Paige Atwood Design, Moscow, ID

Scripture quotations in this publication are taken from the *Holy Bible: King James Version.*

Library of Congress Cataloging-in-Publication Data

Wilson, Douglas
    Mother kirk : essays and forays in practical ecclesiology/
    Douglas Wilson.
  p.cm.
  Includes index.
    ISBN 1-885767-72-2 (pbk.)
    1. Church. I. Title.
    BV600.2 .W565 2001
    262 – dc21   00–010090

Mother Kirk

For my mother, Elizabeth Catherine Dodds Wilson, who prayed with me when I first called on the Lord, and who throughout my life has faithfully modeled for me what it means to be the Church.

Contents

✝ FOREWORD ✝

Reformed theology, especially in its late twentieth-century American variety, emphasizes the comprehensiveness of Christian faith. The notion that Christianity offers a worldview embracing every area of life has never been more explicitly affirmed or more elaborately detailed. Related to this is the claim that every calling is good and noble, that all work can be devoted to the service of Christ, that all Christians are called to seek first the kingdom of God.

This good and necessary emphasis is often accompanied, however, by a corresponding denigration of pastoral ministry: All Christians, it is said, have a "full-time" ministry, so the pastor has no higher a calling than the plumber or homemaker. But this corollary does not follow. Though all callings can be equally devoted to Christ's service, not all callings are equal. And Reformed Christians have always recognized that the pastoral office is the highest office not only of the church but in the world.

It is the highest calling in part because it is the broadest calling, a vocation to minister to everyone in every circumstance. Sickness strikes, and the doctor is called. Sued or indicted, I contact a lawyer. Fired from my job, I may apply with a placement agency. When labor pains begin, we call a midwife or a doctor, and when we have breathed our last, the undertaker has his say. For each stage of life, for each crisis, we have our specialist.

The pastor is no specialist. His field of activity embraces every known profession: The ideal pastor would combine the dialectical skills of the best attorney, the bedside manner of the most compassionate physician, the rhetorical passion of politicians from ages past, and a breadth of scholarship that befits a student and teacher of the Creator's book.

The pastor is no specialist. He is called to represent Christ in every kind of situation of need or pain. He anoints and prays with the child suffering from leukemia, rebukes and guides the adulterer in the way of repentance, offers counsel and encouragement to the entrepreneur whose business has folded, rejoices with new parents and mourns with those

bereft of friends and family. Beside the doctor, beside the financial con-
sultant, beside the nursing home attendant, stands the pastor. In the
maternity ward, in the jail cell, in the home tense with marital strife,
stands the pastor. At the baptism, at the wedding reception, at the funeral, stands the pastor. He is a generalist in human crisis, a generalist
in moments of passage, a generalist confronted with all of the infinite
varieties of human suffering.

There is a sense in which the pastor is a specialist. For every situation, he has essentially one word, the word of the gospel of Jesus. Among
the sick, the pastor's concern is not only for healing but to indicate how
suffering can be transformed into joyful witness. Among the poor, the
pastor's concern is not just how to pay next month's bills, but to consider how poverty may strengthen faith in the goodness of the heavenly
Father. At the bedside of the dying, the pastor's concern is not just to
ease pain but to hold forth the promise of resurrection life.

Mother Kirk can be read with profit by all Christians, but at its heart
this book is an instruction manual for pastors and elders, and it breathes
the kind of wisdom that emerges only from long pastoral experience
experienced through diligent study of Scripture. *Mother Kirk* is written
by a pastor who knows that pastoral work demands courage, determination, gentleness, vision, patience, self-restraint, insight, shrewdness,
and, above all, faith working through love. It is written by a pastor who
sees that pastoral ministry is man's work. Today, many avoid pastoral
vocation because they think it beneath them. *Mother Kirk* will deter for
exactly the opposite reason.

Mother Kirk highlights the importance of teaching and preaching as
the center of pastoral ministry. That is hardly surprising, since this book
comes from a classical Calvinist. Some Calvinists, however, leave the
impression that the church would function much more smoothly if it
were not for the people. Doug Wilson is not that sort of Calvinist. He
understands that the church is people, and that people can be governed
and led only by other people. He realizes that the ministry of the Word
must be incarnated in the life of the pastor. He has observed that the
biblical qualifications for elders focus on character. He knows there are
no paper pastors.

Perhaps the most impressive thing about this book, and certainly
one of the most impressive things about Doug Wilson's own very impressive ministry, is his realization that Jesus is the Head and Lord of
His Church. Every Christian would agree, but few have grasped as pro-
foundly as Wilson the flip side of this confession: If Jesus is the Head of
His Church, that means I'm not and you're not. And that means that
there is no place in the church's leadership for the domineering benefac-
tor, the manipulative wheeler-dealer, the prima donna, the agenda-mon-
ger. There is room only for those willing to become servants to all, those

willing to lay down their lives for (sometimes intractable) sheep, for those willing to bear the slave yoke of Christ with humility, grace, and gladness. Only such leaders will bring genuine reformation, because only such leaders labor in faith, confessing that the future of Mother Kirk is in the Lord's hands and not their own.

Peter J. Leithart
Feast of St. Lawrence, 2000
Peniel Hall

✤ PREFACE ✤

The subtitle of this book describes it as a collection of "essays and forays." The reason for this is that various portions of the book had a different point of origin. We have tried to keep this from becoming an annoyance to the reader through some diligent sandpapering, but the ancestry of these sections will still show through here and there.

Some sections have previously appeared in *Credenda* and others in *Tabletalk*. Many thanks to Ligonier for their permission to reprint these articles in modified form. Other portions were written "in house" for various issues that our church was confronting, and a sizable remainder was written for this book, trying in the process to make the transitions a little less like epistemic lurches and leaps. The average reader does not like being yanked around on the end of a rope.

I am very grateful to Peter Leithart for reviewing the manuscript and writing the foreword.

Thanks go to Douglas Jones down the hall at Canon. I am also most grateful for the practical help in production provided by Joost Nixon and Holly McBroom.

Throughout, I have had the wonderful privilege of ministering to the saints at Christ Church in Moscow, working together with some very dedicated elders and deacons. The ability to put into practice many of the things discussed within these pages has been the direct result of their godly wisdom and patience. Through the grace of God we have been given a fruitful result, and we thank Him for it.

Douglas Wilson
Christ Church
Moscow, Idaho

✝ INTRODUCTION ✝

A Manifesto on What Matters

Our culture is haunted by epistemological despair, a despair which cannot be buried, shouted down, turned aside, or simply ignored. It is always there, even when we may prefer to deny it. We have no idea why we are here, where we are supposed to go, and how we are to conduct ourselves on the way. But in the meantime, our government schools solemnly teach third graders how to use condoms. Countless fathers desert their wives and children. Pastors dishonor their calling through their rampant adulteries. Thieving representatives of a thieving people plunder the widow. The drunkards of Ephraim puke on the table. For those who have eyes, the approaching night is clearly the kind which cannot be danced away.[1]

Why? This has happened because, over the last century and a half, the Christian Church has allowed herself to be corrupted by the various forms of unbelieving *-isms* which surround her — egalitarianism, feminism, socialism, environmentalism, you-name-it-ism. The contemporary Church consequently has no answers for those questioning, no light for those in darkness, no life for those who live in death. The Church, which God ordained as the pillar and ground of the truth, now finds herself echoing (although somewhat plaintively) that ancient relativistic aside of Pilate — *quod veritas?* What is truth?[2]

In a world of pagan despair, the epistemological corruptions and compromises of the Christian Church have blurred and distorted the clarity of the biblical message. And as circumstances continue to

---

[1] Capable critiques of the reasons for this are not lacking. See John Armstrong, *The Coming Evangelical Crisis* (Chicago: Moody, 1996).

[2] Some who ask this question do not care for the answer. For those who do care, consult David Wells, *No Place for Truth* (Grand Rapids, MI: Eerdmans, 1993), David Wells, *God in the Wasteland* (Grand Rapids, MI: Eerdmans, 1994), and David Wells, *Losing Our Virtue* (Grand Rapids, MI: Eerdmans, 1998).

deteriorate, the silent presence of a bystanding, impotent Church has merely added to the weight and burden of our cultural despair.

To the extent that the symptoms of our disease are undeniable, the world does offer some suggestions. A common method solves the problem by admitting that it exists, but it is not that serious. As soon as the false prophets and liars see that God's people are on the verge of a deep and real repentance, they will not be long in coming forward. And when they come forward they will heal the wound of the people lightly; they will speak peace when there is no peace. They will do nothing more than take a damp washcloth and dab around the edges of our gangrenous wound. But there will be no peace. Until we see that God is true, though every man be a liar, we will not have any peace worthy of the name.

Christians must obediently and humbly return to the triune God of Scripture. We must return to a fear of the Lord, which is the beginning of all true wisdom. This must be our epistemology, our apologetic, our hermeneutic — thorough-going obedience to the grace of God through Christ in the fear of God. This, and only this, will enable us to become like the men of Issachar, who understood the times and knew what Israel should do. Therefore, the Lord, not man, must control the transformation of culture.[3]

By the grace of the Lord, we must resolve to be faithful to every word that proceeds from the mouth of God. From Genesis to Revelation, we must not be embarrassed by any passage of Scripture, and once we have submissively ascertained its meaning through careful and patient grammatical, historical and typological study, we must seek to put it into practice the day before yesterday.

The reformation of the Church begins with individuals. It will be as individuals that we will appear before the bar of God to be gathered with the sheep, or scattered with the goats. Individuals will give an account for all their idle words, lustful and covetous thoughts, squandered talents, and now vain excuses. Individuals will enter into the blessed rest or be banished to the outer darkness.

All who name the name of Christ must therefore depart from all forms of wickedness, especially the secret sin which has been hidden from every eye but God's. Individual Christians must repent of the sin of autonomous individual*ism*, the belief that our lives and thoughts are our own property and that our relationships with others are simply a matter of our own voluntary arrangements. As the Lord lives, they are not. We have been bought with a price; we are not our own. Having been

---

[3] The first step in this is the toppling of modernity's household gods. For some insight on who *they* are, see Herbert Schlossberg, *Idols for Destruction* (Nashville, TN: Thomas Nelson Publishers, 1983).

redeemed by Christ, we have been placed by God under various governments to obey Him through faithful service according to the law He has
established for the governance of these institutions.

So the reformation of the family is at the heart of the reformation of
the Church. All Christians concerned for the Church must recognize the
importance of structuring the family according to the Scriptures and not
according to the smoke of this world. The husband is established by
God as the head of the wife, just as Christ is the head of the Church. This
position is not to be abused through petty tyrannies; husbands must
diligently imitate the self-sacrifice of the Lord Jesus Christ. Christian
husbands must repent of their countless attempts to ignore this truth,
their abdications, their compromises with the lies and liars of feminism,
their lack of spiritual leadership, and their adulteries.[4] Godly wives are
to delight in their husbands and in their children.[5] There is no shame in
managing a household well, and a great deal of shame in deserting it.
Children are to honor their parents in the Lord; it is the right thing to do.[6]

In a godly culture, the first social manifestation of grace is found in
the family. But our culture is so rebellious that we have institutionalized
our rebellion and cannot even conceive of how a genuine obedience
would appear. We must nevertheless begin; Christians must insist on
the abolition of the government school system, our nursing home system, our government welfare system, and countless other agencies and
bureaucracies designed by the godless to replace the family. The family,
and only the family, is the ministry of health, education, and welfare.
Christians must hasten the destruction of this godless system of salvation by works through separating themselves from it. Christians must
take their children out of government schools and day-care centers, their
parents out of rest homes, and food stamps out of the budget.[7]

And this brings us to the point of this book, which is the reformation
of the Church. The first duty of all Christian churches is to proclaim
clearly the gospel of Christ as Scripture has revealed it to us. Our preachers must therefore repent of their ignorance, slothfulness, timidity, and
prideful "wiser than God" assumptions, and return to a bold proclamation of the truth of the gospel. We need have no fear in preaching this
message, for it abases man and exalts Christ. We need to tremble for
having neglected it.

---

[4] Of course, we will do our best to keep incestuous footnotes to a minimum. But please see Douglas Wilson, *Reforming Marriage* (Moscow, ID: Canon
Press, 1995).

[5] Nancy Wilson, *The Fruit of Her Hands* (Moscow, ID: Canon Press, 1997),
and *Praise Her in the Gates* (Moscow, ID: Canon Press, 2000).

[6] Douglas Wilson, *Standing on the Promises* (Moscow, ID: Canon Press,
1997).

[7] James Burnham, *Suicide of the West* (Chicago: Regnery Books, 1985).

This message is that man by nature is a deserving object of God's wrath, utterly without hope of saving himself. Dead in his filthiness, he is without God and without hope in the world. But before all worlds, God the Father selected by name a people to be called by His name, the number of whom cannot be increased, diminished, or counted by man. When the appointed time for their redemption came, God the Son took on human flesh and was born of a woman. According to the predetermined plan of God, the eternal Word of God died on a tree as a perfect and efficacious substitute for His people, those whom the Father had given Him. As the message of this gospel progresses throughout the world, God the Spirit comes upon the men and women selected for salvation and in a wonderful and effectual way, regenerates them; those whom God has ordained to eternal life believe. This being the case, what shall we say to these things? If God is for us, who can be against us? No true child of God will ever fall from the everlasting arms.[8]

The message of this gospel is clear in Scripture. We must confess that our sinful neglect of the Bible has blurred it for us. As the Church returns to a clear understanding of the gospel message, other important doctrinal reformations will follow.

The point of this book is the reformation of the Church, and not the reformation of nations and cultures. Nevertheless, if the Church *were* to be reformed, it would have a dramatic impact on the surrounding nations and cultures.

The state is the third institution in shambles. At the very beginning of the coming cultural reformation, our civil magistrates must repent of their blasphemous delusion that the civil government is in any way competent to be a savior for man. This blasphemy is ours, for our magistrates represent us to God in the civil realm. Through them, we have sinned in rejecting the biblical doctrine of God's predestination. Not surprisingly, unbelieving man seeks to fill the void of what he calls "chance" with his own form of total and absolute control—bureaucratic predestination by man. The result is an all-encompassing totalitarian state at war with the living God. But our God is a God of battles and such teapot rebellions never last very long; the Lord in heaven laughs.[9]

God requires the magistrate simply to be a deacon of justice, to punish the wrongdoer with the sword. The duty of the magistrate is to make it possible to walk across town safely in the middle of the night. Generalizing somewhat, this is the extent of their responsibility. But because they have attempted to usurp the position and prerogatives of the

---

[8] David Hagopian, *Back to Basics* (Phillipsburg, NJ: Presbyterian & Reformed, 1996), pp. 6–64.

[9] For background on this, see C. Gregg Singer, *Theological Interpretation of American History* (Greenville, SC: A Press, 1964) and R.J. Rushdoony, *The Politics of Guilt and Pity* (Fairfax, VA: Thoburn Press, 1970).

sovereign God in salvation, they have been too overwhelmed and distracted to do the one thing God requires of them.

All Christians must repent of this, for we have been content to have them represent us by such blasphemous folly. The taxes we currently pay and the persecutions we currently experience are a just chastisement for our disobedience. As unbelieving civil magistrates preen themselves on their omnicompetence, our response must not be rebellion or anger. We live under a civil government which is better than we deserve. Our response must be patience in our suffering; we are responsible for what we receive. If the rod is for the back of fools, we must not complain when God administers the beating. We may confess our sins with patience because we know that when the chastisement is done, God will rise up and use His purified Church to scatter His enemies.

So here is the task before us. The Christian faith calls us to nothing short of world conquest. In order to be faithful to our Lord's great command, we need to take seriously the task of world evangelization. The need is great. But before we send missionaries across land and sea, we must take care that we send out the gospel and not our own sins and follies. Part of our need is to see modernity for the cul-de-sac it is.[10]

So our great need is a second Reformation. We must recover the teaching of Scripture and know it to be the teaching of Scripture. Related to this, our second need is spiritual renewal. Without the power of the Spirit anointing it, all the doctrinal reformation in the world will simply be words and more words.[11] And the third great need is the evangelization of the world, undertaken by a purified and empowered Church. The Lord God has promised that day, and we must pray that He hastens it.[12]

While a lost world has been wandering blindly in the arrogance of sin, we have taken our ease in Zion, seeking our own pleasure and comfort, rather than seeking first the kingdom of God. And those Christians who have been "activists" have sought to do the work of God in the world according to the words and wisdom of men. Our failure has been as great as our folly. We must confess our impotence.

Jesus warned us about these dangers. "Ye are the salt of the earth: but if the salt have lost his savour, wherewith shall it be salted? it is thenceforth good for nothing, but to be cast out, and to be trodden under foot of men" (Mt. 5:13). And here we are, the trampled Church.

No thoughtful Christian can consider the state of our culture today without considerable grief. The lawless are in power, the innocent

---

[10] Thomas C. Oden, *After Modernity . . . What?* (Grand Rapids, MI: Zondervan Publishing House, 1990). The answer to the question is *not* postmodernity. Gene Edward Veith, *Postmodern Times* (Wheaton, IL: Crossway Books, 1994).

[11] Arturo Azurdia, *Spirit Empowered Preaching* (Ross-shire, Great Britain: Mentor, 1998).

[12] Kenneth Gentry, *He Shall Have Dominion* (Tyler, TX: ICE, 1992).

suffer, the gullible believe, the taxable pay, the sages are befuddled, and everything gets progressively worse. One political party wants to drive us toward the cliff at seventy miles per hour, and the loyal opposition wants to go fifty. In such a situation, it is perilously easy for Christians (*always* in the back seat) to begin to think that we have an obligation to "get involved," change our country, turn this thing around, and so on.

And so we do have an obligation—but not in the way most frequently suggested. The humanists who currently run the show believe that politics is our savior. It would be unthinkable for a major political figure to state publicly that some widespread cultural problem (drugs, say) had "no political solution," and that he, Sen. Snoutworst, was therefore going to "do nothing" about it. The ensuing commotion would be a sight to behold, the good senator having blasphemed against the reigning god. For unbelievers, politics provide the only possible answer. The problem is that many of the Christians who have "gotten involved" have assumed that the difference between the believers and unbelievers concerns simply the agenda for action—"what should our leaders do?" But they agree on the fact that there is a political solution. But for Christians who seek to think biblically, the problem is far more fundamental than this.

Any serious attempts at cultural reform, based upon "traditional values," which precede a reformation and revival in the Church, should be considered by Christians as worthless reforms. As a pretty woman without discretion is like a gold ring in a pig's snout, so is a reformation of law without a reformation of the people. Our nation has progressed as far as she has in her moral corruptions because the Church has diluted her message and consequently finds the surrounding culture baffling.[13] She was appointed as the pillar and ground of the truth, and she has found the task wearisome. Contending for the faith delivered to the saints has become too much of a nuisance, and too likely to bring on controversy. We can't have *that*.

Our civic leaders who have not believed God, and who have plunged our nation into this flood of dissipation, were simply acting according to their unregenerate natures. They are without God and without hope in the world. The only way the unbelieving world can be constrained in its external actions, in a way contrary to that unregenerate nature, is when the Church is *salty*. Christ taught that His followers were the salt of the earth—applied to an ungodly society in the same way salt was applied to perishable meat as a preservative. When salt loses its savor, it

---

[13] A delightful exception is found in Harold O. J. Brown, *The Sensate Culture* (Dallas, TX: Word Publishing, 1996). For some fascinating counterpoint from an unbelieving perspective, see Thomas Frank, *Conquest of Cool* (Chicago: University of Chicago Press, 1997).

does no good for the salt to start blaming the meat. Jesus taught that when salt had come to this point, then the salt was due for trampling. It was good for nothing else.

The central problem in America today is the refusal of the Church to act as salt. Salt is controversial. Salt is troublesome. Salt is a nuisance. Salt is divisive. Salt is too doctrinal and theological. Salt is a pain in the neck. Salt is — well, salty. Why can't we all just love Jesus, whoever He is, and try to provide the folks who wander in with a seeker-friendly atmosphere? In the first place, this is pragmatism and not Christianity. In the second place, pragmatism can be readily condemned out of its own mouth. Pragmatism doesn't work. This means that unless God is merciful to us, we will continue to be trampled. If given, His mercy will be shown through a great reformation in the Church — a theological reformation. Many Christians are praying for revival, but we need to be careful how we pray. The Church today is a lightweight operation, like a stack of balsa wood, soaked in lighter fluid. The consuming fire of the Holy Spirit would therefore not burn for long and would not leave much. We must pray for a doctrinal reformation that will cut and split a lot of hard wood — wood that will burn for a long time.

The Puritans are remembered (rightly) for the political impact they had.[14] Hundreds of years after their time, we still owe many of our civil liberties to their teaching and to the sacrifices they made for the sake of their Lord and ours. But the Puritans got their name not because their first goal was to "purify" the politics of the day, but rather because they wanted to purify the Church. The Church of their day needed it, as does ours. But there should be no confusion on this point; the Churches that need to be reformed are not the liberal and apostate Churches. The greatest need for reformation is with the evangelical church.

> Because thou sayest, I am rich, and increased with goods, and have need of nothing; and knowest not that thou art wretched, and miserable, and poor, and blind, and naked: I counsel thee to buy of me gold tried in the fire, that thou mayest be rich; and white raiment, that thou mayest be clothed, and that the shame of thy nakedness do not appear; and anoint thine eyes with eyesalve, that thou mayest see. (Rev. 3:17–18)

Modern evangelicals in our culture have gotten money, power, and influence, and it has been like giving whiskey to a two-year-old. But the need of the hour is theological, not political. The arena is the pulpit and the table, not the legislative chamber.[15] The message is Christ crucified and risen for His chosen sinners and now acknowledged Lord of all.

---

[14] Douglas Kelly, *The Emergence of Liberty in the Modern World* (Phillipsburg, NJ: Presbyterian & Reformed, 1992).

[15] Peter Leithart, *The Kingdom and the Power* (Phillipsburg, NJ: Presbyterian & Reformed, 1993), pp. 107–126.

This risen and conquering Christ is the Head of the Church. Before we are equipped to proclaim His lordship to the inhabitants of all the earth, we must live as though we believed it in the Church.

We must therefore study the Scriptures and reform our doctrines and beliefs according to the Scriptures. We must then pray, seeking reformation and doctrinal renewal from the sovereign Lord Who alone can bestow it. When the household of God has been cleansed, according to His Word, we will be qualified to preach the triumph of the Lord Christ to the nations of the world. And there were loud voices in heaven, saying, "The kingdoms of this world are become the kingdoms of our Lord, and of his Christ; and he shall reign for ever and ever" (Rev. 11:15).

✠ CHAPTER I ✠

WHAT IS THE CHURCH?

The True and Ancient Church

In addressing the question of which is the true and ancient Church, we have to see how important the question is. The issue is important because the Church is our *mother*, and the law of God requires us to honor our mothers.

> But Jerusalem which is above is free, *which is the mother of us all*. For it is written, Rejoice, thou barren that bearest not; break forth and cry, thou that travailest not: for the desolate hath many more children than she which hath an husband. (Gal. 4:26–27)

Christians know that God is our Father (Eph. 3:14–15) and that Christ is the Bridegroom (Eph. 5:25). But few modern Christians know that we have a spiritual mother. The Christian Church is called the New Jerusalem and is the bride of Christ. "And I John saw the holy city, new Jerusalem, coming down from God out of heaven, prepared as a bride adorned for her husband" (Rev. 21:2). In the same chapter the Church, again, the new Jerusalem, is called "the bride, the Lamb's wife" (v. 9). And in Hebrews 12:22–24, the Church is called "the city of the living God, the heavenly Jerusalem."[1]

Put all together, we see that our mother is a holy city, a lovely bride. In the passage quoted already from Galatians, this Jerusalem above is plainly identified as the mother of us all.

The people of God have always had a mother; this lovely woman was Abraham's mother. So when we talk about identifying with the true and ancient Church, we are not talking about an abstraction, but rather about *her*, our glorious Mother Kirk. However detailed and theological

---

[1] Understanding the difference between corporate piety and individual piety at this point is crucial. See Leon Podles, *The Church Impotent* (Dallas: Spence Publishing Company, 1999).

the discussion gets, we should still stand up in respect when she comes in the room.[2]

With this introduction, what then? If we are calling for a return to the true and ancient Church, we should begin with an understanding of what this all means. Since the time of the Reformation, evangelical Christians have struggled with the problems caused by the concepts of the invisible Church and visible Church.[3] The distinction is a valuable and necessary one and was made in response to the claim of the papal church to be the one true Church. For the Roman Catholics, such a distinction between visible and invisible was spurious—they saw the boundaries of their institution as being identical with the boundaries of the one and only Church.

But the Reformers saw that some such distinction was necessary. Without it, men fall readily into the trap of thinking that all that is necessary for salvation is to be in good standing with the visible Church. And because *that* is something they can readily arrange, they think that all is well with their souls. They start to think that their position on Christ's tree is eternally secure, and that they, dry twigs, support the root. Such vanity obviously had to be rejected, as the Reformers did.

At the same time, this classical Protestant distinction can be applied in such a way as to cause some problems of its own. While it was a valuable distinction, it was still not an inspired distinction. For example, are there really two Churches, one invisible in heaven and the other visible here on earth? The assumption can easily be made, and has been, that the invisible Church is the true Church. But this means that the Church below is, at best, a mere human attempt to approximate that heavenly Church. And so we undertake, on our own authority, and by various ecclesiastical schemes, to "copy the pattern we think is up there on the mount." In doing this, we tend to one of two extremes. We either identify the two Churches, falling into the error of Roman Catholicism, or we separate them completely, and follow the path of gnosticism. The difficulty is not that we have made a distinction, but rather that we have made an ontological distinction instead of an historical distinction.

Our problem is that we have tended to think in the Platonic

---

[2] Note how important John Calvin considered this to be. "As it is now our purpose to discourse of the visible Church, let us learn, from her single title Mother, how useful, nay how necessary, the knowledge of her is, since there is no other means of entering into life unless she conceive us in the womb and give us birth, unless she nourish us at her breasts." This, and an impressive collection of other citations from Calvin, can be found in Ronald Wallace, *Calvin's Doctrine of the Christian Life* (Eugene, OR: Wipf and Stock Publishers, 1997), p. 195ff.

[3] For a good discussion of this, see John Murray, *Collected Works of John Murray, Vol. I* (Carlisle, PA: Banner of Truth Trust, 1976), pp. 231–236.

categories of the Greeks instead of the historical and eschatological categories of the Jews. That which is heavenly is true, we assume, and that which is earthly can at best be only a dim shadow of that which is true. Thus, because we think of the heavenly and earthly as two separate and distinct ontological realms, and because we *tend* to think of a Church in each realm, we find ourselves stuck with two separate and distinct Churches.[4] But Christ is the Head of only *one* Church.

The biblical teaching is that earthly history is eternally significant. Just as our individual sanctification occurs over the course of our earthly lives, so the sanctification of the Church occurs throughout the process of earthly history. Consider the feeble strength of the Church when it was first visibly organized in the household of Abraham — an old man and woman, childless. Consider it today, as countless thousands are calling upon the God of Abraham in truth. And for those who have the faith of Abraham, consider it in the centuries to come, when all the ends of the world shall remember and turn to the Lord, and all the families of the nations shall worship before our God (Ps. 22:27).[5]

Instead of thinking of the elect as composing an invisible Church in hyper-space (a category which neglects the importance of history), we should think of the full number of the elect as composing the eschatological Church — the Church as it will visibly be on the last glorious day of *history*. At that day, all the fruitless branches will finally be detached from His tree, and all the permanent branches will be there, bearing abundant fruit.

And rather than thinking of a visible Church, we should think of the historical Church. Obviously, not all of this historical Church is visible to us now. The saints of seven hundred years ago, or the saints five hundred years from now, are all part of the historical Church, the Church as it grows, develops, and matures throughout all history.

A doctrine of an eschatological Church does not neglect the importance of history; this Church is the culmination of the entire process of redemptive history. Those who are in the historical Church should not see that Church as defiled because it is earthly, but rather as immature because it is *early* .

This distinction helps us to understand the relationship of unregenerate professing Christians to the Church as well. The Bible teaches clearly that in the historical Church there are fruitless branches (but real

---

[4] Too often we debate early church history as an ideological abstraction, and not as something that *happened*. See Charles Norris Cochrane, *Christianity and Classical Culture* (Oxford: Oxford University Press, 1940), R. A. Markus, *The End of Ancient Christianity* (Cambridge: Cambridge University Press, 1990), and Peter Brown, *Augustine of Hippo* (Berkeley, CA: University of California Press, 1967).

[5] John Jefferson Davis, *The Victory of Christ's Kingdom* (Moscow, ID: Canon Press, 1996).

branches nonetheless) which will not be there in the eschatological Church. Jesus sternly warns that "If a man abide not in me, he is cast forth as a branch, and is withered; and men gather them, and cast them into the fire, and they are burned" (Jn. 15:6). And Paul says the same. "For if God spared not the natural branches, take heed lest he also spare not thee" (Rom. 11:21).

This does not mean that the elect can lose their salvation. But it *does* mean that branches can lose their position on the tree. The elect always bear fruit, and their fruit remains. And yet some false professors, with a genuine historical connection to the tree, never bear fruit, and consequently fall under the judgment of God.

So what is the true Church? The true Church is the Church in history, the gathered throng of all professing households, assembled in covenant around the Word and Christ's sacraments. At the end of all history, *this same Church* will be revealed to an astonished universe as a bride of extraordinary beauty. Many times throughout her history, she did not seem a suitable bride for our Lord. But then, on that last day, she will be presented and given away, without spot or wrinkle, or any other blemish. As we look at this wonderful eschatological conclusion to history, it reminds us that we should also look to the past. Since we have defined the true Church as one which extends throughout all history, we also have to see that the true Church is an *ancient* Church.

We do not know who the first church member was. It may have been Adam, or perhaps Eve. Scripture does not say explicitly. But at the very least, God had called out a people for himself by the second generation of mankind. Abel is identified by Christ as "righteous," and the author of Hebrews tells us he was a man of faith. "By faith Abel offered unto God a more excellent sacrifice than Cain, by which he obtained witness that he was righteous, God testifying of his gifts: and by it he being dead yet speaketh" (Heb. 11:4).

We also do not know who the last church member will be — the final sinner washed and sanctified before the Lord raises the dead at the time of the last judgment. Whatever *his* name, he will count himself fortunate indeed. But the Lord is longsuffering, and is not willing that any of His people should perish — He will delay that final day of judgment until all His people are safely saved.

Between these two, the first and last sinner forgiven, exists one and only one Church.[6] That Church is the Church of all the redeemed, throughout all time. When we repent and believe, into this one Church we come.

---

[6] James Bannerman, *The Church of Christ* (Edmonton, AB: Turbulent Waters Revival Books, 1991 [1869]).

But ye are come unto mount Zion, and unto the city of the living God, the heavenly Jerusalem, and to an innumerable company of angels, to the general assembly and Church of the firstborn, which are written in heaven, and to God the Judge of all, and to the spirits of just men made perfect, and to Jesus the mediator of the new covenant, and to the blood of sprinkling, that speaketh better things than that of Abel. (Heb. 12:22–24)

If a man is redeemed by Christ, then he is a member of this one Church — a Church founded in God's decree before time existed, and by the grace of God manifested in history as long as sinful heirs of Adam have lived.

Enter the modern rootless evangelical, who, with a bemused detachment, is able to tell you only that the church he attends was founded in the late fifties by a gifted biblical expositor, an honors graduate of Bison Breath Bible College. Historically isolated from other periods of the Church, this church member's faith is very much anchored to the present moment and his own present needs and concerns. For many modern evangelicals, this historical provincialism is perfectly acceptable to them; they enjoy life in the provinces. They have not been taught to appreciate the importance of history, and so, for them, it falls easily to the ground.

But for others, such ecclesiastical rootlessness is intolerable — and rightly intolerable. In search of roots, and not wanting to belong to any denomination that apparently has no more of a historical pedigree than the average cult, they begin to look around.[7] Not surprisingly, they soon encounter a church which lays claim to antiquity — a church which claims continuous existence back to the time of the apostles. Against such a claim, what can a church founded in the late fifties say?

This desire to belong to an old church is certainly a noble and scriptural one. "Remember thy congregation, which thou hast *purchased of old*; the rod of thine inheritance, which thou hast redeemed; this mount Zion, wherein thou hast dwelt" (Ps. 74:2). But at the same time, caution is in order. Someone with a pressing need, even if the need is legitimate in itself, is someone with low sales resistance. If an historically naive American wants to belong to an old church, it does not take much to impress him. We must remember that we Americans think *Sears* is old.

The Church which Christ purchased with His blood is not the only thing which is "of old." Scripture shows us the serpent has been lying from the *beginning* (1 Jn. 3:8; Rev. 12:9). The truth is ancient, but within the experience of our race, lies are almost as ancient. The antithesis

---

[7] For a good example of this kind of thing, see Frank Schaeffer, *Dancing Alone* (Brookline, MA: Holy Cross Orthodox Press, 1994).

between true righteousness and self-righteousness, between the right worship of God and idolatry, has existed since the time of Abel and Cain. So raw historical data, mere antiquity, does not provide the criterion for evaluating that history. After all, Cain was the eldest.

It is therefore not surprising when rootless evangelicals, who have not been taught this biblical approach to the history of the Church, prove themselves to be incredibly naive in historical matters. When confronted with the historical distortions which claim the mantle of apostolic antiquity, they quietly submit. After all, they reason, the one who speaks so confidently about the past must be right, while the one who says nothing about it must be wrong.

But the problem with Eastern Orthodoxy, and also with Rome, is *not* their antiquity. The problem is that they are not old enough—they are not part of the Ancient Church, characterized in all ages by the righteousness of faith.[8] Abel lived under a different administration of the grace of God than did Moses, or the apostle Paul, or Polycarp. But all of them wore the white livery of Christ—the righteousness of faith.[9]

Every age has seen the mummeries of self-imposed worship, and in every age God has been pleased to call out a people for the sake of His name. How may we distinguish the two? The answer has always been the same: God's people are always marked by the righteousness of faith. So just as Israel did not obtain what they sought—righteousness by law—so the Orthodox and the Romanists have not obtained what they prize above all—the righteousness of *old*. In the wisdom of God, the simplest evangelical, provided he is clothed in the righteousness of Christ, however distressingly ignorant of the antiquity of his faith he may be, nevertheless remains a member of that ancient congregation. And in the judgment of God, those who naively want only the feel and smell of antiquity are condemned to continue to act as though they were born yesterday. "Thou wilt perform the truth to Jacob, and the mercy to Abraham, which thou hast sworn unto our fathers *from the days of old*" (Mic. 7:20).

This ancient faith is going to last until the end of the world, and through it Abraham and his heirs will inherit the earth. "For the promise, that he should be the heir of the world, was not to Abraham, or to his seed, through the law, but through the righteousness of faith" (Rom.

---

[8] Again, it must be emphasized that our theological pursuit of these truths must shake loose of that great context distorter, modernity. See David W. Hall, *The Arrogance of the Modern* (Oak Ridge: The Covenant Foundation, 1997), C. S. Lewis, *Studies in Medieval and Renaissance Literature* (Cambridge: Cambridge University Press, 1966), pp. 41–63, C. S. Lewis, *The Discarded Image* (Cambridge: Cambridge University Press, 1964), and David Chilton, *Power in the Blood* (Brentwood, TN: Wolgemuth & Hyatt, Publishers, Inc., 1987).

[9] Martin Luther, *Commentary on Galatians* (Grand Rapids, MI: Baker Book House, 1979).

4:13). So in the providence of God the steady stream of rootless American evangelicals converting to eastern Orthodoxy and Roman Catholicism is not entirely a bad thing. The exodus does serve one valuable function: it reveals the theological bankruptcy of contemporary evangelicalism. The sooner mainstream evangelicalism abandons the generic and vanilla faith it has drifted into, the closer we will be to a second Reformation — which is desperately needed.[10]

Of course this should not be taken as anything like approval of any form of sacerdotalism. But if a man is going to base his worship around ceremonies and traditions of human devising, then it makes far better sense, humanly speaking, to opt for the traditions that were invented in the fourth century, as opposed to those traditions which were invented in Dallas in the early seventies. But of course this is a false dilemma.[11]

We are prohibited from worshiping God according to the word of man, regardless of what theological label man uses, or which century forged that idolatry. We modern Protestants must, therefore, begin our discussion by admitting (with grief and repentance) that the idolatries of modern evangelicalism are not spiritually better than the idolatries of Eastern Orthodoxy or Roman Catholicism, and they tend to be inferior aesthetically.[12] Having lost our ability to see the glory of the gospel in the proclamation of the risen Christ, we have done what men have always done in this situation — we have turned to baubles and trinkets, programs and gimmicks. And if our worship were supposed to be sensual, then aesthetics would make a difference, and aesthetic superiority would count for something. But the Bible teaches us that the Father is seeking those who will worship Him in spirit and in truth.

Now, of course, all this will invite the retort, "Why is it any better for evangelicals to revert to the traditions of the Reformation?" The answer is that it is *not* better, which will no doubt bring the question, "What, then, are we debating? Why all the fuss?" Those who worship the Lord in spirit and truth are those who can trace their spiritual lineage back to Abel. If a man is not a member of the oldest Church on earth — the Church of those justified by faith alone — then he is not saved. Abel was put right with God, as the author of Hebrews tells us, because of his faith. This faith of Abel's was placed in God long before the Reformation. And millennia before the Reformers preached the gospel of Scripture — *sola*

---

[10] John Armstrong, *The Compromised Church* (Wheaton, IL: Crossway, 1998).

[11] But also, of course, there is a big market for false dilemmas among evangelicals. Mark Noll, *The Scandal of the Evangelical Mind* (Grand Rapids, MI: Eerdmans, 1994).

[12] In addition, we certainly also lament the current fragmented condition of the Church. See D. Martyn Lloyd-Jones, *Christian Unity* (Grand Rapids, MI: Baker Book House, 1980), John M. Frame, *Evangelical Reunion* (Grand Rapids, MI: Baker Book House, 1991), and Thomas McCrie, *Unity of the Church* (Dallas: Presbyterian Heritage Publication, 1989).

gratia, sola fide — Abraham believed God, and it was imputed to him as righteousness. Abraham obviously did not use the Latin phrases to describe what had happened, but as Paul teaches us, it was faith from first to last (Rom. 1:17). The language does not matter; the faith does.

As Christ pointed out, those who are related to Abraham spiritually carry with them a spiritual family resemblance. And what is that mark? What is it that shows a man's relation to Abraham? It is his faith — with absolutely no admixture of human effort, striving, deciding, altar-calling, church-attending, willing, or running. Many admirable things will always proceed from faith alone, but nothing *mixes* with faith alone.

The fact that the Reformers recovered this gospel of "grace alone through faith alone" hardly makes what they taught a theological novelty. Things were falling to the ground long before Newton described how they did so, and men were being put right with God long before the Reformers were included in their number. Every man who has ever been justified was put right with God on the basis of a covenant — an ancient covenant — between the Father and Son, and revealed to men from Genesis on.

But rootless evangelicals, who bear the name Protestant, have no concept of this ancient covenant, and they are consequently an easy mark for those who present to them a church which looks ancient from the human vantage point. God has put eternity in the heart of man; we do have a hunger for antiquity and eternal roots. Moreover it is a hunger we are commanded to satisfy; but the means of satisfaction must always be faith. Classical Protestantism stands by faith alone.[13] If that is lost, then everything is lost — everything but the name Protestant. And if everything but the name is lost, it does not much matter where you go, or what you bow down to after that.

The Bible teaches us that the word of Christ should dwell in us richly. We are standing in the midst of a theological ruin because this has not been true of us. But if the word of Christ does not dwell in us richly, something else will. And because the only alternative to God Himself is some created thing, the result of this fall into sin will always be idolatry. This is the essence of idolatry — the substitution of a created thing for the Creator. When idolatry can occur in an "informal" way through the sin of greed (Eph. 5:5), how much more obvious should it be to us when a created thing is the object of religious devotion and worship?

So whether the idolatry is Roman Catholic or Orthodox or "evangelical" does not really matter. When this idolatry has happened (and it has), the church is named Ichabod — the glory has departed from her. Where once the lampstands burned brightly, there is now nothing

---

[13] J.C. Ryle, *Knots Untied* (Cambridge: James Clarke & Co. Ltd., 1977).

but spiritual darkness. Where once the Lord was pleased to inhabit the powerful preaching and celebrating of His Word, we now have nothing remaining but the word of man — a verbal haunt for owls and jackals.

Because of all this, the modern evangelical portion of the Church is in an embarrassed condition, and this embarrassment is made excruciatingly evident whenever Roman Catholic apologists pose certain difficult questions about the source of our authority. Without a coherent doctrine of history and the place of the Church within history, the Bible necessarily becomes a book that is suspended, in good arbitary fashion, in midair. And thus it is that a collection of books about the meaning of history, given within history, by various historical means, including the historical Church, has come to be revered by a group of evangelical saints with virtually no historical sense whatever.

But when we open our Bibles, before we come to the Word of God at Genesis 1:1, we come to the word of the Church at the Table of Contents. No one holds that the Table of Contents is part of inspired Scripture; rather it *points* to inspired Scripture, in a similar way that John the Baptist pointed to Christ. However, it is necessary for us to see that the Table of Contents page is important, and that on that page someone or something is authoritatively identifying for us the boundaries of Scripture. Our full persuasion and assurance of the infallibility and authority of the Scriptures does come from the inward work of the Holy Spirit. The Scriptures are self-authenticating. But we sometimes forget that there is a necessary objective work of the Spirit as well — the work of the Spirit in history, as He has led the Church to make that wonderful confession of faith that we call the Table of Contents.

The problem with contemporary Protestants is that they have no real doctrine of the Table of Contents. With the approach that is popular in conservative evangelical circles, one simply comes to the Bible by means of an epistemological lurch. The Bible "just is," and any questions about how it got here are dismissed as a nuisance. But time passes, the questions remain unanswered, the silence becomes awkward, and conversions of seduced evangelicals to Rome proceed apace.

But this is an inconsistency among modern Protestants and is not at all an inconsistency within the historic Protestant position. Or course, this should not surprise us; if Protestants do not understand the history of the Bible, how can we expect them to understand their own history as Protestants? The problem here is modernity, and not *classical* Protestantism.

Now all this is just to set the stage; the point of this portion of the argument is not to lament current evangelical inconsistencies, but rather to point out that the Roman Catholic Church shares those inconsistencies in remarkably similar ways. I think part of the reason many evangelicals are attracted to Rome is that they have discovered they really have so much in common. When men go over to Rome they believe they have answered these great historical questions, but what has actually happened is that they have joined a communion which is old enough for them to assume that the answers have to be "around here somewhere." But if we investigate, we soon discover the same embarrassed silence that is so characteristic of modern evangelicalism.

Those who have submitted to the Roman *magisterium*, the teaching office of the church, have actually submitted to an historical abstraction. The *magisterium* is the doctrinal application of the *depositum fidei*, itself revealed in both Scripture and Tradition. The Roman church, according to her doctrine, is guaranteed infallibility as the bishops, in concert with the bishop of Rome, teach the faith. According to this position, the Church has been performing this service for two thousand years. So the question is this: where is the Table of Contents for this work which they have done? Put another way, what are the precise boundaries of the *magisterium*?

Conservative evangelicals know what they are submitting to, but they do not know why. Roman Catholics know why they are submitting, but they do not know what they are submitting to. Evangelicals should be asked, with regard to the Bible, "Why is your Table of Contents?" Roman Catholics should be asked, with regard to the *magisterium*, "Where is your Table of Contents?" Why has the Church not performed for the *magisterium* the same service she performed when she testified to the canon of Scripture? Does the *magisterium* have canonical boundaries, and if so, what are they? Anything with an *imprimatur*?

This is why debates on church infallibility between Protesting Catholics and Roman Catholics are debates about the issue in the abstract. We do not have a complete list of infallible pronouncements anywhere that we can discuss in concrete terms. In this, the Roman church has been specific about this or that doctrine, but has not been specific about the historical boundaries. Mark the point well. The *magisterium* as it is being exercised *today* may be clear enough to some, but I am raising an historical question, and on this question of history, the Roman church is just as blurry as the modern evangelicals. Put simply, my challenge contains two questions. Has the Roman Catholic church made infallible pronouncements throughout her history? And may we have an infallible and complete list of them?

Given the nature of history, and what the Bible teaches about the nature of historical growth and development, this problem is not a surprising one. All these issues revolve around genuine church authority, and this leads to another great question, one prompted by a much neglected warning delivered by the apostle Paul.

The Roman church teaches that her lampstand cannot be removed. This is maintained on the strength of the promises made to Peter in

Matthew 16:13–20. Now it is quite true that Christ promised to establish His Church, and to build it, and we do believe that nothing can ever stop this process. At the same time, precisely because this promise to the true Catholic Church stands firm, the Bible is clear that particular churches may be removed from that Catholic Church. This is done by God as a very important means of fulfilling His promise to the universal and apostolic Church.

For example, the church at Ephesus is no more — her lampstand was removed — but this in no way nullifies God's commitment to the greater Church. Actually, this was done in fulfillment of His promise. A gardener prunes in order to save, not destroy. The tree remains; not every branch remains. The true Church of which Ephesus was once a part continues to this day. And because of this, true saints today maintain complete communion with the true saints who were in Ephesus in the first century. But in history, the tree has been pruned. A lampstand has been removed from a particular place.

Such discipline of particular churches is a wonderful example of God's faithfulness to the greater Church. God will not tolerate gross immorality or doctrinal corruption indefinitely — although in His great mercy He often tolerates it for a season. The illustration of the Jewish church is *apropos* at this point. Caiaphas was a true high priest, despite his wickedness and unbelief, and even prophesied concerning the Christ (Jn. 11:49–51). And yet, just a few years after Caiaphas held that office, the apostle John writes of some of the gatherings of the Jews as "synagogues of Satan." So while we agree that corruption is not the same thing as apostasy, the Bible is very clear that complete apostasy of particular churches is a very real possibility.

This pattern is given to us in the New Testament in the form of a very stern warning. Paul used the illustration of the olive tree in Romans 11 to show that Gentiles can be removed from the covenant in just the same way that unbelieving Jews were removed. The olive tree is the Catholic church, the true Israel of God, and the Lord Jesus Christ is the root. That tree will never be chopped down; we have God's word on it. Moreover, we have His word that the tree will grow and flourish, as a visible Church, until the earth is filled with its fruit.

Does it then follow that no branches can ever be removed? As Paul might say, "May it never be!" This sin of covenantal presumption was exactly the sin that was the downfall of the Jews, and Paul warns the Gentiles not to think that what happened to the Jews was impossible for them. The church at Rome has many ancient glories, but what does it have that Jerusalem did not have? It was the Lord Jesus Himself who told the church at Jerusalem that not one stone would be left on another. And again, Paul: "Well; because of unbelief they were broken off, and thou standest by faith. Be not highminded, but fear: For if God spared not the natural branches, *take heed* lest he also spare not thee. Behold therefore the goodness and severity of God: on them which fell, severity; but toward thee, goodness, if thou continue in *his* goodness: otherwise thou also shalt be cut off" (Rom. 11:20–22). To join a church which maintains, as a point of dogma, that it cannot be cut off, appears to be a very perilous course of action.

Now in response to this, Rome would maintain that she is far more than just a particular church in a particular city, that she is not just a branch on the tree, but rather that she is the tree itself. This is internally consistent, but this is not what Paul tells them. These words from Romans 11 are not just being applied by me to the church at Rome, they were written by Paul *to the church at Rome*. Paul expressly warns the Gentiles *at Rome* (Rom. 1:7; 11:13) that their removal from the Catholic Church was a very real possibility. "Boast not against the branches. But if thou boast, thou bearest not the root, but the root thee" (v. 18). What we have here is a letter from Paul the apostle to the church at Rome, telling her that she is not the root, but simply another branch on the tree. He states further that if she becomes haughty and proud, she could be removed as completely as previous branches were removed.

The point here is not to attack the insolence and wickedness of some of the Renaissance popes, Alexander VI, for a good example. Good men in every communion know wickedness when they see it. The question here is what such wickedness potentially means. The issue is whether or not the apostle Paul warned Rome of what could happen to her status *as an ancient church* when she began to produce men who looked more like Caiaphas than Peter. Do not be haughty, he said, but fear. "Fear what?" the question comes back. The apostle told Rome to fear *removal*.

But as a point of doctrine, Rome says she has nothing of this nature to fear. She could produce a hundred Alexanders and a thousand more just like Caiaphas, and she would nonetheless remain permanently on the tree. The doctrine of the apostle was a little different, and the doctrine was given first in a letter *to Rome*, a lesson that was first neglected, then forgotten, and now formally denied.

Now this is why we must return to the question of the identity and nature of the true Catholic church, a question addressed earlier in our discussion of the righteousness of faith. And this is why we remember the words of Irenaeus who said, and said well, that "where the Church is, there is the Spirit of God; and where the Spirit of God is, there is the Church." Where is the olive tree? The answer of Scripture is plain: Where there are olives.

> For we are the circumcision, which worship God in the spirit, and rejoice in Christ Jesus, and have no confidence in the flesh. (Phil. 3:3)

✝ CHAPTER II ✝

REFORMATIONAL IDENTITY

What Are Reformed Evangelicals?

We approach the subject reluctantly, because labels are always dangerous. Still, we live at a time when corruptions in the modern evangelical
church are rampant, and consequently certain key distinctions must be
made, and made carefully. If language is to be used at all, and it must be,
such an endeavor requires the use of names and labels. Nevertheless, if
any name is ever used or applied within the churches of Christ in a
spirit of ungodly strife or competition, then sin resides in the use of any
such names. The apostle Paul sternly forbids the factionalism of a striving sectarian spirit (1 Cor. 1:10; 3:1–8).[1] At the same time, we should
remember this spirit of striving is found in the heart and not necessarily
in the action of naming. At Corinth the ostensible "spiritual" party of
Christ had the same problem everyone else had (1 Cor. 1:12). My desire
and intention in this chapter is to use various names without apology,
but in a manner fully consistent with Christian charity. And this requires careful definition.[2]

With this in mind, the point is to recall the reader to the ancient
biblical faith, which, as it has fought faithfully down through the ages,
has acquired many different names as the war progressed — Catholics,
Waldensians, Huguenots, Calvinists, Methodists, Puritans. Some names
have been corrupted and lost, and others made irrelevant by the flow of
events. No virtue is found in any given name, but if we are to understand the history of the Church, we should seek a name which takes all
of the battles into account, and which stands in unity with all the brethren. We are seeking to explain where we are now, and what must be
done now, through a call for a return to classical Protestantism. We are
doing so as reformed evangelicals. These phrases are not intended as

---

[1] Thomas McCrie, *Unity of the Church* (Dallas,TX: Presbyterian Heritage,
1989).
[2] D. Martyn. Lloyd-Jones, *What is an Evangelical?* (Edinburgh: Banner of
Truth Trust, 1992).

party labels, and we have no business cards embossed with either phrase. At the same time, the chapter is written in the imperative mood — *shoulds* and *musts* abound. Our purpose here is to explain the phrases *classical Protestantism* and *reformed evangelicalism* in some detail and with clarity, and hopefully charity as well. Those who are of one mind may grow further in that unity (Eph. 4:3). It is also offered so that those brothers who differ at various lesser points may understand more clearly the nature and extent of our differences. Our prayer should be that, in both cases, the Lord will use these efforts to hasten the day when the entire body of Christ is bound together in unity according to the truth of Scripture (Eph. 4:11–16). In no way does this explanation separate us in any way from other believers who serve the Lord Jesus according to the basics of His Word.

And while we are indebted to the work done by the leaders of what is historically known as the Reformation, and while we are self-consciously building on their doctrinal foundation, we do not intend the phrase *reformed evangelical* to be limited to this. This phrase also expresses our desire to see a great reformation and revival in the evangelical world today. Over the course of the last century, we believe evangelicals have lost their previous orientation to historic Protestant orthodoxy, an orientation which must be recovered if "evangelicals" are to remain Christians. Consequently, as evangelicals, we desire to see a reforming zeal return to our churches. The spiritual condition of the evangelical church today demonstrates the pressing need for such a reformation.

An essential part of such a reformation requires a return to a rigorous doctrinal integrity.[3] In an age which does not value systematic doctrinal clarity, we must learn that a personal love for Christ requires us to tremble at His Word, and to take great pains to understand it *clearly*. Having taken pains to understand, it becomes our responsibility to articulate that understanding to our fellow Christians.

Reformed evangelicals must be dedicated to the authority of Scripture. Our solitary rule of faith and practice is to be found in the sixty-six books of the Old and New Testaments. Scripture alone is sufficient as an ultimate authority to teach us what we must believe and what we are called to do (2 Tim. 3:16–17).[4] In an unbelieving generation, the temptations to compromise at this point are legion. This is true in the realm of science, so believers must assert the account of a six-day creation in Genesis, and reject the various mythologies surrounding evolution, and do so root and branch (Rom. 5:14; 1 Tim. 2:13–14).[5] Few things are as

[3] Samuel Miller, *Doctrinal Integrity* (Dallas,TX: Presbyterian Heritage, 1989).

[4] Richard Muller, *Dictionary of Latin and Greek Theological Terms* (Grand Rapids, MI: Baker Book House, 1985).

[5] For a great treatment of the evangelical special pleading in this regard, see James Jordan, *Creation in Six Days* (Moscow, ID: Canon Press, 1999).

funny as the spectacle of grown men asserting a family resemblance between a sea lion and a bright yellow canary, and doing so in the name of *wisdom*.

This same assumption about the Bible must govern our attitude to humanistic psychology. Pastors, when they are well-equipped in the teaching of Scripture, are also well-equipped to meet all the spiritual needs of God's people (2 Tim. 3:17; Rom. 15:4).[6] The sufficiency of Scripture also excludes the idea that there is any continuing revelation from the Holy Spirit given to the modern church—whether that revelation purports to come from charismatic "prophets," the *holy-ghost-uh* inspiring an utterance from the pastor's wife, an impressive succession of bishops and popes, or from inner leadings, leanings, impressions, or promptings (2 Pet. 1:16–21).[7] We must affirm the sufficiency of Scripture alone.

This sufficiency refers to the sufficiency of Scripture as an ultimate and infallible authority. The Bible teaches us that God has established religious authorities other than Scripture (the church and parents being two obvious examples), but these other authorities are not ultimate and they are not infallible. Ultimacy and infallibility are reserved to Scripture alone. Unlike the Roman Catholics we must not elevate other authorities to the level of Scripture, and unlike modern evangelicalism we must not deny these subordinate authorities which Scripture establishes. We must recover a proper understanding of *sola Scriptura*, an understanding which is essential to any reformation of the Church.

At the same time we do not hold that a mere portion of Scripture is sufficient for the needs of the entire Church. Our commitment to the revealed Word of God must extend to Scripture in its entirety—i.e., we must seek to teach the whole counsel of God (Acts 20:27). We therefore affirm the continuing authority of *all* Scripture. Particularly, we may not hold that the New Covenant set the Law and Prophets aside, but rather revealed and fulfilled with a gracious clarity what had been seen and known, although in a shadow, by faithful believers throughout the history of the world (Gal. 3:19–4:5; Rom. 11:11–36).[8]

In proclaiming the gospel to the unbelieving world, our starting point must be the self-revelation of God in Scripture (Gen. 1:1; Rom. 1:18–21). We do not appeal to any neutral or autonomous field of study in order to buttress our faith in God and His Word.[9] We do not depend

---

[6] Jay Adams, *Competent to Counsel* (Grand Rapids, MI: Eerdmans, 1994).

[7] Walter Chantry, *Signs of the Apostles* (Carlisle, PA: Banner of Truth, 1973).

[8] See Vern Poythress, *The Shadow of Christ in the Law of Moses* (Grand Rapids, MI: Eerdmans Publishing Co., 1994) and Edmund Clowney, *The Unfolding Mystery* (Phillipsburg, NJ: Presbyterian & Reformed, 1988).

[9] Cornelius Van Til, *Defense of the Faith* (Phillipsburg, NJ: Presbyterian & Reformed, 1955).

upon textual criticism, science, archeology, or Tarot cards. At the same time we also reject a pietistic anti-intellectualism, which denigrates the role of God-honoring study and scholarship (Mt. 22:37).[10] We consequently affirm the ultimacy of Scripture. We must self-consciously presuppose the triune God of Scripture in all that we teach and preach. Sinful mankind comes before the bar of Scripture as the accused, and emphatically not as the judge. If we affirm the ultimacy of Scripture, we must then hold that no area of human endeavor falls outside scriptural authority (2 Cor. 10:1–4). Consequently, it is the duty of Christians to seek to understand the world in the light of biblical revelation. This means that a Christian worldview is clearly necessary.[11]

Our possession of the text of Scripture depends upon the providential faithfulness of the Holy Spirit to Christ's Church throughout history, and not upon the authority of academic or ecclesiastical experts (Rom. 3:2; 1 Tim. 3:15). We affirm the infallibility of the God-breathed original autographic text (2 Tim. 3:16), as well as God's faithful preservation of that Word in the apographic or copied texts. We therefore affirm our faith in the infallible Word of God.[12]

Believers must affirm the need for the Word of God to be translated into the common languages of God's people (Acts 2:6). At the same time, we must recognize that any translation, however good, cannot be accorded the status of the autographic or apographic texts. This means that the ministry of each local church must have men who understand the original languages through which God revealed His Word.

Reformed evangelicals are reformational in their understanding of the doctrines of salvation. The Bible teaches that God is the Almighty One, and that His sovereignty is manifested most gloriously in the salvation of sinners. In our doctrine of salvation, we must hold that God is the sole author of sovereign grace (Eph. 2:8–10). We therefore must hold to the biblical truth of sovereign election. Before the foundation of the world, the Father chose a people for Himself, and He did so without any regard to any choices, merit, or boyish good looks on the part of those chosen (Rom. 9:16). The ground of that sovereign choice was not to be found in man, but rather in the good pleasure of God (Eph. 1:5).[13]

When the time was right, the Son of God was born of a woman, born under the law, in order to accomplish the will of God (Gal. 4:4). That will

---

[10] R.L. Dabney, *Discussions, Evangelical* (Harrisonburg, VA: Sprinkle Publications, 1982), p. 651ff.

[11] Abraham Kuyper, *Lectures on Calvinism* (Grand Rapids, MI: Eerdmans Publishing Co., 1943).

[12] Theodore Letis, *The Ecclesiastical Text* (Philadelphia: Institute for Renaissance and Reformation Biblical Studies, 1997).

[13] Martin Luther, *Bondage of the Will* (n.l.: Fleming H. Revell Company, 1957) and John Owen, *Display of Arminianism* (Edmonton, AB: Still Waters Revival Books, 1989 [1642]).

was to secure the salvation of God's elect through the vicarious death of Christ on the cross (Eph. 5:25).[14] We may call this aspect of Christ's death the doctrine of efficacious redemption. It refers to the nature of Christ's death as an effective substitute for His people (Rom. 5:6). Christ died in order to secure the redemption of His people, and that act of obedience was powerful and efficacious (1 Jn. 2:1–2). When Christ died, the salvation of every sinner to be saved was at that point secured — not merely made possible, but actually secured. But while the purchase price had been paid, it was not yet applied in each individual case.[15]

This application is made by the Holy Spirit at the regeneration of each sinner (Jn. 3:8). We may call this application resurrecting grace. Our salvation is therefore gladly ascribed to our Triune God: sovereign election is the work of the Father; efficacious redemption is the work of the Son; and resurrecting grace is the work of the Spirit.

The regeneration of sinners must be counted as a resurrection from the dead because Scripture teaches that unregenerate men are *dead* in their sins, not sick in their sins (Eph. 2:1–3).[16] In his own nature, apart from the grace of God, each descendant of Adam is dead in trespasses and sins (Ezek. 37:1–14). Every descendant of Adam shares the guilt and corruptions of a fallen, rebellious nature (Rom. 5:12–14). Sin is pervasive in his being and utterly debilitating in its effects. The result is a total inability on the part of each sinner to seek after God unless God first enables and draws him (Rom. 3:9–12).[17]

Although each sinner is unable to come to Christ on his own, much less persevere in following Him on his own, the Bible teaches that not one of the elect can fall away (Rom. 8:31–34). Every forgiven sinner may be assured that God will complete the work of redemption He has begun (1 Thes. 5:24). No true saint, numbered among the elect, can ever fall away from the protecting and sustaining grace of God (Jn. 10:29). We call this precious doctrine the preservation and endurance of the saints. This endurance of ours is maintained by God's sustaining grace through trials, in holiness, before the face of God (Phil. 2:12–13).[18]

---

[14] Although he differs with the perspective presented here, a good place to begin is with Leon Morris, *The Cross in the New Testament* (Grand Rapids, MI: Eerdmans, 1965) and Leon Morris, *Apostolic Preaching of the Cross* (Grand Rapids, MI: Eerdmans, 1955).

[15] John Owen, *Death of Death in the Death of Christ* (Edinburgh: The Banner of Truth Trust, 1952) and John Murray, *Redemption Accomplished and Applied* (Grand Rapids, MI: Eerdmans, 1955).

[16] For a powerful description of this process, see Thomas Scott, *The Force of Truth* (Edinburgh: The Banner of Truth Trust, 1984 [1779]).

[17] For a better understanding of this doctrine, please see George Thoroughgood and the Destroyers, "Bad to the Bone."

[18] B. B. Warfield, *The Plan of Salvation* (Boonton, NJ: Simpson Publishing Company, 1989 [1915]).

With a right understanding of this gospel, reformed evangelicals
are evangelical and evangelistic. A sound understanding of the word
evangelical connects it to the five *soli* of the Reformation. We affirm *sola
Scriptura, soli Deo gloria, solus Christus, solum gratum,* and *sola fide.* Salvation is to be understood according to Scripture alone (Gal. 1:8–9); the
glory from salvation is to be ascribed to God alone (Rom. 11:36); it was
accomplished in a sacrificial death through Christ alone (1 Tim. 2:5);
this blessing is given to us by grace alone (Eph. 2:8–9); and we receive it
through the instrument of faith alone (Rom. 1:17). These five phrases
taken together mean that salvation is not mediated to man through the
manipulation of a religious machinery operated by various priests or
religious experts. Man comes to God through Christ by grace through
faith, that the name of God might be glorified.[19]

Before Christ ascended into heaven, He gave an evangelistic commission to His church. That commission required that we preach the
gospel to every creature, in order to bring the nations into a glad
submission to the lordship of Jesus Christ (Mt. 28:19–20). We understand that the Christian church was constituted by Christ as a missionary church, and that the Christian faith is a religion for all nations (Rev.
7:9). Until the Lord returns to judge the earth, the evangelistic task of the
Church is therefore clear. We must hold to this appointed task of the
Church passionately — and despise the idea of a dead "orthodox" church
(Mt. 23:1–3). Dead orthodoxy is oxymoronic. But these truths, as held
throughout their history, have been anything but dead.[20]

The tools to be used by all God's people in the fulfillment of this task
are many. They include literature distribution, evangelistic Bible studies, Bible translation, etc. Nevertheless, we must return to the conviction
that the primary instrument for the conversion of the nations will be the
preaching of the Word and the faithful administration of the sacraments
(Mk. 16:15). Our prayer, therefore, must be that God will raise up thousands of reformed evangelistic preachers, and will cause His church to
send such preachers out to their appointed task. Such preachers will
minister both within the church as ministers or pastors, and outside the
church as evangelists and apologists.[21]

As the Word is preached, the only saving response to the gospel is
that of true evangelical faith. With the Reformers, we hold that justification by faith is the article upon which the church stands or falls (Rom.
3:28). Saving faith is not to be understood as our autonomous response

[19] John Calvin, *Concerning Eternal Predestination* (Cambridge: John Clarke
& Co., 1961).
[20] N. S. McFetridge, *Calvinism in History* (Edmonton, AB: Still Waters Revival Books, 1989 [1882]).
[21] D. Martyn Lloyd-Jones, *Preaching and Preachers* (Grand Rapids, MI:
Zondervan Publishing House, 1971).

to the message of what God has done. Rather, it is the *gift* of God, so that no one can boast (Eph. 2:8–9). Faith is not the ground of our justification—the only ground of justification is the death of Christ (Jer. 23:6). A man is justified when God, because of His good pleasure, imputes the obedience of the Lord Jesus to that man. Faith is the instrument whereby our justification is received, an instrument in its own turn given to us by God (Acts 18:27; Phil. 1:29). Saving faith is a gift of God. That this removes all boasting can be seen in how controversial the assertion is. Proud men do not want the gospel to be *entirely* grace.

As the gospel is preached throughout the nations, we fully expect that God will bring into salvation a countless multitude that no one can number (Rev. 7:9) and that the earth will be as full of the knowledge of the Lord as the waters cover the sea (Is. 11:9).[22]

This doctrine of the triumph of the gospel encourages, and the fact that we need encouraging should be evident. "Wherefore lift up the hands which hang down, and the feeble knees" (Heb. 12:12). A modern Christian has been watching the news on his nineteen-inch color TV set, in the living room of his home. He switches the set off and comments to his wife that the world is in horrible condition. He wonders how long it can go on—he is very discouraged as he goes to the refrigerator for a cold drink.[23] An old Puritan is tied to a stake, and is about to be burned alive for his faith. He lifts his head to heaven and rejoices that Christ is on the throne, and that He will be worshipped from the river to the ends of the earth.

What is the difference between these men? Very simply, it is a matter of faith in the promise of God to save the world. One sits in ease and is overwhelmed with troubles. The other is surrounded by troubles, and yet speaks the word that goes forth conquering, and to conquer. The first has won his life in what he thinks is a losing battle. The second is losing his life in what he knows to be a winning battle.[24]

When the twelve spies went into the land of Canaan, ten of them were like our modern Christian, and fell into the sin of unbelief. They saw that the land was good, but in their sin they saw only the strength of the enemy. There were giants in the land, and they saw themselves as grasshoppers in comparison. But Joshua and Caleb—troublemakers both—saw the Word of God and the opportunity for obedient conquest.

Now unbelief is not necessarily simple; it can be complicated by

[22] J. Marcellus Kik, *An Eschatology of Victory* (Phillipsburg, NJ: The Presbyterian and Reformed Publishing Company, 1971).

[23] Speculation about the end times is a favorite modern evangelical hobby. Gary DeMar, *Last Days Madness* (Brentwood, TN: Wolgemuth & Hyatt, Publishers, Inc., 1991).

[24] Roderick Campbell, *Israel and The New Covenant* (Philadelphia, PA: The Presbyterian and Reformed Publishing Company, 1954).

many factors. We have our reasons, and our theologies, and our church traditions, for remaining in the sin of unbelief. But Christ told us that our job was to lead the nations to faith in Him; consequently, any theology that rejects our duty to do so is therefore on some level an unbelieving and disobedient theology.

A man says that he has his dispensational charts and diagrams which prove we are living in the last generation. We say that if he would rather sit on the roof doing calculations than obey his Lord in subduing the earth to His glory, he had better hope that Christ doesn't come back right now. Another man says that Satan is the god of this world. "The task can't be done—Satan is too strong." But we say that the God of the Bible is stronger than any creature, including Satan, and God is the one who has given us this task. And if God has given the task, accompanied with a promise, then the task is not impossible.[25]

Still another says that an optimistic eschatology is a point of view, certainly, but there are various schools of thought on all this. He just happens to belong to the more pessimistic school of thought. But who gave any of us permission to be an eschatological pessimist? Not Jesus Christ. He said that all authority in heaven and on earth was His, and that our job was to disciple the nations. He wasn't giving us something to shoot for; He was giving us something to *do*.[26]

Yet another says there is not enough time. Christ is coming back any moment, and the task of evangelizing the world before then is hopeless. But it is not hopeless. We have enough time to do what He commanded, and He commanded us to bring the message of His salvation to the world effectually. We are to do more than *tell* the nations; we are to disciple them, baptizing and teaching obedience. And the job is to be done, not attempted.

We do not have the authority to disobey Christ for the sake of an unbelieving systematic theology. Several very popular systematic theologies (dispensationalism and amillennialism) say that effective world evangelization is impossible, while Christ says that world evangelization is our duty. The one we follow is the real authority in our lives, and in this case, we can't follow both. It is not fashionable to speak in this way. We live in an age when it is considered rude to speak the plain truth, but the plain ungarbled word is what we need. Christ is King, not our theologies, and our task is to proclaim His advancing and invincible kingdom throughout the world.

Mark it well: the point is not that every detail of eschatological chronologies is a matter of obedience and disobedience. This is not a question of chronological *detail*. It is a matter of attitude and submissive

---

[25] David Brown, *Christ's Second Coming* (Grand Rapids, MI: Baker Book House, 1983).

[26] David Chilton, *Paradise Restored* (Tyler, TX: Reconstruction Press, 1985).

obedience. The Scripture promises a glorious future for the progress of the gospel throughout the world; consequently, pessimism about the Church's future is sin — the sin of unbelief. As a corollary, any method of interpretation that results in such pessimism is also sin. Bad trees bear bad fruit. In this case an unbelieving theology bears unbelieving fruit.

What has Christ told us to do? He has told us to make the Christian faith the faith of the entire earth. Because it is His command, *this* issue is one of obedience or disobedience. We have no authority to transfer the responsibility for accomplishing this back to Him. That is, we have no right to say the world will be brought to Him after the Second Coming, but not before. He tells us to refrain from adultery. Do we have the right to interpret Scripture in such a way as to make this only our responsibility after the Second Coming? Of course not. In a similar way, He has commanded us to subdue the earth through the preaching of the gospel. We do not have the authority to say the task is impossible until after He comes back. It is our assigned responsibility *now*.

The question is really a very simple one. We must ask ourselves this: Do we believe that the Great Commission will be fulfilled by the Church of Jesus Christ, with the nations discipled, baptized, and obedient as a result? *Yes or no?* If *yes*, then the task of world evangelization awaits us. If *no*, we must remember that duties do not disappear because of disobedience. Sin or no sin, the same task awaits us, but with sin to confess first.[27]

And this leads to the next point, which is that reformed evangelicals must be experimental. This word *experimental* does not mean that we should operate on a system of trial and error. Rather, we should take the word *experimental* in its older sense, that of practical applied obedience to the requirements of God's Word. In Scripture an emphasis on doctrine does not exclude a concern for righteous living and practical obedience (Rom. 6:2). Our churches must therefore seek to follow the scriptural pattern of setting a solid theological doctrinal foundation, upon which the saints will be exhorted to build in various practical ways — in their families, businesses, communities, etc. This process of edification will exhibit a concern for personal holiness in the lives of all who profess faith in the Lord Jesus Christ (Heb. 12:14). Personal holiness must begin with individuals, but it does not end there. We must affirm the need for personal holiness to affect the proper ordering of our corporate life together as well as our individual lives.[28] It is too easy to follow the Pharisees, who sat in Moses' seat and mouthed his words, and at the same time refused to obey what they mimicked (Mt. 23). Be-

[27] Arthur Hermon, *The Idea of Decline in Western Culture* (New York: The Free Press, 1997).
[28] J.C. Ryle, *Holiness* (Greensboro, NC: The Homiletic Press, 1956).

cause the elders of the church are required to set an example for the people of God in this regard, we must emphasize the practical qualifications for eldership set forth in Scripture (1 Tim. 3:1–7; Tit. 1:5–9). These qualifications are primarily concerned with the character of the elder concerned. But while character must be emphasized, in no way should it be set against other requirements; the ministry of the church must be educated and exhibit doctrinal maturity, particularly in the teaching ministry. But strictly speaking, dead orthodoxy does not exist. A man who truly understands the teaching and doctrine of Scripture will exhibit a godly character. Consequently, we seek to keep the emphasis where Scripture places it — on the required godly character for elders (1 Pet. 5:1–4).[29]

Reformed evangelicals are also confessional. We do not set aside the great historic confessions of the Christian church. Reformed evangelicals affirm the key doctrines of the Christian faith found in the Apostles' Creed. We confess our faith in the triune God of Scripture, also witnessed at Nicea. We affirm the divine and human natures of our one Savior Jesus Christ articulated at Chalcedon.[30] We also affirm the system of doctrine in the great confessions of the Reformation. With these affirmations, we are not claiming that these confessions of faith are infallible, or binding on the conscience of the individual Christian. Still less do we place them on the level of Scripture, which is our only ultimate and infallible rule of faith and practice.

We recognize that qualification for membership in our churches does not require a full agreement with the confessional standards of our churches. The doctrinal standard for membership in a Christian church should be a biblical confession that Jesus is Lord, coupled with a Christian manner of life. The confessional stand of our churches should represent our standard for *teaching*, and not our standard for *membership*. We must have fellowship with as many as the Lord Jesus has fellowship with — the standard to join a church must never be higher than the confessional requirement to be included in Christ's Church.

Because these confessions and creeds are an historical indication of the faithfulness of God in bringing His church into an increasing knowledge of the truths contained in Scripture, our churches as churches need to make our confession in this manner.

Further, we understand that as the Church continues to grow and mature, the need for further confessions of faith in the coming centuries will be apparent. These future confessions will not only address issues before the Church that have not yet been addressed confessionally, but

---

[29] John Armstrong, *Can Fallen Pastors Be Restored?* (Chicago: Moody, 1995).
[30] For a wonderful treatment of the importance of these councils, see Rousas John Rushdoony, *The Foundations of Social Order* (Fairfax, VA: Thoburn Press, 1968).

they will also correct some of the mistakes which crept into the older creeds and confessions. While we should see the need for this to be done, we must acknowledge that the Church of the present day is very ill-equipped to make any such corrections now. The need that confronts us at the present day is reformation and recovery of lost ground. We are not competent to set our betters straight, even at those places where we know that they erred. That task must await a more mature Church in the years to come. In the meantime, we reject any attempt to use these trivial blemishes as a basis for overturning the great central scriptural truths exhibited in these confessions. We therefore affirm the need for a sub-missive, but critical, historic confessionalism. If the Lord is willing, per-haps the critical work we do now may lay the groundwork for future generations of the church.[31]

Reformed evangelicals are also covenantal. God has given His people great and precious promises, but He has not given them to us as isolated individuals. His promises are to us, and to our children after us (Acts 2:39). We gather in the presence of the Lord household by household, generation after generation (Acts 16:15; Lk. 1:50). We, therefore, affirm, with much gratitude, the doctrine of covenantal succession.[32]

We acknowledge that our children are born into this world in need of Christ. We do not assume that mere entry into a Christian home is automatically sufficient to secure a child's entry into the kingdom of heaven. Such presumption has sealed the damnation of far too many. At the same time, the Bible teaches that our children are covenantally holy and are to be brought up in the nurture and admonition of the Lord (1 Cor. 7:14; Eph. 6:1–3). When this is done by faithful and believing par-ents according to His Word, we expect our children, and their children's children after them, to follow us in serving and loving the Lord Jesus Christ. This is given in Scripture as the normal pattern for God's cov-enant people.

Reformed evangelicals must therefore exhort the members of their churches to bring up their children in homes characterized by a gracious love for Christ and to provide a biblical education for these children (Deut. 6:4–9; Eph. 6:4). Because the leaders of our churches are required to set a scriptural example, all the children of all elders and deacons must be brought up to love the Lord Jesus Christ. We share Paul's conviction, and submit to his requirement, that elders have well-disciplined and believing children. In the modern evangelical church,

---

[31] O. Palmer Robertson, *The Christ of the Covenants* (Phillipsburg, NJ: Pres-byterian & Reformed, 1980).

[32] Robert Rayburn, "The Presbyterian Doctrines of Covenant Children, Cov-enantal Nurture, and Covenantal Succession.", *http://www.faithtacoma.org/covenant2.htm.*

this is one of the most widely disregarded portions of Scripture, and we believe that the reformation of the Church must in large measure begin here (1 Tim. 3:4–5).[33]

Reformed evangelicals also emphasize the importance of history. We affirm the doctrinal importance of Church history, in particular the importance of understanding God's redemptive and covenantal purposes throughout all history—and not just the portion of history recorded for us in inspired Scripture. However, without an inspired account, we must be exceedingly cautious in how we interpret Church history. This means that we must turn to Scripture for a theological framework in seeking to understand the flow of Church history.[34]

So we affirm the doctrine of a visible historical Church. The Lord made a covenant with Abraham and thus clearly began His practice of dealing with a visible Church before an unbelieving world (Gen. 17:7). We have an inspired history of this Church down through most of the first century A.D. The Lord Jesus was born in the reign of Augustus and was crucified under the Roman governor Pilate. The context of this time should be of great interest to us.[35] After his resurrection and ascension, He renewed His Church through a new covenant with her and sent it out into the world (Acts 1:8). What happened to that Church after the closure of the canon of Scripture—its triumphs and defeats, its corruptions and reformations—is of great interest to us.

We cannot separate ourselves from this history; we must, therefore, hold the mirror of the Word up against the history of the Church so that we might understand it. Such an examination reveals that God is true to His Word, though every man is a liar. When God worked with His Church in the days Scripture was being written, we see His chastisement for the grossest corruptions, as well as His blessing in the great reformations. As we examine the Church since the time of the apostles, we should expect to see the same kind of thing—heresies, immoralities, apostasies, doctrinal corruptions, and wonderful reformations.

The common desire among evangelicals to have a "New Testament church" is often nothing more than a desire to pretend as though the last two thousand years has not really happened. Nevertheless, the fruit of certain great battles of Church history is quietly enjoyed without knowing where it came from (the canon of Scripture, the doctrine of the Trinity, etc.).

Others who seek to emphasize their connection with the early Church often make an historical error as well—they fail to understand the im-

---

[33] Douglas Wilson, *Standing on the Promises* (Moscow, ID: Canon Press, 1997).

[34] R.L. Dabney, *Discussions: Evangelical and Theological, Vol. I* (Carlisle, PA: Banner of Truth, 1967, [1891]), pp. 5–25.

[35] Suetonius, *The Twelve Caesars* (Cambridge, MA: Harvard University Press, 1913).

portance of corporate sanctification throughout the course of our history. God not only saves His Church in history, calling her out from the world; He also *sanctifies* the Church over the course of history. And of course, sanctification is the process of removing sin. This means that it is necessary to understand the course of Church history and to apply consistently one of the great cries of the reformation — *semper reformanda* — always reforming. The historical Church grows and matures over time. This explains how the early Church could be used by God to accomplish some very great things, and how the Church at the same period of time could have tolerated some very dangerous errors.

Until the end of history, the Church will always be characterized by reformations. We are accustomed to use the term "reformed" with sole reference to the reformation of the corruptions in the papacy in the sixteenth and seventeenth centuries. That reformation was a very important period in Church history, and the gains made at that time should in no respect be set aside. At the same time, new issues will always arise, as well as "new" variant corruptions of the old issues. We seek to understand this principle, apply it to our churches, and pray for other churches do the same.

Reformed evangelicals are presbyterial and representative in their understanding of ecclesiastical government.[36] We hold that God has established His Church, and that He has required us to govern His Church according to the general pattern set before us in His Word. We do not hold that a church is necessarily absent if any of these features of biblical church government are absent. We distinguish the *esse* of a church (its being) and the *bene esse* of a church (its well-being).

The existence of a Christian church is the result of the sovereign work of the Holy Spirit in bringing people together around the preaching and teaching of the Word, along with a scriptural use of the sacraments of baptism and the Lord's Supper. Moreover, such a church is maintained over time when the Word and ordinances are protected and kept through a doctrinal and moral church discipline. These things taken together, constitute the esse of the church. A church may be mistaken on matters of church government (as well as many other secondary issues) and still be a true church of Christ. Nevertheless, we do hold that a form of scriptural church government is necessary for the *bene esse* of the church.

The central principle of sound church government is a practical recognition of the headship of the Lord Jesus Christ. The church is managed by *stewards*, called by Christ to this task, but they must never think the church belongs to them, or is in any way owned by them. Still less may they give allegiance to another head over the church, whether that

[36] David Hall, *Paradigms in Polity* (Grand Rapids, MI: Eerdmans, 1994).

head is political or ecclesiastical. Christ is the only Head of the church, thus excluding all popes, kings, patriarchs, or senior pastors from that position (Eph. 5:23).

The headship of Jesus Christ over the church has a very practical application in issues of reformation. If a church is a Christian church at all, this means that it does not "have a right" to its own doctrinal traditions. The headship of Christ means that He is the final authority, and He has set down His requirements in the Scriptures. So if a church names the name of Christ, then it has an obligation to conform its teachings and practices to the requirements of Scripture. It is not possible to say, for example, that "this denomination" was founded in the conviction that it is possible for a true saint "to lose his salvation." The fact that this teaching was present at the denomination's founding does not justify continuing in that error — precisely because the church is a true Christian church. Christ is the Head, and not the founding denominational fathers.

Another important principle is that the highest authority in each local church should consist of a session of elders. The Bible requires this plurality of elders. The idea of a church being ruled by a solitary individual is foreign to Scripture (Tit. 1:5). Moreover the Bible teaches that there is parity among elders *with regard to the rule* of the church. However, there will not be parity of pastoral gifts, teaching abilities, and leadership abilities. Within the eldership, some of the men will be gifted by God and set apart for distinct official callings — some to preaching, some to teaching — but in the governance of the church, *as rulers*, they all stand on an equal footing.[37]

These elders are selected for their office by the people of God. In the choices made for the leadership of the church, the Bible requires popular representation (Acts 6:3; 14:23). In churches, voting for church office should be done representatively, i.e., the head of each household casts a vote representing his family. When the church officers have been selected by the people, they are ordained to office by the existing eldership through the laying on of hands (1 Tim. 4:14). When the office in question concerns the ministry of the Word, the labor of word and doctrine, the ministers of other congregations should be involved in the process. In the multitude of counselors there is wisdom.

Sometimes disputes or disciplinary problems may arise within a local congregation which cannot be resolved at the local level. In such situations, the Bible provides for the means of appeal to the wisdom of the broader Church. No one church should seek to remain an independent island church, separate from other Christian churches (Acts 15:1–35). Just as the dispute at Antioch was settled in Jerusalem, so we expect

---

[37] Mark Brown, *Order in the Offices* (Duncansville, PA: Classic Presbyterian Government Resources, 1993).

that our individual churches will encounter situations where the wisdom and authority of the broader Church should be sought.

Related to this, reformed evangelicals emphasize unity in the universal Church. We are required by Scripture to acknowledge the universal Church, and acknowledge as true Christian churches every congregation which faithfully holds to the Word of Christ, and which faithfully administers the sacraments of baptism and the Lord's Supper. We therefore believe that we are required to join in Christian fellowship with any individuals or churches whom we believe to be in fellowship with Christ, and it is a duty to be embraced gladly (Eph. 4:3). We hold to the unity of the saints.

At the same time, we also hold that the requirements for fellowship and the qualifications for leadership are quite distinct. A concern for the purity of the Church requires that we refrain from endorsing any substantive doctrinal compromise (Tit. 3:10–11). Given the current state of the Church, this means that reformed evangelicals are regrettably unable to join together with other Christian churches in many cooperative ventures. Nevertheless, we affirm that we have a duty to come together with other Christian churches in every situation which would not require a compromise with sin.

Reformed evangelicals seek to recover a good understanding of what it means to be puritanical. And the first thing which must be said concerns this use of the word *puritanical*. When God's people are faithful to His Word, He promises that they will be slandered — a servant is no greater than his master (Mt. 10:24). It is hard to conceive of a better example of this truth than the case of those Christians in history called the Puritans. But as we use the word *puritanical*, we are seeking to represent the Puritans as they were in the history of the Church, at their best, and not how they exist in the fevered imaginations of moderns who thought they heard something bad about the Salem witch trials.[38]

As modern Christians who seek to stand in the tradition of the early Puritans, we affirm the principle of Christian liberty. The conscience of believers may not be bound according to standards contrary to, or outside of, the clear teaching of Scripture (Col. 2:20–23). Christians have been set free by Christ and have been given, by Him, the gift of liberty of conscience. This conscience is free up to the boundaries set by Scripture and even includes the liberty of error on certain kinds of issues. If a brother with a tender conscience has scruples about such an issue unnecessarily, the Word still requires that such a brother be left in peace (Rom. 14:15).[39]

[38] For a good antidote to this bad business, read C.S. Lewis, *English Literature in the Sixteenth Century* (Grand Rapids, MI: Eerdmans, 1994), pp. 1–65, and Leland Ryken, *The Worldly Saints* (Grand Rapids, MI: Zondervan, 1986).

[39] John Van Til, *Liberty of Conscience: History of a Puritan Idea* (Phillipsburg, NJ: Presbyterian and Reformed Publishing Co., 1972).

When it comes to the worship of God, we should consider ourselves bound to limit our service to those things which the Word requires in Christian worship (Lev. 10:1). Particularly, we affirm (generally) what has been known in theological history as the regulative principle. There will be more on this later, but we may not worship God according to our own inventions, but this includes our own inventions about the meaning of the regulative principle. We do not have to affirm every application made through history in the name of the regulative principle, but we do hold that the principle is God's standard for our churches. This does not require a "bare and plain" worship, because our worship is governed by *all* of Scripture, and not just the passage concerning the deaths of Nadab and Abihu.[40]

As reformation gets underway, we will find that our churches will continue to be diverse in many ways. Some will have roots in the Jesus-people movement of the seventies. Others will have a dispensational Bible church background. Still others will have come out of the charismatic movement. In this we will see reformation in churches that have had no clear historic connection to the historic Reformed churches.

In other situations, churches with a Reformation heritage have been busy throwing it all away. In their midst, there will be some who are distressed by the steady drift of these formerly evangelical Presbyterian and Reformed communions into various kinds of compromise, and so have consequently taken a stand.

The principles which bring such disparate groups together are obviously not cultural, but rather scriptural and theological. Together we affirm these key scriptural principles stated here, and expect that they will continue to bear fruit in different cultural ways.

The need for reformation is great. We must believe that in praying for such reformation, we are praying in the will of God. We should be grateful for God's blessing on our work and trust that He will continue to add to it. As long as the need for continuing reformation exists — and we have to believe that this will be the case until the Lord raises the dead at the Last Day — we must affirm the need for churches to seek on-going ecclesiastical sanctification. We pray that God will keep these churches and individual believers with this name — *reformed evangelical* — faithful in this task for many generations.

Nevertheless, if future generations, holding to this name out of mere traditional inertia, drift away from the standard of Scripture, we take heart in knowing that the sovereign Lord of the Church will remove their lampstand as He has done in countless other cases. His Word, and His true Church, are always secure. The name can change, but the management never does.

[40] Steve Schlissel in Andrew Sandlin, ed., *A Comprehensive Faith* (Grand Rapids, MI: Eerdmans Publishing Co., 1994), pp. 53–68.

✢ CHAPTER III ✢

RECEIVE THE WORD

A Church Bible

The Church receives her identity from the Word of God. The Church is gathered around the Word of God, and in accordance with the Word of God. How the Church understands the Bible is therefore a matter of great importance. The problem is straightforward. The Church is under the authority of the Scriptures, and yet, at first glance it seems that the Church created the Bible, determining which books were canonical. So how can the Church be in true submission to something which it fashioned?

The Bible did not "just appear." In the words of the Westminster Confession, the Bible was inspired by God at the initial writing, and since that time has been preserved by His "singular care and providence." Although this supernatural book has come down to us by very natural means, as Christians we know that God is Governor of all things, and this necessarily includes those natural means and historical processes which placed His Word in our hands.

The Church of the Old Testament—that is, Israel—had the initial care of those books corresponding to them. The apostle Paul plainly says that the oracles of God were entrusted to the Jews. "What advantage then hath the Jew? Or what profit is there of circumcision? Much every way: chiefly, because that unto them were committed the oracles of God" (Rom. 3:1–2). With regard to that trust, they did their duty well. The canonical books of the Old Testament are thirty-nine in number. Our Lord referred to this canonical range when He spoke of the death of certain martyrs from the Old Testament. "That upon you may come all the righteous blood shed upon the earth, from the blood of righteous Abel unto the blood of Zacharias son of Barachias, whom ye slew between the temple and the altar" (Mt. 23:35). Abel was killed toward the beginning of the book of Genesis, the first book of the Jewish canon, and Zechariah was killed in 2 Chronicles, which was the last book as they arranged the canon. Christ is referring to all the martyrs throughout Scripture, from A to Z.

Thus our Lord excludes the books commonly called the Apocrypha. Although valuable for history and background, they had no part of the authoritative Hebrew canon. The more liberal Hellenistic Jews of Alexandria allowed those books into the Greek Old Testament, but this was not the view of the Jews who sat in Moses' seat, those to whom Christ bade us listen.

When the time of Messianic reformation came, the apostles of the Lord began to finalize the Scriptures. As they wrote, they fully expected that their words would be received and acknowledged by the Church to be the Word of God. "For this cause also thank we God without ceasing, because, when ye received the word of God which ye heard of us, ye received it not as the word of men, *but as it is in truth, the word of God*, which effectually worketh also in you that believe" (1 Thes. 2:13). Peter acknowledges that Paul's letters are Scripture (2 Pet. 3:16), and in this assumes a knowledge of the limits of Scripture with New Testament writings included. Paul does the same with the writing of Luke (1 Tim. 5:18). Now the word "Scripture" is canonically defined, i.e., without a canon, the term is meaningless. Both 2 Peter and 1 Timothy were written late, when the canon was basically complete.

This common reception of the New Testament was not challenged until the middle of the second century when a heretic named Marcion began teaching that the Old Testament was not the Word of God. According to Marcion, with the exception of Paul's letters, the New Testament was generally to be rejected as well. Now the Church had received the books of the New Testament from the first, since the first century, but had made no authoritative list, or canon, of accepted books—at least that we know of. Marcion's heresy made that necessary, so the discussions began, and in 393 at Hippo and 397 at Carthage, the Church formally testified that the twenty-seven books which we have in the New Testament are to be received as apostolic.

We receive these Scriptures on their own authority. They are the Word of *God*, and they speak to us as such. Nevertheless, God has given us a secondary earthly testimony concerning them. Martin Luther used the apt picture of Christ and John the Baptist. In no way did John bestow any authority upon Christ when he said, "Behold, the Lamb of God." At the same time, even though John's witness did not create "the Christ," his witness was still important.

In a similar way, submissively and authoritatively, the Church points to the sixty-six books of the Bible. During the Christian aeon, the Church is responsible to keep and preserve the same kind of testimony concerning the entire Bible that the Church gave in her younger years, when Israel had been entrusted with the Old Testament books.

When modern groups and sects point to other books than what God has given (e.g., Mormons and the Book of Mormon, Roman Catholics and the Apocrypha, etc.), they are exhibiting more than just their unbelief. They are also showing their radical detachment from the ancient and historical Church.

This witness is not offered by the Church as "something to think about" or as a mere "suggestion." The testimony of the Church on this point is submissive to Scripture but authoritative for the saints. For example, if a minister in a Christian church took it upon himself to add a book to the canon of Scripture, or sought to take away a book, the duty of his church would be to try him for heresy and remove him immediately. This disciplinary action is authoritative, taken in defense of an authoritative canonical settlement. This does not mean the Church is defending the Word of God; the Church is defending her witness to the Word. As the necessity of discipline makes plain, this witness is dogmatic and authoritative. It is not open for discussion. God does not intend for us to debate the canon of Scripture afresh every generation. We have already given our testimony; our duty now is to remain faithful to it.

Not surprisingly, this relates to the much-vexed question of Bible translations. When a young Christian walks into a Christian bookstore to buy a Bible, he is probably unaware of the debate which surrounds his search for a translation. To the extent he is aware of some controversy on the subject, he is likely to interpret it as a collision between a small tribe of mindless traditionalists ("If the King James Version was good enough for Paul, it's good enough for me!") and those intelligent enough to see that the Word of God must be presented in the language of the people.[1]

This is most unfortunate, because the real debate concerns the nature of God's Word and our consequent approach to it.[2] In seeking to understand this, the best place to start is at the beginning. Until the invention of the printing press in the fifteenth century, copies of the Bible were all made by hand. Consequently, all the ancient copies of the New Testament are called *manuscripts*. Most of these manuscripts are very similar, but a handful contain considerable variations.

Now when the Reformers first rejected the abuses of the Roman Catholic church, they did so on the basis of *sola Scriptura* — Scripture alone. The Catholic response to this was to begin assembling collections of all the variant textual readings of the manuscripts in what were called "polyglots." What was their point? The Reformers might want to say they believed in Scripture alone, but in which textual family was it to be

---

[1] At the same time, the anti-intellectualism of many of the KJV's defenders is completely out of step with its glorious literary heritage. See C.S. Lewis, *Literary Impact of Authorized Version* (Philadelphia, PA: Fortress Press, 1963).

[2] Theodore Letis, ed. *The Majority Text* (n.l.: Institute for Biblical Textual Studies, 1987) and Letis, *The Ecclesiastical Text* (Philadelphia: Institute for Renaissance and Reformation Biblical Studies, 1997). A brief glance will reveal my debts to Letis.

found? Without an infallible church, without experts of some kind, there was no way to tell.[3]

The Reformers answered this question, not as neutral scientists, but as confessing Christians. The Word of God, they said, was basically found in the received text, which was representative of the manuscript family containing the overwhelming number of manuscripts. The Reformers asserted this, not on the basis of some neutral science, but on the basis of faith in God's preservation of His own Word. They looked at the history of manuscript transmission *to see what God had done*; they did not look at the manuscripts to see what man had to do. For the Reformers, and for all consistent Christians, the doctrines of the Bible's inspiration and the Bible's preservation are twins. What good is an inspired Bible which no one of us has ever seen?[4]

This answer was accepted generally by evangelical scholars until the last century. At that time, those who believed in the divine inspiration of the Bible came under attack from liberal theologians and textual critics. Unfortunately, the response of evangelical scholars was similar to their response to the theory of evolution—an anemic attempt to have it both ways, i.e., continuing to believe in the Bible while accepting (to a limited extent) the new critical approach to textual studies.

As a consequence, evangelical scholars gradually came to the conviction that the science of textual criticism was in fact "a neutral science." In other words, the worldview of the textual critic and translator does not necessarily matter. The foundation stone of all the modern versions is that textual criticism is a neutral science, and that Christians and non-Christians alike can be good practitioners of this science. The difference between evangelical and liberal textual critics is that the evangelicals have sought to fight off the principles of higher criticism by using the principles of lower criticism, little realizing that the fundamental principles are the same in each case.[5]

So we must understand there are two different approaches to textual work. One expresses confidence that God has protected His Word down through history. This is a faith position—faith in God. The other presupposition says that it is up to man, through neutral, scholarly, and scientific means, to determine what the original text of the Bible was. This is a faith position too—faith in man.

The practical result of all this is that the modern versions are based

<hr />

[3] John Owen, *The Works of John Owen, Vol. XVI* (Carlisle, PA: Banner of Truth, 1968), pp. 296–421.

[4] Edward Hills, *Believing Bible Study* (Des Moines, IA: The Christian Research Press, 1967).

[5] For a hilarious application of modern textual criticism to the stories of Sherlock Holmes, see Dorothy Sayers, *Christian Letters to Post-Christian World* (Grand Rapids, MI: Eerdmans,1969).

upon a handful of texts from the third, fourth and fifth centuries, discovered (for the most part) in this century and the last. In contrast, the Authorized Version is based upon the overwhelming majority of available manuscripts, dating from as early as the fifth century and in continual use since that time. It is a choice between the eighty percent of ancient manuscripts, which are internally consistent, and the twenty percent of slightly older manuscripts, which differ considerably with one another.

Almost all modern translations are taken from an eclectic Critical Text (CT). One common form of this text for the New Testament is that published by the United Bible Societies. The text is accompanied with an apparatus which enables the student to compare all the variant readings of the manuscripts. Another popular form of the CT is the Nestle/Aland text. Virtually all modern translations of the Bible come from some form of the CT. There is no set form of this text, by definition, and so each translation will accept now this manuscript as reliable, and now another. The cornerstone of the CT, called by the NIV translators the "two most reliable manuscripts," are Codex Sinaiticus and Codex Vaticanus. These two manuscripts are Alexandrian in origin, and when compared to the thousands of later Greek manuscripts (belonging to the Byzantine family), are in a distinct minority.

Sinaiticus and Vaticanus are held up as the closest exemplars of what the New Testament autographs supposedly contained. But they differ between themselves in the Gospels alone over 3,000 times. To applaud them therefore as the "most reliable" really means that reliability must now be an elastic term. This means scholars are not really submitting to the authority of these Alexandrian texts, but are actually using them to overthrow any idea of a settled textual authority. The problem for the scientist is not the *textus receptus*, but is really the idea of *any* received text.

At the same time, it is important to remember that antiquity of manuscripts is not really the issue here. It is like two rivers; one is hundreds of yards wide, and you are able to walk upstream for ten miles. The other is a creek ten yards wide, and you are able to go upstream for eleven miles. Nevertheless, you know that the broad river, given its breadth, must begin a lot farther upstream than you are able to go. In other words, the breadth of the received manuscript tradition shows that it is at least as old as the supposedly more ancient written tradition.

Another option is the result of scholars who have accepted the task of a scholarly reconstruction of the text but believe that the widespread acceptance of the minority readings is misguided. They have produced what is called the Majority Text (MT). A modern translation which refers to the MT in its marginal notes is the New King James Version

(NKJV). In other words, they have come up with a traditional answer but with a suspect, modern method.[6]

The third textual option is to use what is called the textus receptus or Received Text (TR). The TR is a collation of readings taken from the majority Byzantine texts, which readings were gathered in the transition between manuscripts and printing. The early collators were men like Erasmus, Beza, Stephens, and in the last century, Scrivener. Variations exist between these texts, but they are a mere handful compared to the thousands of variants in the CT. The Authorized Version is based upon the TR, and consequently the TR remains the true "majority" text— although the plethora of modern translations has challenged that position within the last generation.

So the earliest complete manuscripts belong to a different manuscript family than do the thousands of later manuscripts which are scattered around the ancient world in multitudes, and which were in common use down to the invention of the printing press. But when we consider the facts carefully, nothing is more apparent than that this is actually a battle of the paradigms. In some respects, this is very much like the reconstruction of the evolutionary fossil tree, 98 percent of which is missing. When we consider all the manuscripts we possess, we must still compare them to the number of all the manuscripts ever written— which we do not have. The reconstruction of the autographic text is a task *outside the competence of science*, and any attempt to submit the task to scientific canons will only result in increasing confusion. A process of scholarly reconstruction here makes sense only when undergirded with faith in the living God who controls the flow of all historical events. If, in order to be "scientific," we eliminate this God from our considerations, the end of the road will be no text at all, or radical confusion about the text. The autonomous text critic is someone who believes that this problem of the original text is one which admits of a scientific solution, or worse, that there is no solution. But the real solution to this problem is faith in God, and in His providential care for His Word.

Of course, we should not be surprised that this ongoing confusion and debate about the original text has resulted in a less than scrupulous approach to translation. After all, the acceptance of lower criticism means that the *details* of the text are up for discussion. For the most part, modern translations, in the name of getting the "idea" across, are notoriously sloppy about getting what God actually said across. In contrast, in the Authorized Version the translators were very strict about translating every word. And where, for the sake of sense, it is necessary to add a word not in the original, that word was put in italics so that the reader

---

[6] Hodges and Farstaad, *Majority Text?* (Grand Rapids, MI: Eerdmans, 1994). See also Pickering, *The Identity of the New Testament Text* (Nashville, TN: Thomas Nelson Pub., 1977, 1980).

could see that it was added. Because it is a strict translation, such italicized words are kept at a minimum.

So this brings us to translation issues.[7] The phrases we use today to discuss our differences over translation philosophy are *formal equivalence* and *dynamic equivalence*. The way we cast the debate, the formal equivalence school wants to reflect the original languages in English as closely as can be done. The dynamic equivalence school is content to render the idea of the passage in the contemporary idiom. In short, the difference is between a strict approach to translation, and a loose one. Obviously these two phrases represent two poles, between which we find a continuum, with a distinct translation possible at every point. A paraphrase is on the far end of dynamic equivalence. A strict translation sticks as close to the original as it can, and when forced to insert words in order to make good English sense, those words are italicized to mark them for the English reader.

We are not the first to discuss these issues, and the more refined terminology coming out of the Reformation era can be a great help. On this question, we have to distinguish material and verbal authority. A phrase to remember here is *authoritas divina duplex*, which means "twofold divine authority." We must come to see the authority of Scripture in two senses. The first is *authoritas rerum* — the authority of the "things" of Scripture, the substance of the text. This authority pertains to the text of Scripture in the original languages, and also to accurate translations of that original.[8]

As Christians, we also believe in verbal inspiration, which means we must hold to *authoritas verborum*, the authority of the words of Scripture. But this authority belongs only to the text in its original form, in the original languages. The *authoritas verborum* is an external and "accidental" authority which always falls away necessarily in the process of translation. No translation, however good, is capable of preserving this authority. The historic Protestant position is that a good translation of the Scripture preserved the authority of Scripture with regard to the substance of the text (*quoad res*). The same cannot be said with regard to the words of the text itself (*quoad verba*).

This means that the words of an English translation, even a good one, do not carry inspired *verbal* authority. But if the English translation is poorly done, it does begin to adversely affect the material authority. For example, the English word *world* in Jn. 3:16 has material authority, but not verbal authority. In order to grasp the verbal authority, we have to see and understand the Greek word *kosmos*. If the word *kosmos* were

---

[7] Robert Martin, *Accuracy of Translation* (Edinburgh: The Banner of Truth Trust, 1989).

[8] Richard Muller, *Dictionary of Latin and Greek Theological Terms* (Grand Rapids, MI: Baker Book House, 1985).

translated into English poorly, say, as *shopping mall*, the translation would lose its material authority as well.

All these distinctions are necessary in order to remember that a strict formal equivalence translation is not an attempt to acquire strict verbal authority for a translation (which cannot be done), but rather to preserve material authority for that translation. This is because material authority can be forfeited or greatly diminished whenever the translation is done poorly. Given the nature of language, material authority could be lost in one fell swoop (e.g., translating *kosmos* as *toaster oven*), or it could be lost by gradations (e.g., translating *kosmos* as *land*).

Our acceptance of English translations does not mean that verbal authority is unimportant to us. On the contrary, this is why the historic Protestant position held that the ministers of churches were to be skilled in the original languages. No church should be without access to the full verbal authority of the Word of God.

When we take this criterion and apply it to various translations, we get a mixed bag. Versions like the Living Bible and the NIV have not lost material authority, but have significantly damaged it. But because of "dynamic equivalence," the popular NIV feels very free to insert many words to convey what the translators believed to be the "sense," and the inserted words are not marked in any way. They have also felt free to omit, without any indication, many words in the original. At the very least, we can say that the NIV approach to the Bible's inspiration (as indicated by how it is handled) is a little fuzzy around the edges.

So through a series of complicated circumstances, we have come to the last point, which concerns the handlers or marketers of the text. We see that text of Scripture is now established by the neutral Academy, and is afterwards packaged, copyrighted, marketed and sold by hustling and enterprising entrepreneurs. The Church today has no authoritative role in the process whatever. When it comes to the Word of God, the modern Christian Church fancies herself as a shopper only — a consumer. Our collective interest in these spiritual things is simply one more itch for Adam Smith's invisible hand to scratch. We think the Church's duty is to send parishioners off to find the Bible section in the Christian gift center, right next to the case of small glass figurines, and there to make a dutiful purchase.

A more biblical vision would see the Church as guardian or custodian of the sacred text. Just as the Jews, the Church of the Old Testament, discharged their obligations with regard to the Scriptures, so should the Church under the New Covenant. What God had spoken through His prophets was entrusted to His covenant people. They had received, as part of their covenantal inheritance, the covenants, the law, and the promises (Rom. 9:4), all of which were contained for them in the Scriptures. As we saw earlier, they had been given the oracles of God

(Rom. 3:2). This is in sharp distinction from the view held by many in the modern Church, which says that the oracles of God should be committed to the scholarly unbelievers down at the University of Whatzit, and marketed by the very important suits and ties down at Zondervan and Thomas Nelson.

Contrary to what many conservatives may think, the recent dust-up over the ongoing move of the popular NIV to gender-neutrality is not really the problem. This current silliness simply illustrates one small snippet of the problem. The problem is that the Church no longer has anything to do with the administration of the oracles of God. But the *Church*, Paul says, is the pillar and ground of the truth (1 Tim. 3:15), not the pillar and ground of a greater market share. Entrusted with something precious, we were foolish enough to set it down somewhere and have now lost track of it.

We are distressed at the trendy foolishness which swirls around the Bible, but given the current custodians of the Word, what did we expect? We still do not have the confessional backbone to suggest a biblical solution. Sober-minded Christians have always objected to the way the Bible is handled by her current hawkers. "How can we get people to buy the same old thing, over and over?" wonder the suits. "I know," says one up-and-comer. "Let's keep changing it—just like Nike does with their sneakers." This is the origin of more translations than one can shake a stick at, along with ever-new and exciting packaging, like a Study Bible for Husbands with Menopausal Wives, and the Nasturtiums Who Love Them. We object, but objecting and repenting are two different things. I made the title of that particular Study Bible up, but it is getter harder and harder to satirize anything. As I write this, I am (really) looking at a full page ad for a conflation of the Gospels, marketed as *The Story of My Life as told by Jesus Christ*. The four Gospels are combined, and then put into the first person singular. "Reads like a Diary," the copywriter breathlessly informs us.

We should all be realists by now and not expect the solution to come from those who are profiteering off the problem. If a serious reform of this particular publishing travesty ever got large enough for anyone to notice it, the caterwauling of Textual Critic and Businessman, in close harmony with one another, would lead any dispassionate observer to conclude that someone had undertaken the skinning of cats with a butter knife.

But reformation always begins with the Word of God. In our case, this means a recovery of the ecclesiastical text from within the Church. Our situation is a difficult one, and the suggestions given below are therefore not necessarily ranked in any particular order.

First, the historic Protestant Church must reassert her prerogatives with regard to the keeping of the oracles of God. The rights to market the

Bible were not sold by the Holy Spirit to Rupert Murdoch, the current owner of Zondervan. How in blue blazes did Mammon get the publishing rights to the Word of God? Who was involved in the transaction, and why hasn't he been publicly flogged?

Second, the Church needs to encourage the saints to discontinue their patronage of those who perpetuate this $49.95 leather-bound trumpery. Any copyrighted-for-profit version of the Bible (with obligatory threats for excessive storage and retrieval) should be rejected out of hand.

Third, we should pray and labor for a new ecclesiastical translation (or revision) of the Bible. This translation and work should begin with the last true ecclesiastical version we had, which was the Authorized Version (popularly known as the King James). At one stroke this would set right the three principle issues involved: the ecclesiastical (the Church distributing Scripture, as opposed to, say, the devil), the textual (the *textus receptus* as opposed to the tossed salad "who's-to-say?" variant readings we get now), and the translational (formal equivalence vs. dynamic equivalence).

Now it is acknowledged that a good translation also has to go successfully into the receiving language. This is one place where the AV does require some continued revision. The AV was revised regularly up until 1769, and that process should continue. *He speaketh* does not represent the original any more successfully than *he speaks*, and for many contemporary readers, it does take away from its accessibility — accessibility which is faithful to the original is the point of translation. In a good translation no good reason exists for keeping that language. The much reviled *thees* and *thous*, however, do reflect the original better. Greek has a distinction between the singular and plural forms of *you*, which contemporary English does not have. *Thee* is not a special form for talking to God; *thou* and *thee* are the singular form, and *you* and *ye* are the plural. Readers of the AV have access to the original at this point which readers of other translations do not have.

Fourth, the portion of the Church involved with the recovery of the Bible should repudiate, in the strongest possible terms, the Glassy-Eyed Defenders of the King James Version, who are very popular in certain fundamentalist circles. Such know-nothingism has been one of the principle reasons why the Bible-mongers have been able to get away with rejecting the ecclesiastical text without any serious argument.

Fifth, the Church should approach the task of recovery and reformation with considerable cheerfulness. After all, the whole thing is kind of obvious, once you think about it.

Tradition and the Word

As soon as we maintain that our trust in the Word has as its foundation a belief that God has providentially protected the manuscript tradition, this leads us to directly consider the role of tradition in our faith. After all, the Table of Contents in our Bibles is one of the Church's first and most important confessional traditions.

So what is the relationship between the Scriptures and the various traditions of the Christian Church since the time of Jesus Christ? Anyone who has spent any time in church knows the force of inertia in all aspects of decision-making. "We've never done it that way before" has considerable persuasive power for many believers. When this process can even be seen in young churches, how much greater force does it have when older churches contemplate the change of patterns, traditions, confessions, etc., which are centuries old?

The unthinking fundamentalist wants to reduce the whole problem to a very simple equation—"just stick to the Bible." His belief is that fooling around with traditions in the first place is what caused the problem. We may call this the "tradition as demon" position.

"We don't believe in tradition. We have never believed in tradition. The founders of our denomination didn't believe in tradition. We can't start following tradition now. We have always not followed tradition." As the statements above amply demonstrate, the only consistent way to follow the "no tradition" school of thought is to abandon it. We needn't spend any time refuting a church whose tradition is that traditions are bad and evil. As the fellow once said, "We don't believe in tradition. It's contrary to our historic position."

On the other side of things, we have the "exalted tradition" contingent. The traditions of men are frankly acclaimed as the requirements of God. This may be held with doctrinal consistency, as the Roman Catholics do, or furtively, as inconsistent "strict subscriptionists" within the Reformed tradition do. This is the "tradition as monarch" school. The theory may mouth a high view of Scripture, but practically, whenever the traditions, creeds, and practices of a church cannot be brought before the bar of Scripture, then that tradition has assumed the place of Scripture. Now a church does have authority to point to the Word of God *as* the Word of God. But it has no authority to elevate the word of men to the same position.

The biblical stance may be described as "tradition as servant." The Protestant doctrine of *sola Scriptura* does not mean that Scripture is the only religious authority in the lives of Christians. Rather, *sola Scriptura* means that Scripture exhibits two characteristics which define its unique place in the rule of the Church. The Bible, and only the Bible, is the ultimate authority in the teaching and practice of the Church, and the

Bible, and only the Bible, is the only infallible authority in the teaching and practice of the church. These two elements — ultimacy and infallibility — are unique to Scripture.[9]

But notice how this leaves us with room for a necessary doctrine of subordinate spiritual authorities. The elders of a local church, Christian parents bringing up children in the fear of the Lord, and convocations of theologians three centuries ago are all lawful authorities, deputized as such in Scripture. They have the authority to teach and make decisions. They do not do so infallibly, and they are not ultimate. God's deacons, God's ministers, are never God's replacements, but they are in fact His servants. Appeal can and should be made beyond them when necessary. But the fact that a case may be appealed beyond them to an ultimate infallible authority does not mean that the initial authority is no authority.

Still less does it mean that these subordinate authorities can get nothing right. A fallible authority is not defined as one that is wrong all the time. This is a good thing, as it turns out, for it is the fallible teaching authority of the historic Church which pointed us to the canon of Scripture. A fallible Church made an infallible (true) judgment when it determined the boundaries of the canon. In the same way, John the Baptist, a sinful man, pointed accurately to Christ, the sinless One. The Church, a fallible authority, has accurately pointed to the infallible and ultimate canon of Scripture.

If there is no room for this tradition, the tradition of the Church pointing away from herself to a final Word, then the modern fundamentalist is not left alone with his Bible. He has no Bible.

One of the reasons why the practical authority of Scripture has declined in the Protestant church is that we have not really understood the nature of that authority. The cry of "Scripture alone," misunderstood as it is, does not eliminate our traditions. It just makes them hard for us to see. A modern church cannot base everything it does on "Scriptures solitaire" without any reference to the testimonies of the historic Church. For one of the central testimonies which the Church has given, and which the historic Protestants continue to give, is that the sixty six books of the Bible are the only ultimate and infallible Word of God. Take that testimony away, and you are left with various lone individuals clutching at a leather-bound book for some mysterious reason. Better not ask them why — that would be asking for their private tradition, and traditions are bad.

Tradition is what the church necessarily hands down to subsequent generations. An essential part of that tradition must be a definition of the ultimate and infallible standard which will serve as the only

---

[9] Ibid., p. 224

criterion for judging the rest of the traditions. And the only tradition which gives that place of honor to *sola Scriptura* is that of the historic Protestant faith.

The Final Word

But ancient traditions of the Church are not the only possible threat to the purity of the Word of God. Another danger is that of new revelation, hot off the press. The men of the Westminster Assembly were certainly alive to this danger when they declared the ultimacy of Scripture. Not only was the Bible senior to "all decrees of councils" and "opinions of ancient writers" but it was also senior to "private spirits." We are to accept the Bible as it is, they said, not adding anything at any time, whether by "new revelations of the Spirit" or "traditions of men." Renegade traditions provide one temptation, but in modern evangelical circles, a pressing problem is created by those who claim that God continues to give revelation. The concern here is not really about worship styles, but rather about the integrity of the Scriptures.

More than a few pastors have wondered whether they are being theologically dishonest in saying that the "sign gifts" are no longer operative in the church today. True, the charismatic movement gives us great reason to be suspicious, and it is a pleasure to be prejudiced and bigoted sometimes, especially when Benny Hinn is involved, but do we not have to admit that such charismatic goings-on were present in the Church of the New Testament? Well, no.[10]

The question goes far beyond the fact of charismatic excesses. The central issue in all of this is the preservation of the doctrine of *sola Scriptura*. The only ultimate and infallible authority in all matters of faith and practice is contained in the sixty-six books of the Bible. If the miraculous gifts are in any way acknowledged, then the doctrine of *sola Scriptura* must necessarily be abandoned. This does not mean that everyone does abandon it who should, only that logical consistency demands it.

The easiest way to illustrate this is to consider the office of prophet, and the nature of prophecy. What happens when someone stands up in a church service and prophesies? He says, in effect, "Thus says the Lord," and then a message follows. A man who hears these words and believes them is obligated to treat the words he heard *as the Word of God*. The only way for him to contradict this is by saying that he believes them to *be* words from God but for some reason he does not really have to treat them *as* words from God. But this is contradictory.

---

[10] See B. B. Warfield, *Counterfeit Miracles* (Edinburgh: The Banner of Truth Trust, 1972 [1918]). See also John MacArthur, *Charismatic Chaos* (Grand Rapids, MI: Zondervan Publishing Co., 1993).

When I have offered this objection in the past, the answer has frequently been an appeal to the lost prophecies of Philip's daughters, or
something else in a similar category. In other words, the Bible tells us
that some prophecies from God did not make it into Scripture, and so
therefore not all prophecies from God have to be considered Scripture.
But this misses the point of the objection.

Of course, the words of God can be disposed of by God. If He gave a
word through one of Philip's daughters which He did not want to be
included in Scripture, then He may obviously do what He pleases with
His own words. The point being made here is that we may not do as we
please with His words. A man who has received these words as from
God has no basis for treating them differently from other words from
God (contained in Scripture) unless God sovereignly intervenes.

As long as a man has in his possession words which he believes are
inspired by God, then he has a moral responsibility to treat them as
though they are words inspired by God. This means he has no consistent basis for treating them any differently from the words of Scripture.
Furthermore, on a practical level, he has certain clear inducements to
pay closer attention to them than to the words of Scripture. Jeremiah
lived a long time ago, he spoke a different language, his culture was very
different from what we have to deal with. And now here, in this church
service, God has given us a word in English, in our time, and in our
surroundings. Which is the more relevant of the two?

Charismatic believers can be divided into two groups, corresponding to two responses to this objection. The first group agrees with the
reductio posed here, and runs with it. These are the groups which have a
prophecy of the week posted on the bulletin board, and every so often
they publish the Bible II, and then the Bible III. These groups are cultic,
and we need not concern ourselves with them, except for purposes of
evangelism.

But the other group does not like this dilemma when it is presented
to them. Because they are genuine Christians, they know that the Bible is
unique. However, because of this false and destructive doctrine of continuing revelation, they have no way of consistently maintaining that
the Bible is unique. Fortunately, they are better Christians than logi-
cians, and so they just live with the contradiction. This is not hard,
because it is rarely pointed out to them. But the fact that they are sincere
Christians does not remove the danger they have created. A man should
fear when his convictions, faithfully followed out to their conclusion,
might lead him to abandon the Christian faith.

But a dilemma for the charismatics is insufficient for those who
want to ground their theology and practice in the plain teaching of
Scripture. Can the cessation of the sign gifts, the gifts bearing or

authenticating revelation, be found in the pages of the Bible?[11] In brief, the case for the cessation of sign gifts can be made in a summary fashion. In the former days, God spoke to us in various ways through the prophets, but in these last days He has spoken to us through His Son (Heb. 1:1). This Son was laid as the cornerstone, and alongside Him were the foundation stones of the apostles and prophets (Eph. 2:20–21). No other foundation can be laid other than the one which was laid, namely the Lord Jesus Christ (1 Cor. 3:11). The indicators of this foundational and apostolic authority were signs, wonders, and various miracles, all done according to the Spirit's desire and will (2 Cor. 12:12; Heb. 2:4).[12]

So the issue is not whether we like this gift or that one, or whether we are to duplicate the phenomena of the first-century church. Rather, the issue is whether we understand the nature of blueprints. No real need for doing concrete work while building the attic.

---

[11] O. Palmer Robertson, *The Final Word* (Carlisle, PA: Banner of Truth, 1990).

[12] Jim West, *The Glorious Foundation* (Sacramento: Covenant Reformed Books, 1999).

✠ CHAPTER IV ✠

THUNDER THE WORD

The Foundations of Authority

Any reformation of the church depends upon a high view of preaching. But a high view of preaching by itself, apart from a scriptural basis for that high view, will lead only to puffed-up and conceited preachers. Personal bombast and dogmatism are not the need of the hour. But neither do we need preachers who think that they are in the pulpit on the basis of their own boyish good looks — men who chat, tell anecdotes, or share. Peter tells us in the plainest possible terms that the one who speaks should do so *as the very oracles of God* (1 Pet. 4:11). How is this possible?[1]

Paul tells us that everyone who calls on the name of the Lord, on the basis of the gospel, will be saved (Rom. 10:13). He then turns to the kind of hypothetical reasoning that he loves to use. If they call on the Lord, they will be saved. But how can they call on someone they have not believed in (v. 14)? He then takes the problem a step further. How can they believe in someone when they have not heard Him? The AV renders this "*of* whom they have not heard," but it should really read "*whom* they have not heard." The verb here (*akouo*) takes the genitive, meaning in this instance that the people to be saved must believe the one they are hearing, and not someone they are hearing *about*. Put more simply, we have no reason to translate this "*of* whom they have not heard." Paul is asking how they can believe in Jesus Christ when they have not heard Jesus Christ speak to them. How can they believe the one *whom* they have not heard?

He then goes on to say something quite profound. "How shall they hear [Jesus Christ] without a *preacher*?" In the faithful preaching of the gospel, Jesus Christ Himself speaks, and when His voice is heard, true salvation comes. The word of God is our life (Deut. 8:3; 32:46–47). Paul's

---

[1] For a wonderful summary of Calvin's high view of preaching, see Ronald Wallace, *Calvin's Doctrine of Word and Sacrament* (Grand Rapids, MI: Eerdmans, 1994), pp. 82–95.

chain of thought continues on—the preachers will not be able to preach
unless they are sent (Rom. 10: 15).

Where does true faith come from? It comes by hearing the word of
God (Rom. 10:17). This does not come by hearing *about* the word of God.
God brings us to new life in this way—He uses His word, and the in-
strument in His hand is the word of truth (Jas. 1:18).[2]

Peter teaches us the same thing. We are "born again, not of corrupt-
ible seed, but of incorruptible, *by the word of God*, which liveth and abideth
for ever" (1 Pet. 1:23). We know that the word of the Lord endures forever, not at all like the grass of the field (vv. 24–25). This imperishable
seed which brings us to new life is the word of the Lord. But how does
this word get to us? "And this is the word which by the gospel *is preached*
unto you" (1 Pet. 1:25). In other words, the normal process by which this
happens is not just scriptural truth by itself, not biblical truths between
dusty covers on the shelf, but rather scriptural truth *preached*.

Now this creates a problem for us. If the Bible were simply read
aloud to nonbelievers, the content would certainly be infallible. And
when the gospel is preached, the sermon is most certainly *not* infallible.
But the Bible nevertheless tells us that it is through the fallible sermon
that the infallible word of God is designed to be heard. This means that
to read the Bible aloud to non-Christians as a normal means of evangelism would be a departure from what the Bible tells us to do for non-
Christians, which is to say, *preach* to them. This is the case even though
the reading would be "safer," and not liable to error in the way preaching is.

This pattern does not change once a man has heard the word of God
and has been converted. The preached word remains the way in which
the word of God is brought with power to men. We are generally familiar with the well-known passage in which Paul talks about the Scriptures, and we usually apply it to our discussions of inspiration. "All
scripture is given by inspiration of God, and is profitable for doctrine,
for reproof, for correction, for instruction in righteousness: that the man
of God may be perfect, thoroughly furnished unto all good works" (2
Tim. 3:16). But the central issue here is not inspiration, but rather proclamation. The *man of God* here is the *minister*, the one for whom the pastoral
epistles were written, the one who is assigned to bring the Scriptures to
bear on the lives of those who hear it. The basis of his ministry is to be the
written word of God, so that he, in preaching the word, will be equipped
to teach, reprove, correct, and so forth. The Bible is not being described

---

[2] And of course, preaching with authority is not going to happen unless
there is bedrock for that authority. D. Martyn Lloyd-Jones, *Authority* (Chicago,
IL: InterVarsity Press, 1958) and J.I. Packer, *Fundamentalism and the Word of
God* (Grand Rapids, MI: Eerdmans, 1958).

here as equipping anyone who reads it, but rather equipping the man who is called to preach to them.

Of course, nonministers are equipped by reading the Bible also, but the point is what Paul is primarily addressing in this passage. We know that ministerial preparation is the point here because of how Paul continues the exhortation in the following verses. "I charge thee therefore before God, and the Lord Jesus Christ . . . *preach the word*; be instant in season, out of season; reprove, rebuke, exhort with all longsuffering and doctrine" (2 Tim. 4:1–2). In other words, the preaching of the word is the point at which doctrine intersects with our lives, at which reproof confronts our lives, at which correction corrects. And of course, the point is not that when the Bible is read it *cannot* do this — we have all heard too many great stories from the Gideons to the contrary. But the point is that the ordinary means which God has chosen for the transformation of the world is *the preached word*. And when the word of God is faithfully preached, Christ is preaching.

This preached word is heard differently by those who are saved and those who are lost. "For the *preaching* of the cross is to them that perish foolishness; but unto us which are saved it is the power of God. For after that in the wisdom of God the world by wisdom knew not God, it pleased God *by the foolishness of preaching* to save them that believe" (1 Cor. 1:18, 21). The foolishness of *preaching* saved those who believed, and the preaching of the gospel continues to manifest itself as the power of God after conversion. But to those who perish, preaching is always held in contempt; it is foolishness. Those who believe the Scriptures should not be astounded that preaching today is held in such contempt by the modern Church. Our churches are filled with just this sort of unbelief. People today, we are told, will not sit still for preaching. And this is why we have to have drama, video, smoke, mirrors, laser displays, action!

But the hope of eternal life is manifested in the world, according to the Bible, through preaching (Tit. 1:1–3). The dead must hear the voice of the Son of God in order to be saved (Jn. 5:24–25), but we know they cannot hear it without a preacher (Rom. 10:14). This reality continues throughout the entire course of a disciple's life — every Lord's Day, every time a minister opens the Bible to speak in the name of Jesus Christ. Every Christian must follow the voice of Christ and *only* the voice of Christ. Not only does the Lord call His sheep by name, but He also leads them. "To him the porter openeth; and the sheep hear his voice: and he calleth his own sheep by name, and leadeth them out" (Jn. 10: 3).

Jesus assumes in this teaching that His voice will be heard after He is gone from the earth. After the ascension, as the gospel goes out in the earth, the voice of Jesus goes out, gathering in His sheep. "And other sheep I have, which are not of this fold: them also I must bring, and *they shall hear my voice;* and there shall be one fold, and one shepherd. My sheep hear my voice, and I know them, and they follow me" (Jn. 10:16, 27). How do His sheep hear His voice? The answer given in the Bible is that His voice is heard through the preaching of the Word. This does not neglect the role of the Holy Spirit because it is the Holy Spirit, the Spirit of Christ, who anoints the preaching and hearing of the word so that this great blessing may occur.

This blessing is not something that is true only for individuals in the first century. Throughout the history of the world, everyone who is of the truth has to hear the voice of Christ. "Pilate therefore said unto him, Art thou a king then? Jesus answered, Thou sayest that I am a king. To this end was I born, and for this cause came I into the world, that I should bear witness unto the truth. *Every one that is of the truth heareth my voice*" (Jn. 18:37).

Jesus, of course, commissioned His apostles to speak in His name. "He that heareth you heareth me; and he that despiseth you despiseth me; and he that despiseth me despiseth him that sent me" (Lk. 10:16). And in another place, "He that receiveth you receiveth me, and he that receiveth me receiveth him that sent me" (Mt. 10:40). But He did not do this so that when the last apostle died, His voice would no longer be heard. Rather, the apostles were to ordain faithful men who would continue to preach the Word (2 Tim. 2:1–2). This is the point of Paul's tremendous teaching on this in the book of Romans. The gospel will be preached in true spiritual authority until the end of the world. The authority of true preaching did not diminish after the apostolic era. The ability to write Scripture diminished — indeed, it ceased when the last apostle died. But the death of the apostles and the closure of the canon of Scripture really occurred at the *dawn* of preaching — not the dusk.[3]

We know that the apostles were authorized to speak on behalf of Jesus Christ in the writing of Scripture, and that modern preachers are not. But more is involved than what we understand as apostolic authority. When the apostles speak about their ministry to the early churches, they are frequently concerned with the preaching. "Ye know how through infirmity of the flesh *I preached the gospel* unto you at the first . . . [ye] received me as an angel of God, even as Christ Jesus" (Gal. 4:13–14). When Paul preached to the Galatians, they received him as an angel of God, as Jesus Christ Himself. The issue here is not the inspiration of the book of Galatians, but rather the authority which all true preaching brings with it. The Galatians heard Jesus Christ through the preaching. Paul says something similar about the ministry in Ephesus. "But ye

---

[3] One of the great books available to men who want to give themselves to preaching is C. H. Spurgeon, *Lectures to My Students* (Grand Rapids, MI: Zondervan Publishing House, 1954).

have not so learned Christ; if so be that *ye have heard him*, and have been *taught by him*, as the truth is in Jesus" (Eph. 4:20–21). In the teaching and preaching of Paul, Jesus Christ was teaching and preaching, and the Ephesians had heard Him.

Not surprisingly, the same thing occurred in Thessalonica. "For this cause also thank we God without ceasing, because, when ye received the word of God *which ye heard of us*, ye received it not as the word of men, *but as it is in truth, the word of God*, which effectually worketh also in you that believe" (1 Thes. 2:13). Paul is not talking here about the letter to the Thessalonians, which we receive as part of Scripture, but about his preached messages to them, which they heard. The same kind of thinking shows up in Paul's second letter to the Corinthians. "Now then we are ambassadors for Christ, *as though God did beseech you by us: we pray you in Christ's stead*, be ye reconciled to God" (2 Cor. 5:20).

When the true gospel is presented by one authorized to present it, then that individual is an ambassador of Jesus Christ and may speak in His name. This does *not* mean that when someone who is unordained shares the gospel that the word of truth has somehow become impotent. What it means is that the Scripture gives a promise of authority to those who are faithful ministers of Jesus Christ, to the extent they are faithful. And when these scriptural conditions are met, when the preacher speaks, Christ speaks.[4]

Some may object here, and say that the apostles could lay claim to inspiration and this is why they spoke of their preached messages in this way. I am not maintaining that preachers today can preach sermons that are infallible, tantamount to Scripture. Nor am I saying that pastors should be treated in their persons as though they were Jesus Christ. The point rather is that they should be regarded as Christ speaking when they faithfully discharge their office. This is determined by hearing with faith, one eye on the pulpit and the other eye on the text. When the sermon accords with the text, and it is heard with faith, then Jesus Christ has spoken to His people. This faith is essential. "For unto us was the gospel preached, as well as unto them: but the word preached did not profit them, not being mixed with faith in them that heard it" (Heb. 4:2). But the eye on the text and the eye on the preacher must both be eyes of *faith*.

Christ did not take the apostles out of the world and then throw together a makeshift church, called to make do until the Second Advent.

---

[4] Of course, faithfulness in this respect requires diligence and care. James W. Sire, *Scripture Twisting* (Downers Grove, IL: InterVarsity Press, 1976); D. A. Carson, *Exegetical Fallacies* (Grand Rapids, MI: Baker Book House, 1996); Bernard Ramm, *Protestant Biblical Interpretation* (Grand Rapids, MI: Baker Book House, 1970); Leland Ryken, *How to Read the Bible as Literature* (Grand Rapids, MI: Zondervan Publishing House, 1984).

Everything that He has done is in line with His perfect plan for the Church, which will culminate when the bride is without spot or wrinkle, or any other blemish. And He established offices in the church to bring this about. "And he gave some, apostles; and some, prophets; and some, evangelists; and some, pastors and teachers; for the perfecting of the saints, for the work of the ministry, for the edifying of the body of Christ" (Eph. 4:11–12).

We know that the word of God is powerful. We know that it is living and active. But in the modern church we need to relearn one of the great truths which was recovered in the Reformation. The word does accomplish its work. "So shall my word be that goeth forth out of my mouth: it shall not return unto me void, but it shall accomplish that which I please, and it shall prosper in the thing whereto I sent it" (Is. 55:11). But the word that goes forth is, according to God's declared plan, a word that is carried abroad in the preaching of it.

When God's people understand this, it transforms what they think about the worship service on the Lord's Day. No longer are they bound by their physical circumstances. No longer must they listen to a mere man share his opinions. Rather they ascend by faith into the heavenlies, and they worship God on the mount, and they hear His Son speak to them.

> But ye are come unto mount Zion, and unto the city of the living God, the heavenly Jerusalem, and to an innumerable company of angels, to the general assembly and church of the firstborn, which are written in heaven, and to God the Judge of all, and to the spirits of just men made perfect, and to Jesus the mediator of the new covenant, and to the blood of sprinkling, that speaketh better things than that of Abel. (Heb. 12:22–24)

There are many applications, but two are worth noting here. When a man approaches a pulpit to preach, he does not understand this doctrine if he does not in some manner tremble.[5] And those who assemble on the Lord's Day in order to hear the word need to prepare themselves to tremble in the same way.

Just One Word

This high view of preaching has consequences. Christians are people of the Word, and as a result they are people of words. They are people of the enscripturated Word, and the preached word. We love the Truth, and this is why we must necessarily love truths. The flip side of this is that

[5] John Piper, *Supremacy of God in Preaching* (Grand Rapids, MI: Baker Book House, 1990).

when a love for the Lord Jesus declines, one of the first places it manifests itself is in an obvious contempt for words. Words become little
lumps of neutral playdough, on which a dishonest heart can exercise its
creativity. But really the source of this rebellion in the little things, and
the final direction of it, is hostility to the ultimate Word.

Take the word *evangelical*. It comes from the Greek word for the gospel, *euangelion*, and has been used to describe those individuals who
held a high view of the gospel and the Scriptures which brought us that
gospel. Whatever disagreements existed among believing Christians in
the era after the Second World War, evangelicals at that time were clearly
doctrinal vertebrates of some description. But in recent decades, we have
added more than a little money to the movement, some academic respectability, a lust for influence, and the result is the widespread existence of evangelicals who think that dialogue is a verb, and a promiscuous
one at that.

The unfortunate result of all this is a fundamental dishonesty in the
use and retention of certain names. Years ago, J. Gresham Machen was
exasperated by those theological liberals who were not willing to admit
that they actually had become adherents of another religion. He wrote
his profound book *Christianity and Liberalism* to show that the two were
rival faiths, and not compatible expressions of the same faith at all.[6] But
the creedal dishonesty of liberalism ran deep, and so the good words
were kept, and the guardians of the substance of those words were banished. This same dishonesty is operative today and manifest throughout the evangelical world.

A corrupt hermeneutic is rarely brought to the Scriptures *first*. Those
who want to twist Scripture have to fend off the possibility of any insti-
tutional discipline while they do so, and so they scramble to keep themselves wrapped in the good words. This is why the right to continue to
call oneself an evangelical is quietly assumed, all while denying the
heart, soul, and center of evangelicalism.

A sound hermeneutic of anything can never be sustained without
discipline. If a man wants a garden full of weeds, he does not need to do
a thing. If a man wants his ability to play the piano to get rusty, he needs
to do nothing. And if a church wants its lampstand removed, in a fallen
world, all that is necessary is a little more standing around. A sound
hermeneutic does not and cannot protect itself. Words and names are
protected by honest men or they are neglected by careless men. In the
modern evangelical world, virtually all our words are in the hands of
the careless.

Consider the advertising blurb for a recent non-Christian book,

[6] J. Gresham Machen, *Christianity and Liberalism* (Grand Rapids, MI:
Eerdmans, 1923).

being marketed as a Christian book by a very brazen former evangelical
publishing house. "Many will find things to disagree with in this book,
but everyone should agree that it has significantly raised the level of
discussion." The book in question promotes a new "openness of God"
theology, one which maintains that God does not know the future, thus
enabling Him to be more "relational" — more of a contemporary god.[7]

     Now why would we want to obey the exhortation implied in this
blurb? Did Ireneaus want to raise the level of discussion with the
Gnostics? Did Athanasius want to conduct a cooperative and helpful
dialogue with the Arians? Because the possibility of any kind of creedal
discipline is negligible in our day, those who have abandoned the gospel are now openly seeking to make their distinctives into negotiable
items, and want to be held by all as being "within the pale." Thus we do
not have to agree with them, but we do have to agree to disagree, and to
do so as fellow evangelicals. They do not resist disagreement; in fact,
they welcome it. But the disagreement must come in the form of continuing dialogue, and not in the form of showing them to the door.[8]

     One of the most astounding things about all this is the fact that there
is so little controversy about it in the evangelical world. Our complacency shows nothing more clearly than how cold our love has grown. If
a man were to see his wife being attacked by rapists, all his professions
of love and deep concern are meaningless unless he fights for her. Under such circumstances, a refusal to fight does not stem from a love of
peace, but rather from the now-revealed contempt he has for his wife. In
the same way, a refusal to discipline is nothing but a manifestation of
contempt for that which we refused to protect through the needed discipline. Bringing us back to the point, a refusal to fight over the meaning of
words betrays, ultimately, a contempt for the Savior. Of course we need
fewer church fights over the replacement for the choir director, or the
color of the carpet in the fellowship hall. But we need many *more* church
fights over the meaning of some precious and important words.

     Until we have them, we must begin to realize that modern
evangelicals have become nothing but theological liberals in a varied
guise. Some of them are willing to deny the faith once delivered to the
saints, and the others, more numerous, are willing to let them. In almost
every instance, the problem can be traced back to cowardice and timid
silence in our nation's pulpits.

---

     [7] Clark Pinnock, ed., *The Openness of God* (Downers Grove, IL: IVP, 1994).
For a reply to this foolishness, see Douglas Wilson, ed. *Bound Only Once: The
Failure of Open Theism* (Moscow, ID: Canon Press, 2001).
     [8] For a particularly fruity example of this kind of thing, see Blomberg and
Robinson, *How Wide the Divide?* (Downers Grove, IL: IVP, 1997), pp. 189–196.

A Culture's Prow

The problem, then, is the pulpit, or the place where a pulpit used to be. We live in a time when most believers have less understanding of the cultural impact of preaching than did some unbelievers of another era. For example, Herman Melville once wrote, "What could be more full of meaning? — for the pulpit is ever this earth's foremost part; all the rest comes in its rear; the pulpit leads the world. From thence it is that the storm of God's quick wrath is first descried, and the bow must bear the earliest brunt. From thence it is that the God of breezes fair or foul is first invoked for favourable winds. Yes, the world's a ship on its passage out, and not a voyage complete; and the pulpit is its prow."[9]

Since the resurrection of Christ it has been the case that the Church, in some fashion, leads the world. Christ put His city on the hill, not in the valley, and the light on the lampstand, not under the bushel. Sadly, this does not mean that blessings automatically abound. It means, among other things, that when the Church is in a spiritual declension, the salt is good for nothing but to be trampled upon by men. But even this trampling is an example of how the condition of the Church determines and directs the behavior of unbelievers. Time to trample. When the Church is blessed with a season of reformation and renewal, the world expectantly awaits the messengers of the evangel and listens to the Church respectfully. So for better and for worse, the Church has an inescapable position of influence in the world.

But as the Church sets the agenda for the world, we must further acknowledge that the condition of the pulpit sets the direction of the Church. And this explains quite a bit about the present day. George Whitefield once said that the churches of his time were dead because dead men preached to them.[10] We may expand the observation. The churches today are effeminate because effeminate men with wireless mikes and cardigan sweaters stroll around a platform chatting with the congregants in a nonthreatening and relational way. The churches are leaderless because we are nervous about prophetic preaching, and settle instead for bland and balanced leadership teams. The churches have no sense of the numinous because men refuse to preach the greatness and glory of the living God.

While speaking of the true calling of the preacher, A.W. Tozer once said, "We must not imagine ourselves commissioned to make Christ

---

[9] Herman Melville, *Moby Dick* (Chicago, IL: Encyclopedia Britannica, 1994), pp. 28–30.
[10] There are some grounds for considering this an overstatement. Harry Stout, *The Divine Dramatist* (Grand Rapids, MI: Eerdmans, 1991). See also Frank Lambert, *Inventing the Great Awakening* (Princeton, NJ: Princeton University Press, 1999). Of course, these gentlemen may want to understate it.

acceptable to big business, the press, the world of sports or modern education. We are not diplomats but prophets, and our message is not a compromise but an ultimatum." Of course, some might object to quoting a writer like Tozer, a man outside the Reformed tradition, but we live in confused times. So men like Tozer might be worth half a dozen of our contemporary pretty boys, men who subscribe to the Westminster Confession because they think they might have read it once.[11]

The point of preaching is never to make Christ acceptable. But in a man-centered era, this is automatically thought to be the task of the preacher — how to make God acceptable to man.[12] The problem which confronts us in the Bible is actually quite different. The real problem is one of sin, and how to make sinful man acceptable to a holy God. With this as the true problem, the solution, one which once made the holy angels stop their mouths, was the Incarnation, Cross, and Resurrection. That is how sinners are made acceptable to God. And how do they hear of it? The word must be preached, and preached to every creature.

But reverse the "problem," as we have, and we discover that the "solution" is necessarily reversed as well. And when the solution is reversed, we discover at the end of the day that we still have the gospel in our hands, but it is backwards and upside down. If we try to make God acceptable to sinners, we find that we are busily engaged in altering the faith once delivered to the saints. We should be preaching in such a way that sinners are altered, but never accommodated. We should be preaching in such a way that the truth is adorned, not draped in tinsel.

A thought experiment might help. Suppose for a moment that the current grand masters of secularism and unbelief sent out a fund-raising letter seeking support for a bill in Congress that would ban preaching the gospel in the churches of Christ. The ensuing controversy would be easy to imagine; we have high-volume mailing capacities of our own. The Christian world would be in an uproar, and we would all be yelling about it.

This being the case, why are we not in an uproar now? No, the ACLU and cronies have not made any such attempt. The attempt was made, and accomplished, by our *own* leaders. The gospel is not preached in our churches *now*. The secularists have not passed any such law, but the Church is out there way ahead of them. We are already in voluntary compliance. We have skits, we have synthesized muzak, we have youth ministers on unicycles, we have flag drill teams over by the baptistry (or rather, over where the baptistry used to be before we took it out), we have

---

[11] A.W. Tozer, *Knowledge of the Holy* (Lincoln, NE: Back to the Bible Broadcast, 1961).

[12] Walter Chantry, *Today's Gospel* (Carlisle, PA: Banner of Truth, 1970).

relational and helpful chats from a member of the leadership team, a member who wears a nice casual and nonthreatening sweater, and we have holytainment, but *preaching*? No, no preaching. And we wonder why the nation is in the condition it is in.

Smooth Words for Hard Hearts

Much more remains to be said on the subject of our antipathy to biblical preaching. Far from revealing an excessive tenderness, it reveals just the opposite.

We live in an era which places a high value on hardness of heart. We can tell this by our love of soft teaching. Of course this is not how we describe it inwardly. In speaking to ourselves, when we generally have a most appreciative audience, we have great affection for smooth words, words which go down easily. Jeremiah talked about this. "They have healed also the hurt of the daughter of my people slightly, saying, Peace, peace; when there is no peace" (Jer. 6:14).

We like to believe that this love of soft words, words which will trouble neither the mind nor heart, nor anything in between, is a deep love of tenderness. Such a conviction flatters us, but our love is actually the opposite of tenderness.

If our hearts were a slab of concrete, and we wanted to keep them that way, our desire to have them caressed with a feather duster would exhibit no love of tenderness, but rather the contrary. The one who really wanted a tender heart would be calling for the jackhammer. Hard words, hard teaching, are the jackhammer of God. It takes a great deal to break up our hard hearts, and the God of all mercy is willing to do it. But He always does it according to His Word, and His Word is not as easy on us as we would like. "Is not my word like as a fire? saith the LORD; and like a hammer that breaketh the rock in pieces?" (Jer. 23:29).

When Christians call for smooth words, easy words, the result is hard people. When we submit to hard words, we become the tender-hearted of God. But let soft words have their way in a congregation, let soft words dominate the pulpit, and hardness of heart begins to manifest itself in countless ways—but the common denominator is always that of granite hearts. Marriages dissolve, heresies proliferate, parents abandon children, churches split, children heap contempt on their parents, quarrels erupt on the elder board and in the choir, bitterness, rancor, envy, and malice abound—and all because the people will not abide that loathsome jackhammer, "Thou shalt not."

We have come to the point—both in the church and nation—where anyone who speaks a hard word is automatically assumed to be displaying his own hard heart. He is harsh and divisive. He is unloving. Like Ahab, we do not like the prophet who tends to disrupt the general bonhomie of the courtiers and kept prophets. "And the king of Israel said unto Jehoshaphat, Did I not tell thee that he would prophesy no good concerning me, but evil?" (1 Kgs. 22:18).

We have lost the antithesis and therefore have forgotten that no virtue can be found in an intransitive verb. We think that it is good simply for a man to love, for example, forgetting that it depends entirely upon *what* he loves. After all, John told us to love not the world, or the things in it. We believe it is a sin to hate, forgetting that this depends upon what we hate. Is the hatred according to the Word or not? We think that it is a virtue to tolerate, forgetting that the Lord Jesus rebuked a church for tolerating that woman Jezebel. Everything hinges on what we are tolerating, and our global love for smooth words indicates that what we are mostly tolerating is our own hardness of heart.

Of course, because life is never simple, we must acknowledge that there is a type of harsh language which dishonors God and embitters our neighbor. And we also know that there is a type of soft answer which turns away wrath. We know that many cantankerous Christians have defended their sin in the guise of Valiant-for-Truth. Far from trying to smooth these words into an easy fit for us, we must take them as they come, and simply submit to them. There are certain kinds of hard words which belong to the devil, and our speech should always be gracious and seasoned with salt.

Nevertheless, the one who speaks as Jesus and the apostles did, the one who seeks to imitate the discourse of Scripture, will soon find himself verbally opposed to sin. Sometimes the sin is visible and concrete, and other times it is harder to identify—as when a man sins theologically by refusing to accept what God has taught us in Scripture. And when that has happened, the one who reproves such sin will immediately be condemned as troublemaker in the gates of Zion, a pestilent fellow. We want to keep our hearts the way they were.

But we need men who wake up in the morning knowing what they believe. We need men committed to truth in principle, men willing to be unpopular in certain compromised quarters. We need men committed to the authority of truth over us, men who know that debate and discussion are a moral imperative. In an age as compromised as ours, this can only serve to increase unpopularity. But the authority of truth means that hard study was not just a matter of scholarship chasing its tail. Questions are to be raised for the sake of finding answers. A wise pastor knows that splitting the difference between the right answer and the wrong answer will only result in another wrong answer. This mentality is not the province of a particular personality type. It is the inheritance of all the saints who would contend earnestly for the faith. May God raise up many more such saints within the Church who are hungry for truth, along with men who are willing to preach to them.

Preconditions for Reformation

In the midst of these problems, temptations are numerous. One of them is to begin thinking that if we just start "preaching hard," then reformation and revival will come. But there are other issues as well, undergirded with the foundational understanding that none of them are really in our hands at all.

Although the modern Church is in desperate need of reformation and revival, we must begin with the recognition that we have no control over whether or not God will grant it to us.[13] The central reason that glory has departed from the church has been our unfaithfulness to the central biblical truth that God is God. Consequently, we cannot consistently pray for revival as long as we continue in our man-centered rebellion against Him. All "revivals" organized and put together by man are nothing but religious enthusiasms — tub-thumping and arm-waving enthusiasms.

But as we prayerfully wait on God, asking Him to restore and reform His church, there are certain things that can be done now. Elijah could not, in his own power, make the fire fall from heaven, but he could prepare the altar, and that is what God had him do. So like him, we must be busy with the preparation. Below are a few of the areas requiring such preparation *from the pulpit*. These are the stones that must go into the altar, and it is important that they be stones that men have not chiseled. They must all come straight from the quarry of God's Word.

First, there must be a return to the doctrines of sovereign and efficacious grace. Jesus did not come into the world in order to give men choices and possibilities. He came to bring salvation to the world, not a chance at salvation for the world. The cross, as many preach it today, receives whatever efficacy it has from the decision of the listener. This, of course, is not the cross of the New Testament at all.

There cannot be any powerful preaching of the cross as long as our underlying doctrine is that the cross is impotent without the sinner's contribution. The modern evangelist operates on the assumption that the cross is powerless to save until the listening sinner puts in his share, making a "decision" or "commitment." Such an assumption is dishonoring to God, and it is not surprising when churches which tolerate such man-exalting puffery turn into a haunt for owls and jackals. But God is gracious and omnipotent; it is possible for dry bones to live, and for ruins to be restored. The prayer that this would happen is a prayer for reformation.

Consequently, a precondition for such reformation is a simple and child-like affirmation of the sovereign election of the Father, the efficacious redemption by the Son, and the resurrecting call of the Spirit. We

---

[13] Iain Murray, *Revival and Revivalism* (Grand Rapids, MI: Eerdmans, 1994).

must repent of our idolatrous preferences — common sense over Scripture, and human reason over the gospel — and we must repudiate the idea that man is in any sense a contributor to his own salvation. The gospel will not be preached in power until the gospel is recovered in its purity. And the gospel will not be recovered in its purity until we can, without embarrassment, say that salvation is, from beginning to end, a work of the Lord. It is Christ who saves us, and not we ourselves.[14]

There must also be a return to eschatological optimism. The modern evangelical church careens from one Second Coming scare to the next. But there is a job to do before Christ comes again, and that job is the evangelization of the world. The nations are to be brought to obedience and submission to the Lord Christ.[15]

Of course this is not something that we do on our own for Him. Rather, it is something He accomplishes in and through us. Obviously, this task cannot be done by us in our own power; it must be through the Spirit's work as a recovered gospel is preached in plain power. But as the Spirit works in His people, one of the things He will overcome is the pervasive defeatist assumptions we have about evangelization. We assume that reformation cannot come, we assume that the Church cannot be restored, and we assume that the Church is destined for cultural impotence and spiritual irrelevance.

But as long as we believe that the Church is destined to be defeated and cling to the conviction that the Antichrist is just around the corner, through our unbelief we attempt to reject the Spirit's work in us. But Christ's death was *efficacious*, and Christ died for the *world*.

This means that the day is coming when the Church shall be greatly empowered, and China will be brought and laid at the feet of the Messiah. The Church will be restored, and Europe will be turned from her horrible apostasy. The Church will return to the faith of earlier Christians, and the Jews will have their heart of stone taken away and will be given a heart of flesh — and then the blessings for the Gentiles will *really* begin.[16] There shall be glory, and all flesh will see it together. The living water will flow out from under the threshold of Ezekiel's Temple, and the earth will be filled with the knowledge of the Lord as the waters cover the sea.

Third, there must be a return to hard work in doctrinal and theological study. This point is related to the first two. The modern evangelical has a "convenience store" theology. We don't want to buy anything unless we can consume it easily in less than 60 seconds. We want easy

---

[14] Douglas Wilson, *Easy Chairs, Hard Words* (Moscow, ID: Canon Press, 1994).

[15] Please see all the postmillennial books already cited elsewhere.

[16] John Murray, *Commentary on Romans* (Grand Rapids, MI: Eerdmans, 1959), p. 75ff.

answers, quick solutions, and as one wit put it well, sermonettes for Christianettes.

Peter tells us that there are difficult things in Paul's letters — difficulties which ignorant and unstable people twist to their own destruction. These are things which God wanted the church to understand, otherwise He would not have revealed them to us. The key to understanding these things is humble, diligent, prayerful study. The modern Christian attitude exalts man-centered ignorance — knowledge without study, and wisdom without books!

Our generation of Christians is not stupid, but we are ignorant, and we are lazy. We must return to the Scriptures with a mind to work. And as we do so, we must remember that the time required for growth varies between an oak and a cabbage.

Festina Lente

We read such words, and we get worked up. The temptation then arises to go into the pulpit and create a firestorm. And this is good, if it is the right kind of firestorm.

The form of the advice mentioned above comes from Caesar Augustus — *festina lente*, which means "make haste slowly." As we confront the need for reformation in the church today, those who love the *status quo* are distressed that we are talking of making haste at all, while those who have gone around the revolutionary bend are distressed at our "compromise" in undertaking the work of reformation so slowly and deliberately. Both need to take these words from an old reprobate pagan to heart.

While the form of the advice comes from a pagan, the substance of the advice is thoroughly biblical. Because we have a perfect Word from God, we know exactly what direction we must go. Our goal in the Church's ministry must be the same as Paul's — to present every man complete in Christ (Col. 1:28). Because our worship is to glorify God, and not to please ourselves, we must never rest content until we worship Him the way the twenty-four elders do. We must never rest until the Church returns to the doctrine of Christ's efficacious death for the sins of His people, and the appropriation of that salvation by faith alone. We make haste because we still fall short of the perfection required by God's Word. Even in times of relative purity, the Church needs constantly to reform itself according to the Word. How much more in times of corruption!

But because that same perfect Word also tells us to reject perfectionism, we must be patient as we labor toward this end.[17] Impatience in the

---

[17] B.B. Warfield, *The Works of Benjamin B. Warfield, Vols. VII and VIII: Perfectionism* (Grand Rapids, MI: Baker Book House, 1931).

ministry is a sign of a revolutionary temperament, as opposed to *reformational* commitment. The revolutionary temperament is essentially impatient. The Christian Church is called to disciple the nations over the course of centuries, not to be social engineers for the next three weeks, maybe four. Our message is the cross of Christ, not a systematic and doctrinal bundle of plastic explosives. Our approach must be patient, organic, biblical, and inductive, and never ideological, abstract, and deductive. When a revolutionary mind gets hold of an abstract ideological system (and it does not much matter whether he calls it Marxism or Calvinism) and conducts all "reforms" in terms of deductions made from his abstraction in the sky, he has become what Hoffer pointedly called the "true believer." The "truth" represented by the cause no longer matters, the cause does. And people just get in the way.[18]

The need for balance in this regard is crucial because the corruptions of the modern evangelical church are so great and obvious. But precisely because they are so pervasive, we must reject the temptation to acquiesce in those corruptions, and we must also reject the temptation of seeking "quick fixes." When a man has a body riddled with cancer his options are not limited to dying quietly or flying to Tijuana to get some apricot pit medicine.

Tragically, the modern evangelical church has become an existentialist hodge-podge of liberalism, random experiences, spiritual sensualism, and the blind pursuit of money in the name of sufficiently sibilant Jee-eesus. But the historic, Reformed churches in our country are faring no better. They have long since left their biblical, confessional foundations and are inexorably drifting toward the falls of apostasy, with some of them closer than others. The CRC and PCA are both beyond the help of ordinary means. Just as the PCUSA passed the point of no return decades before they defrocked Machen, so our modern decidedly Reformed churches have become just a shell of what their confessions promise. They have not necessarily ordained any lesbian Buddhists yet, but there will be no way to stop it when they do get to that point. The only haste shown is that of trying to get away from the plain and obvious teaching of Scripture. Some "conservatives" within these churches lament the state of affairs. They disapprove of the sin, but they will never make an issue of it. This is a conservatism which has never successfully conserved anything. It is salt which has never made anything salty.[19] "American conservatism is merely the shadow that follows Radicalism

---

[18] Despite some blunders, this point is made wonderfully by Eric Hoffer, *The True Believer* (New York: Harper & Row, 1951).
[19] R.L. Dabney, *Discussions, Secular* (Harrisonburg, VA: Sprinkle Publications, 1994), p. 496.

as it moves forward towards perdition." The more things change, the more they stay the same.

Some perfectionists look at this dismal state of affairs and conclude that what we need is an additional splinter group — another presbyterian denomination of three people, not counting the stated clerk. The stationery proudly proclaims that they are a continuing presbyterian church, that they sing Psalms through the left nostril, unlike those hardy blasphemers down the street, that other splinter group, I forget their name.

In the name of reformation, schismatic revolutionaries do not present an alternative to the general corruption, but simply echo that corruption in a way which is harder to recognize. By calling for immediate (deductive) reformation now in a loud voice, they mask their refusal to reform themselves. In the work of reformation, they make haste, but not slowly.

The Church is moribund. What is the duty of pastors and teachers then? We must make haste to learn, and learn thoroughly, the efficacy of the gospel; we must make haste to declare and preach it. But we must speak slowly so the words will be understood. There will be no reformation apart from the gospel preached.

Priorities and Peace

At the same time, preaching must be governed by *wisdom*. A high view of Scripture would seem to some to indicate that everything in the Word of God is of equal importance. This view naturally translates to emphases on certain strange homiletical hobby horses in the pulpit. While honoring the Word in form, this "high view" denies it in substance. Indeed, this view denies the teaching of Scripture on Scripture. When Jesus tells us that two commandments are the greatest commandments, He is saying by implication that some commandments are of *lesser* importance (Mk. 12:29).

When Paul comments on how he delivered to the Corinthians that which was of first importance ("first of all"), he intimates by this that some things are *not* of first importance (1 Cor. 15:3). And, of course, love is greater than faith and hope (1 Cor. 13:13). Careful students of Scripture understand this. "At Parbar westward, four at the causeway, and two at Parbar." (1 Chr. 26:18). Such a passage from the Word is not as important as the following: "But if there be no resurrection of the dead, then is Christ not risen: And if Christ be not risen, then is our preaching vain, and your faith is also vain" (1 Cor. 15:13–14). Both are true and both are God-breathed , but both are not equally important. This is no disparagement of any portion of the Word; the Word contains such things in part to teach us our doctrinal priorities. David ate the showbread because he was hungry, and God had it recorded because, in part, He wanted to exasperate tidy-minds (1 Sam. 21:6).

Now it would be nice simply to affirm the general principle, and have done with it. Unfortunately, this would be empty teaching—clouds without rain. There once was an old country preacher who used to preach on heaven and hell constantly. When asked why he did so, he replied that he had preached on chicken-stealing once, but it had dampened the enthusiasm. In the same way, in order to keep peace in the church, those things which are truly important must be taught and insisted upon, while those issues of lesser importance must be discussed and named. Unless they are named, and named in the particulars, we cannot repent of our foolish disputes.

In order to maintain the peace of Christ's Church, we must not only know what is true, we must also know the relative importance of each truth. The Deity of Christ is important; head coverings for women are not important. Justification by faith is important; whether Pastor Smith ought to be drinking Michelob is not.[20] The doctrine of *sola Scriptura* is important; whether the church baptizes by immersion alone is not important. Election is important; wrangles over the color of the choir robes are not. Christians often quarrel, and part ways, over things which ought not separate them. Preserving the unity of the Spirit in the bond of peace is important; whether it is lawful to keep the refrigerator plugged in on the Lord's Day isn't. The ministry of the pulpit must reflect these relative priorities.

The Bible contains a great deal about doctrinal priorities. Some of the most withering criticism leveled by our Lord was directed at religious meatheads who did not know that the altar was more important than the gold placed on it, and honoring parents was more important than contributing to the current pledge drive for the church parking lot. He also had some things to say about people who forgot justice and mercy while tithing the contents of every container in their spice racks. The Pharisees used to strain out a gnat and swallow a camel. In the last two thousand years, the church has perhaps advanced just a little bit. Now we strain out a June bug and swallow a camel.

In order to avoid this problem, we have to ask two questions about every doctrine we seek to present in the pulpit. The first concerns whether the teaching is true. Having established that something is true, it is crucial to determine the relative importance of that truth. Knowing what is important, and what is not as important, is central to the ministry of the Word.

We must consequently know our Bibles, because sometimes doctrinal issues of the greatest moment can hang on apparently trivial

---

[20] Of course, there is a sense in which drinking Michelob can be properly controversial. In modern evangelical circles, drinking Michelob is controversial because it is drinking beer. In more informed circles, it is controversial because it isn't.

matters. Paul faced down Peter at Antioch because the gospel was at stake in Peter's avoidance of certain dinner companions. Other issues are apparently trivial because they are, well, trivial. When forbidden to destroy our brother in a dispute over vegetables, we sometimes obey and then seek to destroy him over some other food group. "Who art thou that judgest another man's servant? to his own master he standeth or falleth" (Rom. 14:4).

"Ah," we say, "but *our* doctrinal hobby horse isn't in view in Romans 14. The Greek indicates . . ." Whatever the secondary issue we use to harass our brothers may be, we must guard our hearts. "But why dost thou judge thy brother? or why dost thou set at nought thy brother? for we shall all stand before the judgment seat of Christ"(Rom. 14:10). If these squabbles and disputes are going to follow us into the throne room of Christ, then our Greek had better be pretty good.

Of course this is not to say we must have no convictions on secondary matters. No pastoral problems result from being fully convinced in our own minds. So how are we to determine what is of less importance, and what is only apparently unimportant? These sorts of disputes exist in Scripture, and so we must study these disputes to discover what they had in common and then apply what we have found, by analogy, to our own squabbles.

The Christian faith has a center. When Christians gravitate to the periphery in order to conduct their fights along the fence, it betrays a lack of love for that center, and perhaps reveals a desire to get over the fence entirely. As we seek to live together in the congregation of God's saints, we must be mindful of what the Lord is seeking to perform in our midst and be jealous for the protection of it. "For meat destroy not the work of God" (Rom. 14:20).[21]

A Farewell to Calvinism

When we recover our priorities in preaching, we will return of course to the basics of the gospel, and it is not possible to do this without addressing the issues that have been nicknamed Calvinism, as we have already done. Now, it is our solemn duty to preach Christ and not Calvin. But depend upon it—if someone preaches Christ correctly, he will be *accused* of preaching Calvin.[22]

So we must therefore answer the question posed by the serpent in Eden, which is, "Hath God said?" If God has not spoken on these things, we must remain silent ourselves. And if He *has* spoken, then there is no

---

[21] Ken Sande, *The Peacemaker* (Grand Rapids, MI: Baker Book House, 1991).
[22] And there may be some who argue that if they are going to hang you for a thief, you might as well steal something. W. G. T. Shedd, *Calvinism Pure and Mixed* (Edinburgh: The Banner of Truth Trust, 1986 [1893]).

possible reason for attributing the invention of these doctrines to John Calvin.

If it is on account of grace and the cross, then it is an honor to be slandered as a "Calvinist." Christ said it was an honor when men speak evil of us, and it certainly is evil for the followers of Christ to be identified as the followers of a mere man, however godly that man was. But just because we rejoice in the slander, it is not therefore necessary to join in the slander ourselves, and call ourselves these names. We are to rejoice in the slander; we are not to do our best to make the slander true. Christ did say to go the second mile, but we don't think this is what He had in mind.

In contrast, if it is on account of an obnoxious and churlish presentation, then there is no honor at all in being called a "Calvinist." Some who call themselves by this name do have a reputation for an approach which is not characterized by Christian charity. As John Newton pointed out, self-righteousness can feed on doctrines as well as works.[23]

Should "Calvinists" seek unity of fellowship with Christians who differ with them on this issue? Absolutely. Why? Because election depends upon the good pleasure of the Father. And if He has bestowed His unmerited pleasure upon "Arminians" (which He most certainly does), then it makes no sense for a "Calvinist" to magnify the prerogatives of divine sovereignty by telling God He is not allowed to fellowship with any "Arminians," and that furthermore the "Calvinist" is going to try to set a good example for God through restricting his fellowship. Some view of divine sovereignty. Some Calvinism. Woe to the pot who strives with the Potter! Woe to the "Calvinist" who objects to the loose fellowship standards of God the Father!

Is this to minimize the seriousness of "Arminian" error? Not at all — it is a grievous error, and it leads to worse.[24] Is this to minimize the truths contained in "Calvinism?" Not at all. As mentioned before, "Calvinism" is nothing more than a nickname for a thorough and right understanding of the gospel.[25] The point is simply to say that God's grace is greater than all human error and sin. And the grace of God is most apparent when true Christians love each other.

But suppose an "Arminian" says that we cannot really love our brother if we say that he is mistaken about the gospel. We would paraphrase Paul and ask, "How are we an enemy simply because we speak the truth?" True Christians may be mistaken in their theology of the

---

[23] John Newton, *The Works of John Newton, Vol. I* (Carlisle, PA: Banner of Truth, 1985 [1820]), p. 272.

[24] R. K. McGregor Wright, *No Place for Sovereignty* (Downers Grove, IL: InterVarsity Press, 1996).

[25] Gordon H. Clark, *Predestination* (Phillipsburg, NJ: Presbyterian & Reformed Publishing Company, 1987).

cross; our duty is therefore twofold. We must love all true Christians as brothers, and we must graciously dissent from all such mistakes about the cross. And at other points of doctrine or practice, where God uses "Arminians" to correct us, our duty is to receive it humbly.

If an "Arminian" is elect and chosen, then his election is not imperiled through his failure to understand the ninth chapter of Romans. Paul did not say, at the end of the eighth chapter, that nothing can separate us from the love of Christ except for shoddy exegesis. And if a "Calvinist" is reprobate, then he cannot earn his way into the approval of God through a self-righteous mouthing of the doctrines of grace. Unsaved "Calvinists" are like Solomon's beautiful woman without discretion—a gold ring in a pig's snout. But when both share in a common election, their duty is to maintain a unity of love, and to strive for a unity of mind which is only possible through diligent study and application of the Scriptures.

Now there are some who take the name "Calvinist," not out of a fractious party spirit, but because they don't want to seem uncharitable. "Mine is the *biblical* position. What's yours?" But however well-intentioned, it is still not within our authority to act as though something revealed in the first century was invented in the sixteenth. Keeping the peace is not an absolute priority. And for those doctrinally-oriented "Calvinists" who are very concerned for the claims of truth, there is important instruction in the early chapters of Revelation. It is good to be concerned for truth; the ancient Ephesian church was not rebuked for that, but rather for abandoning its first love. We must proclaim the truth, *and* we must love the brethren. If we sacrifice the truth for the sake of love, it is not really love; if we sacrifice love for the sake of truth, it is not really truth. The Bible requires unswerving allegiance to both.

So it is not possible to put the issue to one side even to keep peace between Christians. We are commanded to preach the gospel, and all presentations of the gospel must presuppose the truth of one position or the other. So there is no neutrality; there is no third way.

The Bible reveals truth; it does not conceal it. A "Calvinist" is simply one who believes the revealed truth about foreordination as it was written for us. He does not seek to mix the plain statements of Scripture with human reasoning or logical extrapolation. Therefore the label he uses must match what he is doing—the last thing a label should do is mislead. So we should avoid the term "Calvinist" in every way we honestly can. But in no way are we seeking to minimize any biblical truths about the cross. Rather, we are seeking to detach a human name from God's truth. At the same time, the reader should know that whenever we refer in these pages to grace, faith, justification, the cross, election, etc., we are refering to what others call "Calvinism," and what the Bible calls grace.

A Deeper Right

This is a matter of getting the truth down into our bones. Paul instructs us how we are to behave as the elect of God. "Put on therefore, as the elect of God, holy and beloved, bowels of mercies, kindness, humbleness of mind, meekness, longsuffering; forbearing one another, and forgiving one another, if any man have a quarrel against any: even as Christ forgave you, so also do ye" (Col. 3:12–13).

In this passage, Paul does not just tell the Colossians to act in a particular fashion. He tells them to do so *as the elect of God*. The foundation of our behavior is God's electing love for us in Christ; as recipients of that love, we are instructed to live in a certain way. As we saw above, nothing is more incongruous than to see a pastor who affirms the doctrine of election in the pulpit, but whose life is characterized by harsh dogmatism. We are taught here that the uniform of those who understand election is to be tender mercies — the "bowels of mercies."

But after God has initially brought believers into an understanding of the preciousness of sovereign election, they frequently enter what a friend of mine called the "cage" stage — the time when the newly-convinced "Calvinist" ought to be locked into a cage, and not let out until he stabilizes, or the medication kicks in. This is because coming to a "Calvinistic" understanding of Scripture is not a second experience that removes one from temptation and sin. But unfortunately, there are some who never grow out of the cage stage, and this type of personality often thinks he is called to the ministry. He loves to talk about these truths all the time, and what could be more obvious than the fact that he should pursue a calling that would permit him to talk about these truths all the time? In such a situation, many peculiar temptations present themselves to the "Calvinistic" pastor. Below are listed some of the more common temptations and sins of those who hold to the doctrine of efficacious grace, and who are charged with preaching it.

Exasperation: One of the benefits of having one's eyes opened is that one can now see. The temptation associated with this is forgetting what it was like not to be able to see. Everything is now so clear to us that anyone who does not immediately assent to what we see in the Word seems either theologically perverse or a chucklehead. But what does the Bible say? "And the servant of the Lord must not strive; but be gentle unto all men, apt to teach, patient, in meekness instructing those that oppose themselves; if God peradventure will give them repentance to the acknowledging of the truth" (2 Tim. 2:24–25).

These verses are speaking about a confrontation with unbelieving false teachers. That being the case, what should our attitude be toward *brothers* who are entangled in error? How much more must we love our mistaken brothers with kindness and humility! Unfortunately, this passage has commonly been used in debate by an exasperated "Calvinist" to prove that *God does too* give repentance. But is the passage being used or obeyed? To obey a passage is better than to beat someone else over the head with it.

Arrogance: There is a particular kind of vainglory which loves being correct — "being right." We live in an evangelical culture which has debauched the truth, and "Calvinists," by contrast, hold to a pure gospel. What fine fellows we are! But Scripture comes to us again — "For who maketh thee to differ from another? and what hast thou that thou didst not receive? now if thou didst receive it, why dost thou glory, as if thou hadst not received it?" (1 Cor. 4:7).

Paul teaches this in the context of his rebuke to those who glory in human teachers — it doesn't matter whether it is Paul, Apollos, Luther, or Calvin. Of *all* people, those who profess to believe in the sovereignty of grace should understand this. If God had not been pleased to teach us what we now understand so clearly, we would still be saying all the things we used to say. So we need to maintain doctrinal humility before the Lord.

Imbalance: The Bible teaches both the sovereignty of God and the responsibility of man for his sin. There is a temptation to emphasize the "sovereignty" passages, and let the "Arminians" bring up those which teach the responsibility of man. So we have to take care that we affirm everything the Bible affirms — and not just when we are forced to affirm it in a discussion or debate. But this is something that must be done before the Lord. You will not get accurate feedback from your "Arminian" friends on this one. You can preach, with perfect balance, every passage under debate, and as long as it includes Romans 9, you will be thought imbalanced. At the same time, it *is* possible that you are a bit wobbly on it, so keep it before the Lord.

Lack of proportionality: The Lord is God, and all of His Word should be precious to us. But not all of His Word is of equal importance. The Lord taught us that the law contains "weightier matters", and Paul tells us that certain gospel truths are of "first importance." In "Calvinistic" circles, the divine prerogatives of the sovereign God are strongly emphasized. If His Word commands it, then it must not ever be considered a "little thing." This is quite true; no part of God's Word may be set aside deliberately. The temptation here, however, is to set aside the central truths of God's Word for the sake of tithing out of one's spice rack. So if a church is torn apart over a controversy about whether to sing Psalms through the back of the neck, the greater is sacrificed on the altar of the lesser. But as the Lord taught, both the central and lesser truths should be maintained — with the greater given the seat of honor.

When a sense of proportion is lost, minds and attitudes get seized up in a kind of theological vapor lock. This results in a literary genre common among the "Truly Reformed" — single-spaced, typewritten, nasty-gram letters, with typing up the margins. I have seen such letters, written by pastors.

Frustration: One time a friend joked with me that there is one thing that a sovereign God cannot do — change an "Arminian's" mind. The resistance that many Christians have to the teaching of Scripture on the sovereignty of God is very great. After this resistance is experienced for any length of time, the temptation is to give up all hope of our brothers ever coming to understand it. But when we do this, we are not just giving up on our friends, we are giving up our theology. Is God in control or not? Is He in control of *this* or not? And how can we ask our family and friends to affirm with their lips what we deny with our attitudes?

So there is a deeper right than "being right." If we affirm the letter of Scripture, but do not live according to the Spirit who gave it, then we betray the cause of truth.

Of course this is not said to justify setting aside the plain teaching of Scripture through an appeal to the "deeper" truths it contains. As always, we must affirm only what the Bible teaches, and all of what the Bible teaches. And affirming is not enough; we are to adorn these truths with tender mercies.

Legalism: Hatred of God's Law

As we have seen, in addressing how to preach the greatness and sovereignty of God, we find ourselves continually dealing with *shoulds* and *oughts*. And this brings us to the source of every godly imperative, which is the law of God. But pastors who take refuge there will soon find that creates a new set of difficulties.

Pastors cannot preach the necessity of godly attitudes in handling the truth without soon dealing with the law of God. And when this happens, it is the rare pastor who has not at some time encountered criticism of his sermons as "legalistic." And it is very common for Christians to define legalism as taking the law of God "too far." The legalist, the Pharisee, is seen as someone who does not know when to quit. Sure, the law says to do this or that, but why do these guys take it so *seriously*?

This common understanding is really nothing less than total confusion. When Christ rebuked the Pharisees, it was not for keeping the law; He attacked them because they *refused* to keep the law. "Woe unto you, scribes and Pharisees, hypocrites! for ye pay tithe of mint and anise and cummin, and have omitted the weightier matters of the law, judgment, mercy, and faith: these ought ye to have done, and not to leave the other undone" (Mt. 23:23). Notice the last sentence here. Christ did not rebuke them for tithing out of their spice racks; He rebuked them for having no sense of biblical proportion at all. He rebuked them for keeping (with a great deal of fanfare) the periphery of the law, while trashing the heart of the law.[26]

Because of this, Christ says that His followers were to be much *more* scrupulous about how they lived. "For I say unto you, that except your righteousness shall exceed the righteousness of the scribes and Pharisees, ye shall in no case enter into the kingdom of heaven" (Mt. 5:20).

We are creatures; our pattern of life must conform to an external standard. Everyone in the world lives according to law — law-guided behavior is inescapable. As creatures, we are incapable of choosing between law-guided behavior and nonlaw-guided behavior. The heart of legalism, therefore, is the substitution of man's law for God's law. God tells us what His law is, and in His Word He describes the relationship of all believers to that law. If by grace we submit to His declaration, it shows that we have been saved by grace, and through His grace we keep the righteous requirements of the law (Rom. 8:4).

If we do not submit to God's law, we will be submitting to the authority of a creature. It does not matter if the substitute for God is self, some Bible teacher, or a counseling guru. It is always the same; those who will not live by God's law are simultaneously submitting to man's law. For laying aside the commandment of God, you hold the tradition of men (Mk. 7:8).

We are incapable of turning away from God to nothing. We cannot worship the void because we cannot escape the world in which we were placed. Consequently, all rebels follow the pattern seen in the first chapter of Romans. *They substitute.* They worship and serve the creature, rather than the Creator.

Of course there are varying degrees of substitution. Some try to rebel against everything God says. For some, salvation (or enlightenment) is the result of the sum total of all a man's work. They make no bones about it: they are going to make it on their own. Once my wife and I were speaking with some Jehovah's Witnesses. One of them, an elderly woman, listened as my wife gave her testimony of how God had graciously saved her. When my wife was done, the woman said, "That's not the way it is with us — we have to work for everything we get." This was a form of legalism, substituting the law and gospel of man for the law and gospel of God.

But there are less obvious forms of legalism. Because they are less obvious, and serpents are subtle, these substitutions are found among professing evangelical pastors. Many who profess to follow the Bible (as the Pharisees also professed to follow it) in effect substitute their own laws for the laws of Christ.

---

[26] Greg Bahnsen, *By This Standard* (Tyler, TX: ICE, 1994).

Some make the substitution for the sake of "holiness" or "sanctifica-tion." They say, for just one example, that Christians must not drink anything containing alcohol. But the Bible contains no such require-ment, and provides many examples to the contrary. Why do people who call themselves Christians want to be holier than Christ was? All such attempts are legalistic.[27]

Others substitute their own wisdom for the gospel of pure grace. It is intolerable, the thinking goes, that God would save us out of His gra-cious pleasure; man must make his contribution. I was once talking with a man who was maintaining that Cornelius was saved because he—on his own—was worthy of the gospel (Acts 10:1–8). When the leaven of this teaching has done its work, the result is another gospel.

All the commands are summed up in the greatest command of all, which is to love God without reserve. Because we are sinners, we cannot obey this command apart from the grace of God. But for those who are recipients of this grace, they find that it works in them to accomplish God's good pleasure. And the good pleasure of God is expressed for us in written form in the law. He who loves keeps the law. He who truly keeps the law is doing nothing more than loving God and loving his neighbor. "Owe no man any thing, but to love one another: for he that loveth another hath fulfilled the law. For this, Thou shalt not commit adultery, Thou shalt not kill, Thou shalt not steal, Thou shalt not bear false witness, Thou shalt not covet; and if there be any other command-ment, it is briefly comprehended in this saying, namely, Thou shalt love thy neighbour as thyself. Love worketh no ill to his neighbour: therefore love is the fulfilling of the law" (Rom. 13:8–10).

Our duty is clear. We are to obey the law in our love for God and man. But all of us are sinners and are incapable of doing this. Because of His lovingkindness, God has provided a means of transforming hearts which hate the law. At this point, our duty is equally clear—it is to obey the gospel.

And when God by His grace makes it possible for us to repent of our sin and believe the gospel, we find that we have been set free to love Him and love our neighbor. Put another way, we have been freed from sin that we may keep the law of God. As Christians, we can accept no sub-stitute. As pastors, we must allow no other standard for behavior to enter our pulpits.

---

[27] Kenneth, L. Gentry, Jr., *Christian and Alcoholic Beverages* (Grand Rapids, MI: Baker Book House, 1986). For a more, ahem, exuberant treatment, see Jim West, *Drinking With Calvin and Luther!* (Carmichael, CA: Jim West, 1995).

✠CHAPTER V✠

OBSERVING THE SACRAMENTS

Sacramental Thinking

Rightly understood, sacramental thinking is covenantal thinking. But many modern evangelicals shy away from a word like *sacrament*. It sounds too *priestly*; the concern is that using words like this leads inexorably to Rome. But our real concern should be the practice of using language that does not do justice to the biblical categories.

In a sacrament we have a covenantal union between the sign and the thing signified.[1] The Roman Catholic position destroys the possibility of having a sacrament through *identifying* the sign with the thing signified. The modern evangelical position destroys the definition of a sacrament through *divorcing* the sign and the thing signified. In this position, the sign is a mere memorial of that to which it points, and thus there can be no sacramental *union* between the two.

This covenantal union is the work of the Holy Spirit, who with divine authority, says that the water is united to the cleansing while distinct from it, and that the bread and wine are united with the body and blood of the Lord Jesus — which body, of course, we are.

There are only two established sacraments in the Christian Church, which are baptism and the Lord's Supper. But the whole world is sacramental, teeming with metaphor. To come to a fuller understanding of this, we should seek to grow in our knowledge of the two formal sacraments that have been placed within the Church.

Baptism and the Lord's Table have the Lord's promises attached to them, and when approached rightly, they nurture and instruct us in this way of thinking. They enable us to see what is occurring throughout the rest of our lives. Thus, table fellowship with friends is not a sacrament, but it is sacramental. Sex is not a sacrament, but it is

---

[1] Ronald Wallace, *Calvin's Doctrine of Word and Sacrament* (Eugene, OR: Wipf and Stock Publishers, 1982), pp. 133–174.

sacramental—a great mystery, as Paul would say. Giving birth is no sacrament, but motherhood is certainly sacramental.

We lives our lives in union with Christ. This is seen and blessed in the richest possible way through the two sacraments of the Church. But having been nurtured there, we do not go out "into life" in order to fend for ourselves. We have been taught that in God we live and move and have our being. We do so as members of Christ—this is covenantal living; it is sacramental living.

The Sacrament of Baptism

Baptism is the doorway of the visible Church.[2] A man who has not been baptized in water is not yet a professing Christian. He may be regenerate—God knows—but he has not yet professed Christ in the way Christ instructed and required. Jesus said, in the Great Commission, that the nations were to be discipled, and that the first step in doing this was to *baptize* them (Mt. 28:18–20). In short, the visible mark of a visible saint is water baptism. This is how Jesus told us to make disciples.

This kind of language makes modern evangelicals nervous, and two responses are necessary. The first response is that we have a fine way of setting aside God's requirement for the sake of our traditions. We do not like the idea of requiring a man to be baptized down in front of the church before we call him a professing Christian—although Jesus commanded such baptism. In lieu of this, we offer a substitute of our devising. Instead of being baptized in front of the church, we say he has to go down in front of the church and sign a little card, and then talk with a trained counselor. In short, practices with *no* scriptural warrant are a better indicator of whether a man is a professing Christian than doing what Jesus Christ said to do. This is baffling. You'd think we would remember that the Christian faith is, after all, *His* religion. Modern evangelistic appeals frequently tell the one who has "prayed the prayer" what to do afterward—that is, "tell a friend." But in the Acts of the Apostles, Paul did not have the Philippian jailor tell a friend. Peter did not have the three thousand at Pentecost scatter throughout Jerusalem, telling their friends. Repent, he said, and *be baptized*. So someone who is not yet baptized has not yet professed the faith, regardless of what human means for making a profession he may have employed.

The second response is to acknowledge an important truth embedded in our modern disobedience. Water baptism by itself does not constitute the gospel. Christ did not send Paul to *baptize*, he said, but to preach the *gospel* (1 Cor. 1:17). Water baptism is the appointed means for professing Christ, but it does not follow from this that every such

[2] John Murray, *Christian Baptism* (Phillipsburg, NJ: Presbyterian and Reformed Publishing Co., 1980).

profession is genuine. In a biblical church, the Word always accompanies the sacrament, and as it is administered faithfully, the Word is received along with the sacrament.

A man who is baptized is a professing Christian. Even if he is unregenerate, he remains a professing Christian. Regardless of what he might say or do, until he is excommunicated or God removes him through death, he is part of the visible Church.[3] The profession made through baptism is *Christ's* profession, the mark of Christ. Of course it is the duty of everyone who bears this mark to make the same profession with his life throughout the course of his life — to say *amen* to what Christ has said in the baptism.

In the baptistic understanding of this, baptism is a profession of a profession. That is, a man has believed in Christ, and has consequently made a verbal profession of faith. He then seeks water baptism in order to point to the condition of his regenerate heart, which prompted him to make his verbal confession. Baptism is an arrow pointing in.

But in the covenantal paedobaptist view of baptism, water baptism points away to Christ, and not to the internal condition of the one being baptized. This is not because the internal condition is irrelevant — it is very important, but it is just not what baptism primarily signifies. To speak autobiographically for a moment, my baptism had nothing whatever to say about Douglas Wilson. My baptism spoke only of Jesus Christ. But because I bear this mark which speaks so loudly of Christ, I have an obligation to add my voice to the testimony, so that every fact may be confirmed in the mouth of two or three witnesses.

In this view, baptism points authoritatively to Christ as the only salvation of sinners, and the fact that this marker was placed on a particular individual places him under a covenantal obligation to say the same thing with his life that his baptism does. A baptized child, growing up in a covenantal home, is taught that his baptism confesses Christ — so must he. His baptism points to Christ — so must he. His baptism testifies faithfully to Christ — so must he. His baptism reflects the gospel — so must he.[4]

Considered from another angle, the circumcision of Esau and the circumcision of Jacob meant exactly the same thing. Both pointed to a coming redemption, and a righteousness that was by faith alone. But Esau, a profane man, refused to confirm what his circumcision declared. He contradicted a true witness. Jacob, a righteous man through faith,

---

[3] Douglas Wilson, *To A Thousand Generations* (Moscow, ID: Canon Press, 1996).

[4] See the work of my good friend, Randy Booth, *Children of the Promise* (Phillipsburg, NJ: Presbyterian & Reformed, 1995). Randy and I got to know each other by phone as we fell down the paedo staircase together, hitting our heads on every step.

made his declaration which lined up faithfully with the testimony of his circumcision.

Thus we see that membership in the covenant community is objective. Pastors do not have to try to read hearts, pick up spiritual vibes, or conduct great experiments in telepathy. If someone is baptized, then they have a covenantal obligation to repent and believe, and to live accordingly. Young children are nurtured in this obligation, church members are strengthened in it, and the rebellious are admonished and rebuked by it.

Because they have come through the door of the visible Church, they are all to be taught their obligations as they live in the household of faith.[5]

Baptism and Culture

It has been said that in the Bible belt everyone is a Christian until they get their driver's license. As soon as a child is old enough to leave his upbringing, he does so. And, after a time of wild living, he frequently comes back to the church so that his kids can go to Sunday School, but no one takes the charade very seriously.

Because consistent Christians are appalled and disgusted with all forms of such nominalism, they often react strongly to this problem. But reactions are frequently overreactions, which lead in turn to new distortions and errors. One such reaction has led us to minimize and underestimate the cultural potency of water baptism.

Because of our opposition to nominalism, it has come about that one of our definitions of the word "baptized" says that it means nothing more than to place a religious veneer on something, always to little or no effect. Thus we talk about baptized secularism, or baptized humanism, or baptized feminism. Baptism is thought to be the whitewash we use to clean the outside of a sepulchre. The only thing it does, we think, is make hypocrisy possible.

Having acknowledged that nominalism is a sin and a great evil, let me suggest that we have greatly misunderstood what kind of sin it is. A culture in which a great number of people are baptized — whether they live consistently with their baptismal vows or not — is a culture which is under covenantal obligation. As we have discussed, this obligation is external and objective and is based upon an external and objective criterion — water baptism.

Too often parents haul their infants down to the front of the church for a feel-good Kodak moment. The baby is cute, the baptism is

[5] For a wonderful treatment of the covenant, see David L. Nielands, *Studies in the Covenant of Grace* (Phillipsburg, NJ: Presbyterian and Reformed Publishing Co., 1980).

performed, and the flesh applauds. But the true meaning of baptism is *objective*, and rests outside of all hypocrisies and doctrinal misunderstandings. It means that the mark of Christ has been placed on that person, and that he now has an additional obligation to repent and believe. A baptized individual has the obligation to have his life point the same direction his baptism does — to Christ and to His righteousness. The fact is that many refuse to do so, but this does not alter their obligation in the slightest. When many individuals in a culture have received the mark of baptism, the presence of this obligation works its way out into the cultural assumptions held in common by all. And this is how a culture can come to be very wicked, and yet be, to use Flannery O' Conner's phrase, Christ-haunted.[6]

Suppose a man marries and he knows that he is going to be unfaithful to his wife — in fact, he already has adulterous plans. But for various reasons, he thinks it expedient to be married, so he goes to the church and makes the vows. Now, is he married? Of course he is — he is under covenantal obligation to keep his vows, *whether or not he meant them.* Using a figure of speech, we might say that he was not being a "real" husband to his wife, meaning that he did not treat his wife the way a husband should. But in another sense, he is very much a real husband. In using the figure of speech, saying he is not a real husband, we are *not* saying that he has no obligation to keep his vows. We simply mean that he is being a scoundrel. In the same way, baptized infidels are not "real" Christians, and unless they repent, they will all perish. But this is where modern evangelicals must take care. These hypocrites remain under the obligations of the covenant, and so in another sense, they *are* real Christians.

This is related to another common misunderstanding of infant baptism, a misunderstanding shared by nominalists and sincere Christians alike. It is thought by the untutored that to have a child baptized is "better than nothing." A child may not make it to heaven because of this, but at least he is off to a good start. But the Bible teaches that to whom much is given, much is required. Those covenant members who despise the covenant are under a much stricter judgment than the pagans outside. Parents who know what the covenant obligations are should tremble at the baptismal font. And parents who do not take the sacrament very seriously should come to realize that they are in reality heaping condemnation upon their children.

So the fact remains that we are living in a country where a great many of the unbelievers surrounding us are *baptized* unbelievers. This should not make us dismiss baptism as a nullity; that would be to make

---

[6] Flannery O' Conner, *Mystery and Manners* (New York: The Noonday Press, 1957), p. 44.

the same mistake that everyone else is making. Rather, we should see the prevalence of baptism as a wonderful tool for covenantal, cultural evangelism. Oddly, many unbelievers have a better sense of this than we do. They know that a claim of Christ rests upon them — they feel the weight of it. They want to ignore this claim, but it still presses on them. Sadly, they are helped in their attempts to suppress this claim by *our* neglect of their status. We ignore the claim of Christ on them too. But Matthew Henry's father said once[7] that, whenever his children misbehaved, the first thing he would do would be to "grab them by their baptism." In our presentation of the gospel to a nominally Christian nation, this is what we must learn to do. We must grab them by their baptism.

The Amount of Water

Baptism can lawfully be administered with various modes, but this does not mean that the Bible gives us no direction on the subject.

Contrary to what many assume, the most biblical mode of baptism is *not* immersion. Where mode is indicated by context, we have no instances of baptism by immersion in the Bible. That is, no narrative of a baptism describes it as an immersion, or in terms which require an immersion. Confronted with this, the response of many immersionists is that the word *baptizo* simply means "to immerse," and so we do not have to have contextual descriptions. Now if "John the Baptist" *means* "John the Immersionist" then the point is well taken.

The problem is that the claim is simply untrue.[8] Many examples of baptism can be shown in the more biblical modes of sprinkling and pouring. We will not have to deal with this at length because the passages concerned are fairly straightforward. The only reason it presents any difficulty at all is that the force of ecclesiastical tradition is a powerful one.

In the ninth chapter of Hebrews, the author is discussing the ceremonial washings of the Old Testament at some length. These washings are described throughout the Old Testament as *sprinklings*, and they are described in the same way in this section of Hebrews. These sprinklings are then called *baptisms*.

---

[7] In defese of non-traceable footnotes. Heb. 2:6, "But there is a place where someone has testified."

[8] James Dale, *Baptizo* (Phillipsburg, NJ: Presbyterian & Reformed , 1991 [1869]). If these three volumes are overkill, then Jay Adams does the job with *The Meaning and Mode of Baptism* (Phillipsburg, NJ: Presbyterian & Reformed, 1975). A good treatment of the mode of baptism can also be found in Ralph E. Bass, Jr., *What About Baptism?* (Naples, FL: Nicene Press, 1999) and in Duane Edward Spencer, *Holy Baptism* (Tyler, TX: Geneva Ministries, 1984).

Which stood only in meats and drinks, and divers washings [*baptismois*], and carnal ordinances, imposed on them until the time of reformation. (Heb. 9:10)

No Jew would have had any trouble recognizing a ceremonial washing, conducted by means of sprinkling, as a baptism. This is a very natural use of the term. And the imagery which points to the cleansing of the new covenant, and the giving of the Spirit, is fully adequate to the occasion.

For I will take you from among the heathen, and gather you out of all countries, and will bring you into your own land. Then will *I sprinkle clean water upon you*, and ye shall be clean: from all your filthiness, and from all your idols, will I cleanse you. A *new heart* also will I give you, and a *new spirit* will I put within you: and I will take away the stony heart out of your flesh, and I will give you an heart of flesh. And *I will put my spirit within you*, and cause you to walk in my statutes, and ye shall keep my judgments, and do them. And ye shall dwell in the land that I gave to your fathers; and ye shall be my people, and I will be your God. (Ezek. 36:24–28)

And so we see that sprinklings are baptisms—but so is pouring. The early Christians were baptized in the Holy Spirit at Pentecost. Whenever the mode in which the Holy Spirit was given is described, it is consistently described as a *pouring out*, or as a *descending*. The disciples are not lowered into the "water" of the Holy Spirit. Rather, the "water" of the Spirit is poured out upon them. They are not placed *in* Him; He is placed *on* them. The evidence for this is overwhelming (Acts 2:3, 16–17, 33; 10:44–45; 11;15–16; Mt. 3:16–17; Jn. 1:32; Lk. 3:22; Is. 44:3).

While the mode of baptism is not the most important thing about it, the image given in these scriptural modes is truly glorious.

Not by works of righteousness which we have done, but according to his mercy he saved us, *by the washing of regeneration*, and renewing of the Holy Ghost; *which he shed on us abundantly* through Jesus Christ our Saviour. (Tit. 3:5–6)

The Sacrament of the Lord's Supper

A good place to begin our discussion of the Lord's Supper is with the scriptural names for the sacrament. We have already referred to it as the Lord's Supper, which is the phrase Paul uses for it in 1 Corinthians 11:20. "Therefore when you come together in one place, it is not to eat *the Lord's Supper*" (1 Cor. 11:20).

He also calls it a cup of blessing: "The *cup of blessing* which we bless,

is it not the communion of the blood of Christ?" (1 Cor. 10:16).[9] We need
to remember the figure of speech called synecdoche, where a part can be
applied to the whole. Obviously, Paul does not want to limit blessing to
the *cup*, excluding the bread. Consequently, we see that the entire Lord's
Supper is a *blessing*. It is also a thanksgiving. When Paul recounts the
words of institution, he says, "For I received from the Lord that which I
also delivered to you: that the Lord Jesus on the same night in which He
was betrayed took bread; *and when He had given thanks*, He broke it and
said, "Take, eat; this is My body which is broken for you; do this in
remembrance of Me" (1 Cor. 11:23–24). The Lord's Supper is a celebration, a feast. We are to remember the Lord, and part of what we remember
is that He *gave thanks* for His sacrifice. The Greek word for thanksgiving
is where we get the word Eucharist.

The Supper is also called the Table of the Lord — "You cannot drink
the cup of the Lord and the cup of demons; you cannot partake of *the
Lord's table* and of the table of demons" (1 Cor. 10:21). Notice that we
have two tables, and the worshippers partake of each one in the same
way — covenantally. In other words, it is not when we come to the Lord's
Table that a covenantal "miracle" happens. The world we live in is
covenantal, and the only choice we have is between sitting at the Lord's
Supper in covenantal obedience or sitting elsewhere in covenantal idolatry. We do not have the option of sitting down at a noncovenantal table.
They don't exist. This shows us that the sacrament is not a covenantal
island in the middle of a noncovenantal world. Rather, everything
around   us   must   be   seen   in   covenantal   categories —
unbelief included — with the Table of the Lord at the center of *believing*
covenantal living.

Another common name is Communion. "The cup of blessing which
we bless, is it not the *communion* of the blood of Christ?" (1 Cor. 10:16)
The word for communion here is *koinonia*, which refers to our *fellowship*
in Christ, and consequently with one another. In the book of Acts, it is
also called the breaking of bread. "Now on the first day of the week,
when the disciples came together *to break bread*, Paul preached to them,
ready to depart the next day." (Acts 20:7). And lastly, the Lord's Supper
may be called the Cup of the New Covenant. "In the same manner He
also took the cup after supper, saying, '*This cup is the new covenant* in My
blood. This do, as often as you drink it, in remembrance of Me.' For as
often as you eat this bread and drink this cup, you proclaim the Lord's
death till He comes" (1 Cor. 11:25-26).

So what does all this mean, taking it together? Consider what we are
doing. *We* do not own the Supper; the Supper is the *Lord's* Supper — He is

---

[9] For any still concerned about the issue of alcohol and the Lord's Supper, see Andre S. Bustanoby, *Wrath of Grapes* (Grand Rapids, MI: Baker Book
House, 1986).

the host. When we approach it properly, we receive a blessing which we cannot receive in other ordinary situations. *This* cup is a cup of blessing, which distinguishes it from all other cups. If our Lord, facing death, was able to give thanks, how much more should we come together in order to celebrate this Supper *eucharistically*. We are to look around the sanctuary as we discern the Lord's body in our fellow saints — this is communion. We signify our loyalty by partaking of the Lord's Table. This is our covenant oath. We break bread, just as the Father broke the body of His Son. And we remember the heart of the New Covenant, which is the remission of sins in His blood.

In the Table of the Lord we have a glorious opportunity to grow in faith, as the Word commands the sacrament and the sacrament enriches the Word. "I speak as to wise men; judge ye what I say. The cup of blessing which we bless, is it not the communion of the blood of Christ? The bread which we break, is it not the communion of the body of Christ?" (1 Cor. 10:15-16). In this text, Paul assumes that he is addressing the wise. He does not speak to those who react to others; his message is for those who submit to the teaching of the Word.

We learn here that the Lord's Supper is a means of blessing; it is very clearly *a means of grace*. Paul identifies the cup as a cup of blessing. This means that when a believer comes to the Lord's Supper, and partakes of it in a worthy manner, he is blessed by God in the coming. This is a blessing the communicant would *not* have received if he had not partaken. Paul says here that there is blessing associated with this cup, and in the next chapter of 1 Corinthians, Paul makes it very clear that abuse of the Supper brings down God's covenantal curses (1 Cor. 11:27–32). Christians in sin are warned about faulty participation in the Supper; those who disregard the warning are guilty of the body and blood of the Lord. They are told that their observance does more harm than good. Such promises and threatenings enable us to see that this is not just some empty religious ceremony.

But the blessing of this sacrament has historically been distorted in two ways. One is the error of the sacerdotalist, who magnifies what happens to the bread and wine to the point of idolatrous superstition. The other is the error of the memorialist, who reacts to the idolatry, and minimizes or denies the reality of the blessing.

The former teaching is that the sacraments perform their function *ex opere operato,* that is, they work blindly and mechanically, quite apart from faith and obedience on the part of the recipient. So some believers, when they have seen this sort of idolatry, have reacted in the opposite direction by saying that the Supper is nothing more than "a mere memorial." Now it is important for evangelical Christians to reject all forms of priestcraft, but we must do so without being reactionary. Biblical rejection of false teaching is not the same thing as mindless reaction to false

teaching. An idolater will say that the observance of the Supper is everything. A reactionary will say, in contrast, that it is nothing. But in order
to maintain his position, the reactionary must do just as much violence
to the biblical data as does the idolater.

The teaching of Paul cannot be reconciled with either extreme. There
is true blessing here, and it is the result of *covenantal identification*. This is
a blessing that is poured out on the believer by a sovereign God in a
providential response to the believer's obedience. The blessing does not
come through the elements, like water through a garden hose. But it
does come *on account of* a worthy and faithful use of the elements.

In the Old Testament, the Levites who ate at the altar were partakers
of the altar (1 Cor. 10:18). When they ate the sacrifices, they were consequently covenantally identified with the God of Israel. In order to make
this happen, God did not magically transform the meat. Nevertheless,
the Levites were blessed when they faithfully kept the sacrificial ordinances God had commanded them to keep.

This sort of covenantal participation is not limited to the godly.
Something similar happened to the idolaters of Corinth. They were partakers at a demonic table, but no sacerdotal miracle was occuring there
either. But by eating at an idolatrous feast, those worshipers were
covenantally identifed with the demons behind their idols (vv. 20–21).

So we must see that the elements are not an automatic channel of
blessing. There is no magic in the Supper. No mystical substance flows
to the believer through the elements. We must remember that in the previous verse (v. 14), Paul warns the Corinthians to avoid idolatry. As the
sacerdotalist error makes plain, one of the ways this warning has been
neglected in the history of the church has been through the sin of looking at the bread and wine as though *they* contained the blessing.

But for most modern evangelicals, the opposite error has been far
more common. The Supper is considered as nothing more than a memorial. Now this is partially correct: it is a memorial, but of what? What is
it that we gather to remember? The obvious response appears to be that
we gather to remember the Lord's death. And it is here that the rampant
sentimentalism about the Lord's death has obscured the very point of
the memorial. It is very common for Christians to think of His death as
an act of love for individual sinners, and nothing more. It is almost
never seen as a covenantal act, establishing a covenantal people.

But how did Christ think of His death? "After the same manner also
he took the cup, when he had supped, saying, *This cup is the new testament* in my blood: this do ye, as oft as ye drink it, in remembrance of me."
(1 Cor. 11:25). When Christ laid down His life, He did so in order to
establish the new covenant with His people. So those who gather to
remember His death, but who neglect the covenantal aspect of it, are
missing the entire point. When we gather at the Supper, we do so in

order to demonstrate our continued understanding of, and faithfulness to, the new covenant. So participation in the Supper is an act of covenantal allegiance. Participation in the Supper is an act of covenant renewal.

This understanding helps us with another problem that has been perplexing to many believers, and that is the question of the "real presence" of the Lord in the Lord's Supper. Because of a long-standing difficulty with Hellenistic categories, the debate has usually centered on whether the Lord's presence is "spiritual" or "physical" or "spiritually physical" or "physically spiritual." But these are not scriptural categories. There is a real presence of Christ in the Supper, but His presence is *covenantal.*

The importance of this would be hard to overestimate. A lot of ink has been used in the discussion of Christ's statement that the bread was His body. Comparatively little has been said about His statement that the cup was the new *covenant.* Thus we will not have a full understanding of the Supper until we recover an ability to think in covenantal categories. And, not surprisingly, the Lord's Supper is a good place to work at this recovery.

Consequently, the backslidden Christian should come to the Supper with trembling, and confession had better be on his lips before the bread and wine is. The one who has been walking faithfully under the covenant should also come with trembling, and in utter humility look for the undeserved blessing. "Open your mouth wide, and I will fill it" (Ps. 81:10).

Bread and Wine

As if the theology of the Supper were not difficult enough in its own right, our modern traditions have created additional questions. And we do have some complicating traditions. What does the Bible teach about the elements of the Supper? What are we required to understand and do?

The elements of the Lord's Supper are bread and wine. Our purpose always is to remember that He has invited us to His Supper, and we are to study to determine how *He* has set the table. And at the same time, we are also to study what manners are appropriate whenever we sit down at His table. How does He want us to treat His other guests?

We must remember the context of Passover. Christ instituted the observance of the Lord's Supper on the 14th of Nisan, at the annual Passover festival of the Jews. In the course of that meal, Christ set apart some of its elements for the establishment of a new meal, the meal of the New Covenant. Christians were to take these elements and remember Him, proclaiming His death, until the Second Coming. At the same time, it is a memorial in the Old Testament sense, in which we are asking God to remember us, for Jesus' sake.

The bread used was the middle loaf of three, and was called the *aphiqomon*.[10] This bread, because it was at the Passover, happened to be unleavened. Christ took it, and broke it, and gave to it a new significance. "This is my body."

During the course of the Passover, there were four cups of wine. The third cup was called the "cup of blessing." This is the cup Paul refers to as being the cup from which Christians would drink until the end of the world. Now this cup was a cup of *wine*—fermented grape juice. The practice of the Jews was to mix water with their wine, usually at a ratio of two to one, so the cup was one of diluted wine. The common evangelical practice of substituting grape juice for wine, simply for the sake of keeping our own pietistic traditions, is scripturally unwarranted, and more than a little impudent.

The questions concerning leavened and unleavened bread are not so simple. Contrary to popular opinion, leaven does not always represent sin in scriptural imagery. The basic idea behind leaven is neither a representation of sin or righteousness, but rather that of *growth*. That growth may be for good or ill, depending on what kind of leaven it is. The imagery of leaven shows that basic religious commitments have consequences over time. Leaven shows us the dominion of a faith. The only question is *whose* faith.

> Another parable He put forth to them, saying: The kingdom of heaven is like a mustard seed, which a man took and sowed in his field, which indeed is the least of all the seeds; but when it is grown it is greater than the herbs and becomes a tree, so that the birds of the air come and nest in its branches. Another parable He spoke to them: The kingdom of heaven is like leaven, which a woman took and hid in three measures of meal till it was all leavened. (Mt. 13:31–33)

The unleavened bread of the Passover meal was a representation of the break with *the leaven of Egypt*.[11] Consequently, the unleavened bread was called the bread of affliction. "You shall eat no leavened bread with it; seven days you shall eat unleavened bread with it, that is, *the bread of affliction* (for you came out of the land of Egypt *in haste*), that you may remember the day in which you came out of the land of Egypt all the days of your life" (Deut. 16:3). The meal was also eaten with bitter herbs to remind the people of the horrible time they had had in Egypt, and to

---

[10] Alfred Edersheim, *Life and Times of Jesus the Messiah* (Peabody, MA: Hendrickson Publishers, 1993), p. 822.

[11] Gary North, *Unconditional Surrender* (Tyler, TX: Geneva Press, 1994), pp. 118–122.

help them look forward to the times of the Messiah. They were not to take any of the leaven of Egypt with them as a "starter." That would simply have built them another Egypt. We may say, on the basis of this passage in Deuteronomy, that the missing leaven from the Passover was to show the *affliction* of Egypt, and the *haste* in which Israel left.

Consequently, many have an assumption that leaven in the Bible always represents sin. Certainly it *sometimes* represents sin: "Your glorying is not good. Do you not know that a little leaven leavens the whole lump? Therefore purge out the old leaven, that you may be a new lump, since you truly are unleavened. For indeed Christ, our Passover, was sacrificed for us. Therefore let us keep the feast, not with old leaven, *nor with the leaven of malice and wickedness*, but with the unleavened bread of sincerity and truth" (1 Cor. 5:6–8). Here leaven represents, as it did in the Old Testament, the principle of sin working through the entire loaf. But as we saw above, leaven is also symbolic of the Kingdom of God (Mt. 13:33), working its way through the world. Thus leaven can represent sin, the leaven of Egypt, as it works at corrupting something good, or it can represent God's leaven as it works at establishing righteousness throughout the world. This is found in the Old Testament as well.

When Israel came into the promised land, they were to begin serving the true God. One of their offerings was the peace offering, a picture of the coming reconciliation which the Messiah would accomplish. "Besides the cakes, as his offering he shall offer *leavened bread with the sacrifice of thanksgiving* of his peace offering" (Lev. 7:11–13). This leaven is a picture of thanksgiving, just as a lack of leaven is a picture of affliction under sin and hastening away from sin. Of course it is better to be in haste while fleeing sin than at rest and leisure in sin. But the point of bringing the people of Israel into the promised land was to liberate them from sin and *give them rest.* This meant they were to offer back up to God offerings which had the leaven of *Israel* in it, a thanksgiving leaven, and not the leaven of Egypt.

We see the same truth at the offering of the first-fruits at Pentecost, or the Feast of Weeks — also gloriously fulfilled in the coming of Messiah. "Even unto the morrow after the seventh sabbath shall ye number fifty days; and ye shall offer a new meat offering unto the Lord. Ye shall bring out of your habitations two wave loaves of two tenth deals: they shall be of fine flour; they shall be baken with leaven; *they are* the firstfruits unto the Lord." (Lev. 23:16–17).

Interestingly, the first recorded instance of Christians celebrating the Lord's Supper after its institution was at this festival, at the time of Pentecost (Acts 2:46). At Passover, no leaven could be present. But at Pentecost, the presence of leaven was required. In other words, the first celebration of the Lord's Supper was not held in the strictness of Passover, but in the liberty and joy of Pentecost.

Our celebration of the Supper must therefore be *unleavened* in the sense that we reject all worldliness and sin. Our celebration of the Supper must be *leavened* in the sense that we proclaim a gospel which will transform the entire world. Both are true, and both are necessary and legitimate statements to make at the Supper. But which kind of physical bread should we use? The question should be answered based upon which of these two truths we want to have *preeminence* in our observation of the Supper. First, the Christian Church should stay away from worldliness. Second, Jesus Christ died to save the world.

The tenor of the New Testament is conducive to the latter statement; leavened bread represents a *potent* gospel.

Preparing for the Supper

As we come to the Supper we want to understand it, and we want to understand what we are coming to *do*. In order to do this we must pay special attention to the words of our Lord Jesus:

> Now there was also a dispute among them, as to which of them should be considered the greatest. And He said to them, "The kings of the Gentiles exercise lordship over them, and those who exercise authority over them are called 'benefactors.' But not so among you; on the contrary, he who is greatest among you, let him be as the younger, and he who governs as he who serves. For who is greater, he who sits at the table, or he who serves? Is it not he who sits at the table? Yet I am among you as the One who serves. But you are those who have continued with Me in My trials. And I bestow upon you a kingdom, just as My Father bestowed one upon Me, that you may eat and drink at My table in My kingdom, and sit on thrones judging the twelve tribes of Israel." (Lk. 22:24–30)

No thinking Christian approaches the sacrament flippantly or casually. The Corinthians did not discern the Lord's body in one another, and consequently Paul says their meetings did more harm than good. We are therefore *required* to be in fellowship with one another as we partake. But what if we are not? Does this mean that one has the authority to suspend himself from the Supper, or to excommunicate himself? Not at all.

If a man is coming to the Table with a bad attitude, then he should *not* hold back from partaking. Rather, he should come confessing the attitude. But what if he remembers his brother has something against him (Mt. 5:23)? The passage is talking about presenting a gift, and not about *receiving* this gift from the Lord. Self-suspension may occur legitimately (once in a blue moon), but the common practice among evangelicals of routinely removing themselves from communion is simply unwarranted. Unless Christ has prohibited a man from coming through his ministers, that man should come.

Preparation includes our children, who are here with us.[12] They sing the psalms and hymns, they say *amen* to the prayers, they listen to the sermons. They also ought to partake of the Supper with us *in faith*. Parents therefore should ask themselves two questions with regard to their children taking the Supper. The first concerns baptism. Many disagreements exist among Christians concerning baptism, but there is no disagreement that baptism is the ordinance or sacrament of *initiation* into the visible body, and the Supper is the ordinance of *nourishment* within that body. This means that no one should be taking the Lord's Supper unless he has been baptized. Someone who has not come through the door should not be sitting down at the table.

The second concerns the fact that the Word should accompany the sacrament. When baptism and the Lord's Supper are observed apart from the instruction of the Word, *superstition inevitably results*. Children are not mature, but nowhere does Scripture require *mature* faith in order to be built up by the grace of God. We speak English to our children before they understand it. This is how they come to understand it. We should instruct them through the Supper in a similar way. If children are mature enough to receive simple instruction from their parents as they take the Supper, then they should be included in it. If the children are consistently bearing bad fruit (rebellion, defiance, etc.), then the parents should bring the concern to the elders, who should consider suspension from the Supper, accompanied by instruction.

A last concern has to do with a preparation of the congregation as a whole. The Lord's Supper is not a funeral. The authority of servanthood embodied by Jesus at the Last Supper was placed by Him on all His followers. He gave to them a kingdom, which was designed to be a kingdom of *servants*, but a kingdom nonetheless. A contrast is seen with lordship among the Gentiles. A certain kind of authority is the most natural and carnal thing in the world. As the quarrels among Christ's disciples made plain, that desire for that kind of authority can creep in among the people of God; it can come into the presence of Christ Himself.

Appearances can be deceiving. Who is greater? The one who sits or the one who serves? In the kingdom of heaven, the one who serves his brothers is the one who sits in authority. The lesson must be mastered in order to understand the Lord's Supper. The Lord's Supper is where the Lord makes His servants into kings.

We are eating and drinking at His table, and so we should notice that Jesus gave the Twelve their authority in the kingdom in the context

[12] Peter J.Leithart, *Daddy, Why Was I Excommunicated?* (Niceville, FL: Transfiguration Press, 1992, 1998).

of the first communion meal. What did He say to them? He gave these His servants a *kingdom*, so that they could eat and drink at His *table*, in order that they might *rule* the twelve tribes of Israel. We are seated at that same table today, in order to eat and drink. Do we have the hearts of servants as we do so?

This celebratory meal is the place where we as Christians proclaim the Lord's death. What is the meaning of His death? His death means dominion. His death was how the conquering servant came into His inheritance. We proclaim His death, not with saddened funereal looks, but while seated on a royal dais, in the presence of the one who conquered everything. We begin with confession, but move on to solemn thanksgiving.

When we eat and drink at His table, with a servant's heart, we are not attending a gloomy memorial, sitting in the dark, feeding on a dry cracker. We are engaged, by the mercy and grace of God, in the extension of Christ's kingdom. We are conquering the world *through sitting down in the peace of God*. No more will a man learn war; we are seated in spiritual peace.

Weekly Communion

Of course we know that Word and sacrament go together. But how do they go together? In the minds of many believers, the two go together like ham and eggs, two disparate but complementary elements combining in a pleasing way. But perhaps they go together in another way entirely — one suggestion is that they go together more like cooking and eating.

Before beginning this portion of the discussion, let's pretend for a moment that we have no traditions on frequency of communion to maintain (a big pretend!) and that advocates of every position share the same biblical burden of proof. We know that we are to observe the Lord's Supper, but how often? — daily, weekly, monthly, quarterly, or annually? When we come to this question, we should note initially that virtually no biblical case can be made for our most common practices — monthly and quarterly. While perhaps this is par for the course, it should at least excite some comment.

Annual communion could be defended on the basis of the Lord's Supper being established in the context of Passover which was an annual festival. Jesus said of "this cup," speaking of the cup of blessing in the Passover meal, "As oft as ye drink it" (1 Cor. 11:25). It could be argued that He simply intended this symbolic meaning of the new covenant be added to the annual celebration of the Passover meal. While it is possible that His meaning included this application, subsequent apostolic practice shows that they drank from that cup of blessing far more frequently than this.

Another option is daily communion. In the heady days following Pentecost, the believers broke bread daily, and from house to house (Acts 2:46). As Luke uses this phrase it almost certainly refers to the Lord's Supper. From this we learn that if daily communion is not normative, it is at least lawful. The Lord's Supper should not be *restricted* to the Lord's Day.

But after the situation stabilized, we can see the practice of the early church, settling in for the long haul. "And upon the first day of the week, when the disciples came together to break bread, Paul preached unto them, ready to depart on the morrow; and continued his speech until midnight" (Acts 20:7). They gathered together on the Lord's Day, and they did so for the purpose of breaking bread. Paul assumes the same kind of thing at Corinth. "When ye come together therefore into one place, this is not to eat the Lord's supper. For in eating every one taketh before other his own supper: and one is hungry, and another is drunken" (1 Cor. 11:20–21). The assumption here is that when the Corinthian church came together, it was not to eat the Lord's Supper, even though that is what they thought they were doing. In other words, the Lord's Supper was being abused at Corinth on a weekly basis. (And, as detailed word studies by teetotalers have shown, the abuses had gone so far that Corinthian believers were starting to act silly from drinking too much grape juice.) In other words, they came together weekly on the Lord's Day (1 Cor. 16:1–2). They should have been doing so in order to eat the Lord's Supper, but instead, they were doing more harm than good through their behavior.

It is therefore fair to say that weekly communion, while not mandatory in any absolute sense, is biblically normative. We have as much evidence for weekly communion on the Lord's Day, for example, as we have for meeting on the Lord's Day to do anything else. We have more evidence for weekly communion than we have for weekly sermons, or weekly singing. But why choose? Why not do it all?

And this brings us to consider the theology of the thing, and the initial question of how the Word accompanies the sacrament. We know that a sacrament is both a sign and seal of the covenant promises (Rom. 4:11). Whenever we think of those things which we seal, we should note something about the natural order of things. We write the letter, *then* seal the envelope. We negotiate the contract, and then seal it with signatures. The marriage is conducted first, and sealed sexually that evening. In short, that which seals follows that which is sealed. A seal is, by its very nature, a culmination.

In the prayers, psalms, and sermons of a worship service, the terms of the covenant are praised, noted, explained, and acknowledged. In the sacrament of the Lord's Supper, the covenant is sealed, and because this sacrament (unlike baptism) is repetitive, each sealing is a covenant renewal. Given this, why would we want anything other than a weekly communion service as the culmination of the worship service? We have already seen that this was the general pattern in the time of the apostles, and the theological logic points in the same direction.

We gather in the name of Christ, assembled as His people. We present our praises and petitions to Him, we sing and chant to God the Father in His name, we hear His Word proclaimed, and then, in the most natural way, we sit down with Him at Table. The covenant is explained when we talk. But it is not renewed when we talk. That occurs when we take and eat.

✠ CHAPTER VI ✠

THE LORD'S DAY

Sabbath Rest

The Puritan John Owen once remarked that through various controversies the sabbath itself had been given very little rest. We should pray that this will not be the case in our treatment of it. No question but that sabbatarianism has a bad name. Just say the word *sabbatarian*, and images of purse-lipped Pharisees rise before the mind's eye. In part this has occurred through effective slander in fiction, but it must also be admitted that numerous purported friends of the sabbath have done their favorite day few favors over the years. Too often questions about the fourth commandment deteriorate into whether or not we can ride bicycles in the park on the Lord's Day, rather than asking the question positively — what are we called to *do*?

> Keep the sabbath day to sanctify it, as the LORD thy God hath commanded thee. Six days thou shalt labour, and do all thy work: But the seventh day is the sabbath of the LORD thy God: in it thou shalt not do any work, thou, nor thy son, nor thy daughter, nor thy manservant, nor thy maidservant, nor thine ox, nor thine ass, nor any of thy cattle, nor thy stranger that is within thy gates; that thy manservant and thy maidservant may rest as well as thou. And remember that thou wast a servant in the land of Egypt, and that the LORD thy God brought thee out thence through a mighty hand and by a stretched out arm: therefore the LORD thy God commanded thee to keep the sabbath day. (Deut. 5:12–15)

The heart of the command is to keep the day holy through *rest*. Six days were given for labor, and the seventh is set aside for rest. We learn more about the nature and boundaries of the commandment elsewhere in Scripture, but we must take care not to rush to these other places before noting what the commandment itself expressly requires. We keep the day holy through ceasing from our own vocational business and resting from our labors in the presence of the Lord. The fourth commandment requires that we *abstain* from our normal labor and work. This is defined by what we do in our vocation six days out of seven. The requirement is that we *rest* before the Lord. The definition of work comes from the pattern of our lives, and not from physics.

Once we have settled this, we ask what the possible relations of work to the Lord's Day is. What kinds of work are lawful on the sabbath? First, one type of work is *mandatory* on the sabbath — the work of worship. In Leviticus 23:3, we see that part of the sabbath observance was a weekly convocation and feast. This shows us the development of synagogue worship in the Old Testament was not an arbitrary action on the part of the Jews. They were being obedient to His requirement to assemble on the sabbath, and when the Jews had settled throughout the land, it was not practical to assemble at the Temple weekly. This is why local houses for meeting developed. We have a reference to such meeting houses fairly early, quite apart from the Temple. "They said in their hearts, Let us destroy them together: they have burned up all the synagogues of God in the land" (Ps. 74:8).

In many ways, we can see how the synagogue was the precursor for the church. The Temple was in Jerusalem, but weekly worship was in the local synagogue. The Temple is now Jerusalem above, the mother of us all, but worship on the local level is still necessary. So we still have these meeting houses, these churches. As we gather in these places to worship on the sabbath, pious work is necessary. But the Lord tells us that while such works of piety can profane the sabbath, those who do so are guiltless (Mt. 12:5–7). — "And immediately *on the sabbath* He entered the synagogue and *taught*" (Mk. 1:21).

We are also taught in Scripture that works of necessity and mercy are *permitted* on the Lord's Day. The disciples harvested grain in order to eat on the sabbath (Mk. 2:23–28). When the Jews attacked Christ because his disciples plucked grain on the sabbath — they were doing "what was not lawful" (Mt. 12:2) — Jesus does not dispute with them by maintaining that it really was lawful. Rather he told the story of David and the showbread, which was, on one level, *unlawful* for David to do. At the same time, it was necessary, and hence justified. This means that it was lawful when all of God's law was considered.

With regard to mercy, our Lord was not reluctant to heal on the sabbath (Mk. 3:2–5). "Therefore," Jesus said, "it is *lawful* to do good on the sabbath" (Mt. 12:12). From this we may gather that works of necessity (e.g., food preparation) and mercy (e.g., visiting the sick or hosting guests) are fully lawful.

Consequently, putting this together, we see there are four aspects to proper observance of the Day: rest, worship, maintenance and mercy. Some sabbatarians, unfortunately, leave out the first component, that of rest. They believe that the entire day should be taken up with works of piety, necessity and mercy, making the taking of a nap, for example, unlawful. Not only is this erroneous, but it is an error that overthrows a central point of the commandment. In essence, this declares a restful obedience to be sabbath-breaking. But man was not made for the sabbath — the sabbath was made for man (Mk. 2:27–28). God does not command us to work one way for six days and work hard another way on the seventh. The Lord's Day is a day of *rest*. But, lest we forget the meaning of our rest, we worship the Lord so that the Word might accompany the sabbath ordinance in the same way the Word should accompany the sacraments. The day of rest without the word would soon become something else entirely — a day of recreation and not rest.

When we observe the Lord's Day rightly, we adorn it with our actions, and we make it lovely. When we make it lovely, there will be those who ask us (honestly) for our reasons for this observance. They are not accustomed to sabbath observance, and so they have some questions. But if we have been pursuing a cranky sabbatarianism, then the questions are likely to be adversarial or hostile. This reveals that many of the sabbath's worst enemies have been those who observed it without understanding it.

For those who have questions, the answers are available. When the apostle Paul is discussing the law, he says that love is the summary of the law (Rom. 13:10). He lists a number of the commandments by name, but goes on to include "whatever other commandment there may be." Love does no harm to his neighbor, and therefore love keeps the sabbath. Modern Americans have very little idea how we are wearing one another down, tearing one another apart, through our 24/7 lifestyle. The more I have reflected on this, the more convinced I am that a truly humane and Christian culture is simply impossible unless we learn to keep the sabbath *as a people*. Paul tells us that we do not love if we don't keep the day holy. Of course, as part of the first table of the law, this commandment is primarily directed toward God, but, at the same time, we remember that the sabbath was made for man. We love one another through righteous sabbath keeping. Love is the fulfillment of the law.

This is in keeping with a basic assumption we should have about the New Testament. We should not require that every law or precept in the Old Testament be relegislated in the New in order to have binding authority. Too many Christians today think that requirements of the Old Testament are not binding unless the New Testament says that they are. Rather we should assume that the Word of God given in the Old Testament is authoritative unless the New Testament says that it does *not* remain in force. Thus, on this basis, we continue to tithe, but we do not sacrifice animals. The same is true about keeping the sabbath holy. This commandment remains in force (albeit modified by the New Testament), because the New Testament does not negate observance of the day.

Some object to the very idea of a change in the day because the fourth commandment is one of the Ten Commandments, and it seems that the Ten Commandments have to be inviolable. They were written on tablets of stone, after all. But we may not object in principle to changes within the Ten Commandments (provided they are changes made by *God*). First, remember the Ten Commandments are summary law (Exod. 34:28). They summarize *all* of God's covenant with Israel. This means that the Ten Commandments summarize both creation law and redemptive law — remember that in the new covenant some obedience looks the same, and some looks different. In addition, the sabbath command is a positive ordinance, meaning the visible appearance of obedience can vary while the heart of the commandment remains.

As a summary of both kinds of law (creation and redemptive), we should *expect* changes. Further, this particular commandment changes in its form in the short time between Exodus and Deuteronomy. We can also see that a clear change is made elsewhere in the Ten Commandments (see Exod. 20:12; Eph. 6:3). So the idea of change in form should not be excluded at the outset.

But on what basis do we say there has been a transfer of the day from the seventh to the first? Christians have observed the first day of the week as holy since the first century. Why? We should begin with the basis of the transfer, which is the Lord's resurrection on the first day of the week (Mk. 16:9; Jn. 20:1). He then made a point of appearing to the disciples on the following Sunday (Jn. 20:26). He was establishing a pattern for them to follow, which was reinforced again by the giving of the Holy Spirit at Pentecost, also a Sunday. The disciples were not spiritually slow as they had been during the Lord's earthly ministry, having been now enlightened and empowered by the Holy Spirit. They led the Church in establishing worship on the first day of the week. They met together to break bread in the Lord's Supper on the Lord's Day (Acts 20:7), also gathering for the teaching of the word. Paul required the Corinthians to take a collection on the first day of the week so that they would not have to scramble to get the money together when he arrived (1 Cor. 16:2). The apostle John received the vision that we call Revelation on a day which he called the Lord's Day (Rev. 1:10).

The author of Hebrews puts everything in theological perspective when he says this: "For he that is entered into his rest, he also hath ceased from his own works, as God did from his" (Heb. 4:10). The passage is admittedly vague because of the use of many pronouns, but we can still understand the point through examining the context.[1] Just as God accomplished the work of creation and then rested from His labors, so the Son of God accomplished the work of redemption (*recreation*) and

---

[1] Walter Chantry, *Call the Sabbath a Delight* (Banner of Truth, 1991), p. 95.

then rested from His labors. In the Old Covenant, the pattern was work followed by rest; in the New Covenant, the rest is on the first day, and is followed by work.

An alternative understanding of this passage, which is that a sinner repents of the work of trying to save himself, in a comparable way to God's resting after creating the world, is too much of a stretch. It depends upon a maladroit metaphor — God's work of creation being compared to a life of self-righteous striving, and His satisfied rest compared to a repentant rejection of what had gone before. In the first sabbath, God said it was good. In repentance, a sinner says it was pretty bad.

Now we are in a position to understand Paul's teaching to the effect that every day is alike (Rom. 14:5), and his point is that sabbath observance is part of the old Jewish calendar of sabbaths, new moons, and annual festivals (Col. 2:16–17). We have already seen that for the apostle John, every day was not alike, because he was in the Spirit on a special day, called the Lord's Day. When we remember this we can reconsider the *context* of Paul's teaching in Romans, which was his opposition to a continuation of particular levitical observances. His statement was not an absolute, requiring us to say that no day is special. This would bring him into collision with John. But if he is simply opposing the Jewish ceremonials, there is no conflict with John at all. It was John, remember, who saw the water of the Jewish ceremonial cleansing turned into the wine of the gospel.

The same is true of the passage in Colossians. The triad of sabbaths, new moons, and festivals is a common one in the Old Testament, referring to the sacrificial calendar. We must not forget that the Jews had more sabbaths than just the weekly sabbath. These are the sabbaths (plural) which are fulfilled in the coming of Christ.

In churches which have a commitment to the sabbath, or in churches which are moving toward such a commitment, it is important to remember that the sabbath has often been wounded in the house of its friends. As a minister sets himself to preach on the fourth commandment, he must take great care to avoid encouraging the wrong kind of question from the people. Of course, at some point, certain behaviors will be excluded by a right view of the Lord's Day. But everything depends on *how* they are excluded. The carnal mind naturally gravitates to a list of rules — don't do that, and don't do the other. After his first sermon on the topic of the Lord's Day, the minister will likely be asked by a concerned mom if it is all right for her teenage boy to shoot hoops in the driveway on the Lord's Day. Of course the question must be answered sometime, but it is being approached from the wrong end.

The day should be filled with rest, worship, things necessary, and things kind. In the time left over, the time should be filled with activities that are consistent with the first four, and which the person wants to do having been disciplined and instructed by the first four.

In our home, we celebrate the Lord's Day from 6 pm Saturday night until 6 pm Sunday night. My wife prepares a sabbath feast during the day on Saturday, and when it is ready, the Lord's Day begins. The work of preparation was largely done on Saturday. The point is to fill the day with godly celebration, rest, feasting. Sabbath keeping is the best wine, not tepid water. Observed the right way, the children in the home should grow up longing for the Lord's Day to come. Remember that in obeying this commandment, we must not turn aside either to the right or to the left (Deut. 5:32). Those who carry on business as usual (Neh. 13:15), and those who are "righteous over-much" about sabbath concerns (Ecc. 7:16), are *both* sabbath-breakers.

This is the Lord's Day, and that means that in our minds it should be the best day. More than anything else, this is the tone which a minister should seek to establish in the church concerning the best of days.

The Sabbath As Gospel Rest

Too many Christians have allowed various controversies surrounding the fourth commandment to distract and tangle them up. But in this section, we want to sidestep all the typical "sabbath questions." If we are seeking to live out the gospel, a different approach is needed.

> The stone which the builders rejected has become the chief cornerstone. This was the LORD's doing; it is marvelous in our eyes. This is the day the LORD has made; we will rejoice and be glad in it. Save now, I pray, O LORD; O LORD, I pray, send now prosperity. Blessed is he who comes in the name of the LORD! We have blessed you from the house of the LORD. (Ps. 118:22–26)

This is one of the most frequently quoted passages of the Old Testament in the New. The disciples of the Lord learned the messianic application from the Lord Himself (Mt. 21:42; Mk. 12:10–11; Lk. 20:17; Mt. 21:9; Mk. 11:9; Lk. 13:35; 19:38; Jn. 12:13). Of course, all the Old Testament speaks of Christ, but this portion of this psalm speaks plainly and loudly. The disciples learned their lesson well (Acts 4:11; 1 Pet. 2:7). But which day is spoken of here? It is the day the Lord has made.

The cornerstone was laid on the day of Christ's resurrection. The stone had been rejected three days and nights prior, but now Christ has been declared with power to be the Son of God by His resurrection (Rom. 1:4). This day, the day of His resurrection, is the day the Lord has made, and it is the day on which we should rejoice in the gospel.

As we have seen, Christ rose from the dead on the first day, He appeared again on the eighth day, the next Sunday, He sent His Spirit on Pentecost, a Sunday, He established apostles who met with the Church on the first day. Taking all Scripture together, when we say *this* is the day the Lord has made, which day are we talking about?

> There remains therefore a rest for the people of God. For he who has entered His rest has himself also ceased from his works as God did from His. (Heb. 4:9–10)

Two key words are important here. The first is *sabbatismos*, or sabbath rest, and the second is the word for remains. If Joshua had given the people rest, then there would be no need to speak of *another* day (v. 8).

God created the heavens and earth in six days, and on the seventh He rested. God *re*created the heavens and earth in the death, burial, and resurrection of Christ, and when His work was completed, Christ rested again just as God had rested at the earthly creation. And this is the resurrection rest that we are to enter by faith.

This helps us as we seek to get the gospel right. All the various forms of what we might call cranky sabbatarianism are simply ways of breaking the sabbath, and consequently are ways of misrepresenting the gospel. Cranky sabbatarianism preaches a false gospel. But we must remember that if we say nothing about resurrection and rest, we are acting as if there is *no* gospel.

We are called to a clear declaration of the gospel. As we seek to grow in grace, these are some aspects of the gospel message we are privileged to preach in how we live our lives, and particularly how we live out the gospel in sabbath resting.

It is a time for holy convocation. "Six days shall work be done, but the seventh day is a sabbath of solemn rest, *a holy convocation.* You shall do no work on it; it is the sabbath of the Lord in all your dwellings" (Lev. 23:3). The gospel *gathers* the saints of God.

The sabbath sets sweet rest before us. "Six days you shall do your work, and on the seventh day you shall rest, that your ox and your donkey may rest, and the son of your female servant and the stranger *may be refreshed*" (Exod. 23:12). The gospel *relieves.* Far from bringing burdens, the Lord's yoke is easy, and the burden is light.

Another important part of this practice is redemptive remembering. Even in the Old Testament, the people of God were to remember by this means, not just their creation, but also their salvation. "And remember that you were a slave in the land of Egypt, and the Lord your God brought you out from there by a mighty hand and by an outstretched arm; therefore the Lord your God commanded you to keep the sabbath day" (Deut. 5:15). The gospel *saves,* and the right kind of sabbath keeping is a declaration of this salvation.

We are creatures; although we are redeemed, we still live in the world God made. "Then God blessed the seventh day and sanctified it, because in it He rested from all His work which God had created and made" (Gen. 2:3). The gospel *restores*, and because we reject a gnostic understanding of our salvation, we realize that it restores us physically as well. The physical rest given by sabbath-keeping is also a gospel blessing.

And then we come to feasting — this is especially to be remembered: The Lord's Day is *not* a day of fasting. The gospel is to be heard in a spirit of joy, gladness, and *feasting*. On the day of resurrection commemoration, how did our fathers in the faith act? "These are spots in *your love feasts*, while they *feast* with you without fear, serving only themselves" (Jude 12). The gospel brings *joy*, and the weekly commemoration of that central event to the gospel should do the same thing.

But What About...?

Obviously, questions about the fourth commandment have been controversial for Christians over the years. These controversies have not been manufactured out of whole cloth; an exegetical basis does exist for the questions which arise around the fourth commandment.

But first we have to set the stage. One very common assumption about Old Testament law is that God's law is not binding on us today unless the New Testament expressly says that it is. The other assumption, and the one which we make, is that God's law is binding unless the New Testament shows us the change of application. So the question then becomes, "Has the New Testament set aside, or shown the fulfillment of, the physical observance of the fourth commandment?" Our answer, with the reasons given above, was *no*. But many conscientious Christians answer by pointing to some key passages in the New Testament.

> So let no one judge you in food or in drink, or regarding a festival or a new moon *or sabbaths*, which are a shadow of things to come, but the substance is of Christ. (Col. 2:16)

> One person esteems one day above another; another esteems *every day alike*. Let each be fully convinced in his own mind. (Rom. 14:5)

> But now after you have known God, or rather are known by God, how is it that you turn again to the weak and beggarly elements, to which you desire again to be in bondage? *You observe days* and months and seasons and years. (Gal. 4:9–10)

Let us briefly address these passages in turn. In Colossians, Paul says that we are to let no one judge us "in food or in drink, or regarding a festival or a new moon or sabbaths." First, he says that they are a shadow: In Hebrews, the shadows were *sacrifices* (Heb. 10:1). He then refers to food and drink. In the Old Testament, these two words brought together refer to *sacrifices* (Ezek.. 45:17). Paul refers to "festival," "new moon," "sabbaths." In the Old Testament, these refer to official *sacrifices* (1 Chr. 23:31; 2 Chr. 2:4; 8:13; 31:3; Neh. 10:33; Hos. 2:11). The foundation of all this is Numbers 28. God commands the people of Israel to offer sacrifices on the weekly sabbath (vv. 9–10), on each new moon (vv. 11–15), and on each of the annual festivals (vv. 16–31). This understanding fits with the broader context of Colossians. Gentile Christians are not to allow themselves to be judged by a Judaic asceticism. It has no reference to the fourth commandment when considered *apart from the sacrifices*.

In Romans, Paul says that in disagreements about observance of a "day," each believer is to be fully convinced in his own mind. First, he does not mention the sabbath by name. There were many days observed in the Old Testament law. The context of these disputes at Rome appears to have concerned things closely connected to Jewish scruples and observances. Remember that the relationship between Jew and Gentile is one of the central themes of the New Testament. I believe we see it here.

Now if, from the apostle's standpoint, every day is alike, then what do we do with the scriptural evidence concerning *some* distinction of days? John refers to the "Lord's day" (Rev. 1:10), and the disciples met together on the first day (Acts 20:7; 1 Cor. 16:1–2). Was John a weaker brother? Or was Paul talking about something else here? The latter is clearly more plausible.

Third, for those opposed to sabbath worship, this appeal proves far too much. If it applies to the fourth commandment and not to the ceremonial feasts and sacrifices contained within the law (Eph. 2:15; Col. 2:14), then this gives the church *warrant* to establish the first day of the week as our day of observance, and to be fully convinced about it.

In the passage from Galatians, Paul says that he is worried about the Galatians because they were turning back to Judaism. This is the context of the entire book—the controversy is over circumcision and submission to the entire Old Testament law in its *unfulfilled* sense.

Paul does not mention the sabbath here either. We need to remember the sabbath did not begin with the law of Moses, and so an attack on continuing Mosaic observance is not necessarily an attack on the sabbath. In this light, the immediate context of his warning against calendar observance is his discussion of the maturing of God's church from the time of the Old Testament. He is talking about Old Testament calendar observance.

Our keeping of the Lord's Day must therefore not resemble the bondage resulting from a *distortion* of Old Testament law. We have been set free in Christ, and part of that freedom includes the freedom to rest before Him. The change to the first day should be more than an important symbolic statement; it should reflect the reality of our liberation.

✣ CHAPTER VII ✣

THE WORSHIP SERVICE

The Regulative Principle

How should we then worship? One answer to this question comes in the form of what is usually called the Regulative Principle of Worship. Those who want to uphold the regulative principle usually define it this way: With regard to the worship of the church, "that which is not commanded in Scripture is forbidden."[1]

Steve Schlissel has written cogently on the problems inherent with this, and in his analysis little pieces of strict regulativism fly everywhere, reminding one of Luther taking Erasmus into a theological back alley for a doctrinal drubbing. Schlissel has argued for what he calls the Informed Principle of Worship, which is that "if it is not commanded, it might be prohibited: it depends." But the problem here is that some of the essential questions are still before us.

I have argued before that all Protestants must be regulativists *of some stripe*. This can be seen when we flesh out the larger issues contained in words or phrases of each principle. Of course, when we say in the informed principle that "it depends," we can see that our work is not done. We are invited to ask, depends on *what*? If we say that it all depends on whatever our creative little minds can manufacture, which Schlissel would not say, then we have opened the door to pandemonium in worship. But if we say, as Schlissel does, that it depends upon a sanctified common sense, constrained by general, biblical categories, then we are back at a broad view of the regulative principle.

---

[1] It would be too easy to be hard on those who developed what might be called the strict regulative principle. But they were, many of them, faithful martyrs. This issue did not grow out of academic debate. For background reading, see J. H. Merle d'Aubigne, *The Reformation in England* (Edinburgh: The Banner of Truth Trust, 1962 [1853]), Carlos M. N. Eire, *War on the Idols* (Cambridge: Cambridge University Press, 1986), J.C. Ryle, *Light From Old Times* (Moscow, ID: Charles Nolan Publishers, 2000), and Iain Murray, *The Reformation of the Church* (Carlisle, PA: Banner of Truth, 1965).

This is not necessarily an argument against the informed principle; it just means that we are not done yet. The same problem exists with the regulative principle. When we answer the problems or questions created by these two principles as articulated, provided we answer them biblically, we find that we have arrived at the same place. By *problem* I mean something that has to be unfolded and explained before we know what to do in worship. In short, in the regulative principle, what do we mean by "commanded"? What constitutes a command?

There are two directions we may go — narrow or broad. If we go narrow, we have adopted what Schlissel calls regulativism and what I call strict regulativism. The narrow application of the regulative principle is that in worship whatever is not *expressly* commanded is forbidden. The problems with this are enormous, as Schlissel has proven, and consist basically of being unable to do anything if consistent. In other words, going narrow is not an option. There remains the option, however, of *pretending* to go narrow.

The hermeneutic of requiring express warrant from Scripture for all elements of a worship service is essentially a baptistic approach. For example, because we have no express mention of infant baptism in the New Testament, infant baptism is prohibited. Presbyterian strict regulativists try to get away from this by allowing for express warrant through "good and necessary" deductive consequence. But the case for infant baptism (a compelling one I believe) is theological and broad and not analytic and narrow. It is not on the order of "God made all porcupines, this is a porcupine, and therefore God made it too."

The question of consistency has to be addressed here because strict regulativists are quite arbitrary in their pronouncement on what stays and what goes. Examined closely, it is not the regulative *principle* which is winnowing the wheat and chaff, but rather the personality types of the regulativists themselves. Because the principle they articulate is not the basis for their exclusions or inclusions, then we know the decisions are being made on the basis of another principle, a hidden one. In the case of strict regulativists within the Reformed tradition, the inclusions and exclusions are made, not surprisingly, on the basis of various Reformed traditions. What a shock.

Once we accept the constrictions of a (claimed) narrow approach to the regulative principle, what goes (or should go) on the chopping block? We have no express warrant for worship services on the Lord's Day. We have no warrant for women receiving the Lord's Supper. We have no basis for a benediction at the close of the worship service. We have no grounds for singing psalms *out loud* in the worship service. We have no foundation for putting the pulpit in the center. We have no authority for translating psalms into metrical paraphrases. We have no reason to include baptisms in the worship service at all. We have no grounds for baptizing children of any age. We have no warrant for the use of musical instruments in worship. We have no basis for two services on the Lord's Day. We have no reason for a recitation of the creed. Even when we have some element that has warrant, like Scripture reading, we cannot say where to put it, where or how to begin, and what the ending point should be.

Looking at this list, we see some practices which the strict regulativists admit, and others which they hotly deny. But a strict application of the regulative principle excludes all these things.

John Frame has addressed this dilemma as well.[2] As we have seen, the regulative principle, and the various liturgical monkeyshines which provoke ongoing discussion of it, is a major source of controversy. In the midst of the fray, John Frame carefully presents the regulative principle, as well as his declared adherence to it — kind of. "Scripture must positively require a practice, if that practice is to be suitable for the worship of God. . . . This regulative principle reflects a genuine insight into the nature of biblical worship. As we have seen, worship is for God, not ourselves"[3]

But the regulative principle, as it is has been articulated by strict regulativists, states that whatever specific element of worship is not commanded by God is absolutely forbidden. The problem arises, as Frame adroitly points out, when we try to figure out what these constituent "elements" of worship might be. Each basic element requires a separate command from God. Lack of careful definition in this can lead to enormous problems. For example, are instruments in worship a separate "element" in worship, requiring a distinct command to include them, or are they simply a constituent part of the singing, which is commanded? Are we fulfilling the biblical admonition to sing psalms if we content ourselves with singing psalmishly? Is putting psalms in meter an additional element? If the pastor started singing his sermons, would they still be sermons? How much sand can we add to the sugar before it isn't sugar anymore?

Frame is at his best when he reveals some of these dead ends for strict regulativists. For example, the practice of breaking the service up into constituent elements, each of which must be approved separately by Scripture, is a practice which itself cannot meet its own standard. Where does the Bible require us to require biblical justification for each element of the service? Biblically defined, what is an *element*? "Scripture nowhere divides worship up into a series of independent 'elements,' each requiring independent scriptural justification. Scripture nowhere

---

[2] John Frame, *Worship in Spirit and Truth* (Phillipsburg, NJ: Presbyterian & Reformed, 1996).
[3] Ibid. pp. 38–39.

tells us that the regulative principle demands that particular level of specificity, rather than some other."[4]

At the same time, two important deficiencies in Frame's book are that he misapplies the biblical requirement of intelligibility in worship and appears unaware of the broader meaning of cultural events and movements. With regard to the first, he appeals many times to the fact that the worship of God must be in the language of the people, i.e., it must be culturally relevant to them. "There are different 'musical languages,' just as there are different spoken languages. Therefore, if we are to pursue the biblical goal of intelligible worship. . . "[5] Frame refers to 1 Corinthians 14 throughout his book as requiring intelligible worship, which he takes as requiring some elements of contemporary worship. But in that chapter, Paul was discussing the use of different languages in worship. The Reformers dealt with the same issue when they preached to the people in the common tongue instead of in Latin. But the principle of intelligible worship does not require separate services for valley girls or bureaucrats or any other subgroup with its own jargon. Paul was maintaining that services for Americans should not be held in Chinese, not that surfers should get their own church.

No culture is "neutral." This means we must always be concerned not only with the rightness and wrongness of a particular thing, but also with the rightness and wrongness of the cultural trend it exhibits. As it has been well said, you don't need to be a weatherman to tell which way the wind is blowing. One man may be glad for the little breeze that he feels, while another man looks with concern at the horizon, recognizing a distant hurricane. The issue is not the breeze, but rather what it *means*. Jesus rebuked some of His listeners for not being able to read the signs of the times, and the sons of Issachar are commended for the opposite (Mt. 16:3; 1 Chr. 12:32). Far too many contemporary Christians are gathered around the foot of our postmodern golden calf, not because they want to worship the thing, but just because they like to dance — they like the driving backbeat. Questioned by some grim Moses on their presence there, they say, "Why? What's wrong with dancing?"

Returning to the issue of the regulative principle, as was said above, all Protestants must be regulativists of some sort. God is to be worshiped according to His Word, and not some other way. But worshiping God according to the Word is not a simple matter of connecting the dots. With this recognition of scriptural complexity and latitude, we leave room, not for our own "will-worship," but rather for the all-encompassing authority of Scripture.

A great problem exists with how strict regulativists apply the regulative principle itself. We are to be governed by the Word of God alone,

[4] Ibid. p. 53.
[5] Ibid. p. 140.

and not by any "will-worship" (Col. 2:23). But what does will-worship mean? Is the pianist in a "compromised" church nothing more than a priestess of Baal? *This finicky approach is itself a violation of the regulative principle.* It sets the accuser over the authority of the Word of God in his own worship and in evaluating the worship of others. Is a church nursery "will-worship?" This absurdity is reached by basing the regulative principle on merely a portion of Scripture. What happens when we look at the entire Bible?

Was David right to eat the showbread? Was Naaman right to bow in the house of Rimmon? What did God think of those Israelites who worshiped in the high places, contrary to His Word, but refused to serve idols, in conformity to His Word? Was Christ right to worship in the synagogue, a pattern of worship generally required by God (Lev. 23:3; Ps. 74:8), but nowhere regulated in the details? To ask such questions is to answer them. Put another way, the requirements *of* the Word of God are broader than the requirements *in* the Word of God. Our worship is to be authoritatively regulated *tota et sola Scriptura*, by the Scriptures alone, and by all of Scripture.

As Steve Schlissel has pointed out, the strict regulative principle in Scripture is applied to the worship of the Temple (and even that principle is applied less rigorously than some of our regulativist brethren would desire). With the fulfillment of the sacrificial system, and Christ's ascension to heaven, the restrictions are taken with it. The synagogue, meanwhile, which was the prototype of the Christian church, was required by God, but not highly regulated. What is still tightly regulated is the Temple service and the work of our High Priest. We are not to add to, or subtract from, the *gospel*.

This means that controversies over the "regulative principle" often miss the real problem. When we are confronted with worship services conducted by Kuba the Clown, and we marvel at the flag drill team over by the baptistry, we are tempted to attack the weirdness, instead of the doctrinal confusion which preceded it and produced it. That preceding foolishness is always an abandonment, diminution, or alteration of the gospel of Jesus Christ. That is always the real problem. If a friend decided to abandon his wife in order to run off with another woman, it would hardly be a relevant rebuke for me to point out that his girlfriend wears too much lipstick and has a funny laugh. *That* is not his problem. In the vast majority of "bizarre worship" cases, the real problem was that the church in question abandoned a sound understanding of the gospel long before they began their mummeries.

So the regulative principle, biblically understood, is a Person. The Lord Jesus is the Head of the Church; He is our regulative Principal. This is no appeal to mysticism — this Person has revealed His gospel propositionally in His Word. When we are faithful to that, we will be faithful in worship. As we pursue the crucial question of how we worship, we must go well beyond a narrow critique of narrow regulativism.

Cultural Impact of Worship

The issue of worship is crucial because, for good or ill, the Church leads the way in our culture. Long before feminism became the force it is in our general culture, the feminization of the Church was already old news. Long before subjectivism became a way of life for most Americans, Christians had been groping around in the closets of the soul in search of some meaningful inner religiosity. In a similar way, our willing adoption of breezy informality in worship has led to a host of problems outside the Church.

One of our problems is that we have confounded praise and worship. The definition of praise seems obvious, and fortunately, it is. Praise means to adore, magnify, exalt, and honor the Lord. But most of us think that worship is a synonym for praise, and it really is not. When Abraham took Isaac to the mountain in order to sacrifice him, he told the servants as he was leaving that he and Isaac were going to go to the mountain, to *worship*, and then they would return. He did not mean that they were going to break out their guitars and a tambourine and hold a little service. Rather, *they were going there to do what God had said to do*. Worship means obedient service, and when we gather formally to worship the Lord we are gathering in order to make ourselves available for that service. When Isaiah saw the glory of the Lord fill the temple, his response was one of worship. "Here am I, Lord, send me." We tend to think we are instructed only to go to church; rather, we go to church to be equipped and instructed by the Word and sacraments—instructed on what to do and how to live.

When true worship does not occur, when the worshiper does not remember the name of God, the praise naturally deteriorates and becomes wispy and thin. And this is precisely what has happened to us. We talk about our likes and dislikes with regard to "worship" songs, for example, without any regard for the character, nature, and attributes of God. Our problem is that our debates about praise have not been preceded by worship.

Formal worship is a time when we remind ourselves of our constant and standing duties in the light of who God is. On the Lord's Day, our worship reminds us that the rest of the week belongs to Him as well. When we gather in family worship, we are not setting aside God's portion of the day, but are reminding the entire family that the entire day is His. Put another way, formal worship does not create a secular/sacred distinction. Understood in the classic Protestant fashion, formal worship obliterates such distinctions. I give one day in seven because all seven are His. I give ten percent because one hundred percent is His. I give time during the day to recognize Him with the family because the day is the Lord's.

Paul tells us that our bodies are to be a living sacrifice, holy and acceptable to the Lord (Rom. 12:1–2). The next verse tells us not to be conformed to the world, but to be transformed by the Word of God. Understanding this instruction is much more than the key to personal sanctification; it is the key to cultural transformation. This continual sacrifice is, Paul says, our spiritual worship. The reason the Christian Church today does not have any cultural potency is because our formal worship is so poverty-stricken, and we therefore do not understand how our spiritual worship is to apply on a late Thursday afternoon. All our cultural activities, great and small, are inextricably linked to our spiritual worship, which, in turn, is linked to our formal worship. Christians do not know how to lift a glass of beer to the glory of God for the simple reason that they do not know how to sing the *Gloria Patri*. We do not know how to compose concertos that honor God because if the sermon goes longer than fifteen minutes we get a case of the creeping fantods. We do not know what a statesman is because we do not know what a call to worship is.

Most Christians walk out of the church building thinking that something happened in there (Time, after all, was consumed!), but they would be most surprised to discover that anything worthwhile was supposed to have been *done*. A.W. Tozer once remarked that if revival means more of what we have now, we most emphatically do not need a revival. But if revival means returning to the old paths, and recovering the way of worship which our fathers knew, then we most certainly need a revival. A revival of formal worship filled with doctrine, laughter, glory, and light would be the first step to a remarkable transformation of the nation.

Christians often debate whether or not they should throw themselves into the political realm. Some say we should, because Christians should be involved in saving our culture. Some say we shouldn't, because our culture is soon to be perpendicular to the surface and headed for Davy Jones. We should consequently continue to focus on our "man the lifeboats" evangelism. No one appears to be saying that the cultural and political life of our nation can and should be transformed, and that is why we should concentrate on learning how to worship the Lord.

Just One Channel and No Remote

So worship in the modern evangelical Church is, by and large, pathetic. The Church has left her biblical standard of worship, which is to glorify

God, and has embraced a man-centered goal, which is the enjoyment and pleasure of the viewer. A successful service is now thought to be one in which the participants are pleased. In a biblical service, the desire of the worshippers' hearts is fulfilled when *God* is pleased. But once the goal shifts from the pleasure of God to the pleasure of man, the Church has taken the first step towards liturgical idiocy. When that happens, all conservative challenges to this deterioration will be resisted by the ever-sliding *status quo* until God is pleased to grant a reformation to the Church.

Whenever a culture's goal becomes entertainment, a law of degeneration immediately sets in. In the field of economics, Gresham's Law states that bad money drives out good. In the same way, bad entertainment displaces that which is not quite as bad. In a sinful world, poor comedians will go for the easy laugh with dirty jokes, lousy screenwriters go for high ratings through half-dressed sex cookies, and mindless rock bands yell into the mike, using a lot of dry ice and lasers in the background.

In the Church, the principle is no different. When God is the audience, standards will be high. "And if ye offer the blind for sacrifice, is it not evil? and if ye offer the lame and sick, is it not evil? offer it now unto thy governor; will he be pleased with thee, or accept thy person? saith the LORD of hosts" (Mal. 1:8). Biblical Christianity is a serious, intelligent, and demanding faith, because the God we serve is the Most High.

The evangelical Church at large has opted for the superficial in worship. Devotees whoop and holler their way through trite upbeat songs; sometimes the songs are even blasphemous. At a conference, I once saw grown Christians jumping up and down, lustily singing away, with hand motions, splish-splashing in the blood of Christ. And when the moment turns serious, they cooed their way through worship songs that sounded like they were written for somebody's girlfriend. Substitute *Sheila* for *Jesus* in a lot of these songs, and it would not make much of a difference. At other times some good biblical word like *alleluia* is sung over and over and over, as though it were a mantra for the born-again labotomized.

The church building itself often resembles the set of a variety-hour television set. Some members, disgusted with these ecclesiastical monkeyshines, have tried to leave, but they have not really succeeded. Tiring of the circus, they decide to go to the opera. Wanting more serious entertainment, but entertainment nonetheless, they worship with mummeries that resemble an initiation down at the local Moose Lodge. They have simply changed the channel from MTV over to a liturgical PBS.

But the focus of our worship is to be the glory of God. When evaluating a song, or any part of our worship, we should not ask whether we like it, but whether God's name will be lifted up through it. In contrast to this God-honoring evaluation, we often see people visiting various churches the same way a bored television viewer channel surfs, looking for something "he likes."

Because God must be our focus, the standard should be high, not to impress people with a virtuoso performance, but rather to honor His name. This means our lives should be in order, the lyrics scriptural in content, balance, and tone, and the music worthy of Him. This last point is very important, because relativism has invaded the church more successfully in the area of aesthetics than anywhere else. Whenever high musical standards are set, all of a sudden Christians start talking like nihilists. "And who's to say what constitutes good music? *You?*"

The answer is found in Scripture. God is the source of all that is good, and when it comes to music He has said that there is such a thing as skill. "Sing unto him a new song; *play skilfully* with a loud noise" (Ps. 33:3). And this is how those who love Him must strive to serve and honor Him.

The New Testament calls us to have the Word of Christ dwell in us richly as we worship. "Let the word of Christ dwell in you richly in all wisdom; teaching and admonishing one another in psalms and hymns and spiritual songs, singing with grace in your hearts to the Lord" (Col. 3:16). The majesty of our God and the richness of our faith will not manifest themselves in poverty-stricken lyrics and three-chord wonder songs.

The richness of our worship is a good litmus test for the richness of our faith. Tragically, by this standard, the modern evangelical church has sold her birthright. Our name is now Ichabod—the glory has departed. Until the glory returns, the believer can begin consistently to pray for reformation and revival. Or he can shrug it all off, return to Howdy Doody time at church, and scratch a friend's back, a "back next to ya."

Worship Music and Propriety

None of this involves a necessary rejection of more popular forms of music. One of the great problems which modern evangelicals have is their inability to make cultural and social distinctions. The struggle is really over the meaning of the word *propriety*, and this inability to make distinctions is right at the heart of our difficulties in the "worship wars." What kind of music should we use in our worship of the Most High God?

Rejection of a particular kind of music *for worship* is not the same thing as a rejection of that kind of music. I like jazz, I like rock and roll, some of it, I like classical, I like the blues, and I love the psalms. Now given this hash of musical interests and appreciations, you would think that I would be arguing that we should employ all of it in the worship of God. The assumption is that anything we like ought to hauled into the worship service. Not a bit of it, and the key word is *propriety*. I like beer too, but it would be sacrilegeous to have a bottle of beer with me in the pulpit, though it would not be sacrilegious to have a glass of water there.

The problem with many modern evangelicals who automatically insert the kind of music "they like" into their worship of God is the fact that they haven't studied the direction and use of their own music. The problem is not that they like their music so much, the problem is that they think so little of the music they like that they refuse to study what it is *for*.

Music is teleological; it is designed to perform certain functions, to arrive at a certain end. It is not true that any piece of music can be performed for any function, and have the results be at all reasonable or normal. When Saul was in a blue funk, David's music would soothe him (1 Sam. 16:14–17). When the musicians of the Temple came to prophesy, they did it with musical instruments (1 Chr. 25:1). When certain children wanted a jig, they played a pipe (Mt. 11:17). When the prodigal son returned home, the residents of that household broke out the instruments that were conducive for a good bit of dancing (Lk. 15:25), dancing and music, incidentally, that could be heard down the driveway. Music must suit the occasion, and because the tone and mood of occasions vary considerably, the kind of music we play must vary considerably. And as we study the subject of music we see that God has given us an impressive range of musical options to accompany us throughout our lives. The problem with contemporary worship music is not the kind of music it is, but rather the kind of occasion everyone seems to think the service is.[6]

"Wherefore we are receiving a kingdom that cannot be moved, let us have grace, whereby we may serve God acceptably with reverence and godly fear: For our God is a consuming fire" (Heb. 12:28–29). Let those words, *reverence and godly fear*, roll around in the mind and heart while you sing through some inane song, with all the hand motions. The difficulty is not the music, but rather the incongruity of the music and what the Bible says the occasion of formal worship should be like. The music itself, that song itself, might be perfectly fine at a birthday party for someone's kindergarten class. But in the worship of the God of Abraham, it is a wretched insult.

---

[6] The issues surrounding the impact of popular music on worship are complicated and require careful background reading. I recommend John Makujina, *Measuring the Music* (Salem, OH: Schmul Publishing Co., 2000), E. Michael Jones, *Dionysos Rising* (San Francisco, CA: Ignatius Press, 1994), Leonard J. Siedel, *God's New Song* (Springfield, VA: Grace Unlimited Publications, 1980), and Martha Bayles, *Hole in Our Soul* (Chicago: University of Chicago Press, 1994).

Ragtime is not suitable for a wedding march. Complicated operatic music is not suitable for congregational singing.[7] Conversely, swing is suitable for a particular kind of dancing. It might therefore be suitable at a wedding reception, but not during the wedding itself. The preacher tells us there is a time to mourn and a time to dance (Ecc. 3:4). We have music for dancing, we have music for funerals, we have music for military parades, we have music for lovemaking, we have music for a peaceful evening at home, we have music to pump up the crowd at a basketball game, and we have music to write chapters like this by.

Music can be evaluated in two ways. One method is the pure aesthetic evaluation, with teleology forgotten. Considered in this sense, the Brandenburg Concertos are vastly superior to anything in the world of rock and roll—Chuck Berry made this point, perhaps inadvertantly, when he said, "Three great chords and eighteen great albums." This "abstract" evaluation is important but should not lure us into forgetting the teleology of music entirely. Despite this abstract superiority, a performance of the Brandenburg Concertos would not be appropriate in a worship service, any more than some song by Big Fats O' Toole and his Ragtime Seven would be. Superior music is inferior in some settings. Inferior music is inferior in some settings. Music that is poorly done within the constraints of each genre is bad music and shouldn't be tolerated anywhere. Thus, we have good and bad superior music and good and bad inferior music. And surrounding all such distinctions we have the category "appropriate music."

When the role of teleological function is remembered, we see that inferior music can be superior. For an "inferior" social event, that is to say, an informal social gathering, inferior music is better. Blue jeans are better than good clothes if you are chopping wood. Put another way, when chopping wood good clothes are no good. Failure to recognize this can result in serious weirdness. I recall a training film in the Navy which had some machinist mate working on a diesel engine in his dress blues.

The music of Bach and Mozart are the musical equivalents of a great cathedral. And we can all recognize the vast architectural superiority of such a cathedral over the typical suburban house. But it would be a drag to have to make your breakfast or watch Monday Night Football in the cathedral. The fact that it is a superior building does not mean it is superior for every function.

In the same way, congregational worship has a particular function; our corporate goal should be to hallow God's name. This is what we are

---

[7] This is not to say that congregational music should never be initially challenging. Our congregation has had to get over some hurdles in singing Genevan Psalms. But once the Psalm is learned, it is preeminently singable.

doing in worship. And having come to this answer from the Bible, we should ask what music is *fitting*.

Right Pretty

This brings us to our right to make any aesthetic judgments at all. And it may not seem relevant right now, but Abigail was a beautiful and intelligent woman.

Christians are good at fighting relativism when it comes to matters of truth. Those who reject a fixed standard of truth are soon engaged in debate by capable Christian apologists. Believers also do well when the subject at hand is ethics. Those who want moral standards to be set, or set aside, according to the dictates of the current situation are also quickly challenged by Christians. But in the realm of aesthetics we are almost as relativistic as the world outside. Whenever an aesthetic judgment call is made, inside the church or out, the chorus of protests *from Christians* starts in: "But who is to say?" In this, we sound just like the people we debate in matters of truth and ethics. The reason we sound like them is that because, on this issue, we *are* like them. We are seeking to function as though atheism could be true in a limited way, at least on the question of beauty and loveliness.[8]

As a result, we choose churches on much the same principle used in choosing a department store or gas station. In this choice, the criteria are convenience and suitability to our tastes. We function as consumers, and the church is thought of as a service in which religious products are produced, in order to be consumed by us. And, because tastes vary, we drive down "church row" expecting all kinds of worship services— liturgical, traditional, contemporary, odd, bizarre, and so forth.

Beneath this is the assumption that every consumer has a constitutional right to his particular tastes. Some people like contemporary music, and some don't. Some people like complicated music played on a church organ, and some don't. Some like landscapes painted on saw blades, and some don't. All such debates are resolved, at the end of the day, by our free market solution to this dilemma, which is to get in the car and drive around looking for the product which suits you.

Coming from church, we ask whether we liked the music, and not whether it was any good. We ask whether the service met our felt needs, and not whether God was honored in what was sung. We do this because we are relativists, and we might as well say so.

So then, back to Abigail. The fact that the Bible tells us that she was attractive means that such a thing as attractiveness in women exists. The idea that everyone is equally good-looking is consequently

---

[8] Gene Veith, *State of the Arts* (Wheaton, IL: Crossway, 1991).

unscriptural. Extending the point, the fact that a psalm can be played skillfully means that it might not be. It might be played poorly (Ps. 33:3). The musicians selected for the worship of the Temple were talented. Apparently this mattered, but my point is a more fundamental one. Apparently, musical talent *exists* — in just the same way that truth and goodness exist. The Bible says that musical ability exists and is to be preferred in the worship of God.

This is not to say that aesthetic judgments are easy, or that we could flippantly make them without hard thinking and long training. The subject of aesthetics in the light of the Bible's teaching has been long neglected among us, and we cannot expect to recover what we have lost in short order. We cannot throw away a legacy for several centuries, and then expect to get it all back in fifteen minutes. But the fact that the task is difficult does not make it optional.

Given this difficulty, it is not surprising that we are confused. In our debates about worship music, we frequently miss the central point. For example, the issue of *first* importance is not which side is right in the debate over traditional forms or contemporary forms. The thing that really matters is that a true debate be acknowledged to exist. For example, I sometimes jokingly describe the worship service at our church to be "seeker hostile." We do not exactly have what could be described as a contemporary service. This is not because we don't know how; when the church began it was very much a "Jesus people" operation. Over the years, we have come to a different position, and to a different practice. But if someone were to challenge what we are doing because he believed we were not honoring God, I would hail him as an adversary well-met.

This is because the Bible says that an honest answer is like a kiss on the lips. If privileged to debate a brother who said that what we were doing was aesthetically inferior, I would be delighted, because we would share a belief that some standards exist. A man in error will pick up the wrong side of the debate. But a relativist says that all such debates are silly and unproductive. There is no debate, because there is no answer. And this is what I hear from Christians. What I hear is a poor substitute for honest debate, and is, in the final analysis, the counsel of despair. "Who is to say what good music is?" If the question cannot be answered, what shall we sing in heaven?

Our motive for all that we do is to be the glory of God — even if it is something as mundane as eating or drinking (1 Cor. 10:31). How much more, then, should we be seeking the glory of God when we are in the act of, well, *glorifying* Him? Now, of course, Christians would agree that we should sing to glorify God — but the snare comes when we assume that whatever we like is suitable as an offering to God. This was the error of Cain, of Nadab and Abihu, and of those guilty of "self-imposed religion" in Col. 2:23. When we ask what glorifies God, we must seek the answer through careful study of Scripture. Our motive must be to glorify God in our singing, according to the pattern found in His Word. An essential part of this is the necessity of beautiful music.

Of course, church music must not be evaluated aesthetically alone. Men and women express themselves to God through music. This is why it is important for those who sing, whether individually or congregationally, to have hearts prepared to offer the sacrifice of praise. "By him therefore let us offer the sacrifice of praise to God continually, that is, the fruit of our lips giving thanks to his name" (Heb. 13:15). If we do not prepare ourselves spiritually for worship, God is not pleased with our musical offerings. "I hate, I despise your feast days, and I will not smell in your solemn assemblies. Though ye offer me burnt offerings and your meat offerings, I will not accept them: neither will I regard the peace offerings of your fat beasts. Take thou away from me the noise of thy songs; for I will not hear the melody of thy viols. But let judgment run down as waters, and righteousness as a mighty stream." (Amos 5:21–24). We must remember that God takes a dim view of musical hypocrites.

Having said this, we must also add that the aesthetic poverty of much church music really proceeds from our irreverence. Through the prophet Malachi, God protested the blemished offerings being given to Him. "Offer it now unto thy governor; will he be pleased with thee?" (Mal. 1:8). Invited to sing at the White House, how many of us would sing the way we do in our church? The flippancy with which some churches address God is truly frightening. "The LORD reigneth; let the people tremble: he sitteth between the cherubims; let the earth be moved. The LORD is great in Zion; and he is high above all the people. Let them praise thy great and terrible name; for it is holy" (Ps. 99:1–3). We should note the translation here — His name is *terrible*. And this requirement to be God-fearing was not some Old Covenant thing. Paul taught the Philippians to "work out your own salvation with fear and *trembling*" (2:12). But because we do not fear God, we do not worry at all about what kind of music we offer Him.

Our music must be well done, and the Bible says that such beautiful music exists. What is beautiful and what isn't is not simply a matter of personal taste. In Col. 3:16, we are required to have the word of Christ dwell in us richly , and the result of this rich indwelling is to be music. The music that comes forth should reflect the richness of our faith, not the poverty of the faith. If the faith is rich, then the music will be rich as well. Scripture teaches a correspondence between tree and fruit, fountain and water.

Not only must the worship of the congregation be good, it should be good and loud — Scripture does not require the people of God to come before Him in order to mumble. "Sing . . . *with a loud noise*" (Ps. 33:3;

cf. 150). In another place it says, "Make a joyful noise unto the LORD, all the earth: make a loud noise, and rejoice, and sing praise" (Ps. 98:4). Of course instruments are a help here. "Make a joyful noise unto the LORD, all the earth: make a loud noise, and rejoice, and sing praise. Sing unto the LORD with the harp; with the harp, and the voice of a psalm. With trumpets and sound of cornet make a joyful noise before the LORD, the King" (Ps. 98:4–6).

Because the lyrics must have Christ at the center, the lyrics must also be worthy of Him. "Saying with a loud voice, Worthy is the Lamb that was slain to receive power, and riches, and wisdom, and strength, and honour, and glory, and blessing" (Rev. 5:12). An important aesthetic attribute is symmetry; and, in order to be symmetrical, our lyrics must effectively focus on Christ (Rev. 5:9,12), the One in whom all things hold together. They must do so not only in content, but also in form. In order to glorify God as He deserves, the lyrics must be well-written. If they are not, then they will only confuse, distract, mislead, or stumble the saints as they sing to Him. How words go together is not irrelevant to the effectiveness of the communication, and certainly not irrelevant in their effectiveness in giving God glory and honor.

Biblical symmetry results in aesthetic balance. The lyrics should express the doctrine of God's people in a clear, balanced way. This is simply another way of saying the lyrics should be creedal and systematic (Phil. 3:16). Further, the lyrics should express God's truth with the same aroma as found in Scripture (Ps. 95:1–2). Our joy and thanksgiving may not be *pro forma*, but rather an expression of gladness and simplicity of heart.

In short, beauty in our music and lyrics is necessary for this overriding reason—He is worthy.

Solempne

But to many Americans this sounds like a drag. We are a breezy lot; we like to go casual. Whether we are flipping burgers in the back yard or approaching the throne of the Almighty, we want to wear shorts and flipflops. The problem is nearly universal; the only thing that varies from church to church is the extent of the damage.

The one thing needful, as C. S. Lewis once argued, is represented by a Middle English word *solempne*, which expresses something which is desperately needed in our worship.[9] On either side of this *solempne*, we have this error or that one. Either we are right out there on the cutting edge with worship teams, a thumpin' band and all the rest of it, or we are content with our lazy afternoon orthodusty. If the preacher were

---

[9] C.S. Lewis, *A Preface to Paradise Lost* (Oxford: Oxford University Press, 1942). His discussion of solemnity throughout this book is first rate.

ever to whack the congregation with one of those things you use for cleaning rugs, the cloud of dust would look like it had been raised by Jehu's chariot.

Like our word *solemn, solempne* represents the opposite of casual, but unlike solemn, it carries no connotations of austerity, moroseness, or gloom. We moderns have come to associate spontaneity with innocence and virtue, fresh and unsullied. Our adoption of unbiblical criteria means that we frequently overlook those things which the Bible associates with a healthy church, dismissing them as dead simply because they have more formality in the liturgy than we like.

Solempne is out of our reach because we simply assume that formality is deadness. But many different scriptural arguments against the spontaneity assumption could easily be brought — e.g., Christ's worship in the synagogue, the elements of worship required by Scripture, etc. But for our purposes here, one conclusive argument should suffice. God prohibits spontaneity in worship.

In 1 Corinthians 14:40, Paul requires, among other things, that everything be done according to *taxis*, according to *order*. He is not just discouraging chandelier-swinging, he is requiring something else, of a different kind, in its place. The word means "arrangement; order; a fixed succession observing also a fixed time; orderly array [in a military sense]." God requires that everything in the Church should be done according to a set arrangement. Far from "quenching the Spirit," these are the *instructions* of the Spirit. He tells us that our worship service should be planned and predictable. This means that a preset order of worship printed in the bulletin is the result of the Spirit's leading. It is not spiritually stifling.

Paul uses this same word in Colossians 2:5 when he rejoices at what he hears about that church. "For though I be absent in the flesh, yet am I with you in the spirit, joying and *beholding your order*, and the steadfastness of your faith in Christ" (Col. 2:5). How many of us would write to a similar church today, rejoicing to behold their *regimentation*? A vast difference exists between the quenching of the Spirit, which the Bible prohibits, and being quenched by the Spirit, which is the result of listening to His Word.

Of course a worship service may be formal and also lifeless. This is disobedience. "Wherefore the Lord said, 'Forasmuch as this people draw near me with their mouth, and with their lips do honour me, but have removed their heart far from me, and their fear toward me is taught by the precept of men" (Is. 29:13). In the opposite corner, a worship service may be informal and lively. We have no Scripture for this one, other than the implication that the absence of *taxis* did not unchurch the group of saints at Corinth. But we must remember that tolerated disobedience over time always leads to death.

A worship service may be informal and spiritually chaotic, meaning that lifelessness is just around the corner. "Now in this that I declare unto you I praise you not, that ye come together not for the better, but for the worse" (1 Cor. 11:17). If the disorder evident in their worship went unaddressed, the end result of their activity would be final, lasting spiritual inactivity. The activity in a church can simply be a form of pandemonium.

But obedience requires that a worship service be both formal and lively. To say it again, "Though I be absent in the flesh, yet am I with you in the spirit, joying and beholding your order, and the steadfastness of your faith in Christ" (Col. 2:5).

We should therefore see that there are two types of order. When a formal church is unhealthy, it is because their arrangement is the order of china figurines on a shelf. When a formal church is obedient and healthy it is because their arrangement is that of well-disciplined troops preparing themselves for battle. An opposing general would not look at their cavalry, wheeling as though one man, and dismiss them as a bunch of legalists.

The worship of the Church accomplishes work in the world. Battles are won or lost as a result of how our churches worship God. Too often we act as though our differences over liturgy were simply differences over decoration, instead of differences over effective strategy in the midst of a fearful war. There should be no disagreement over whether the warfare of an army should be coordinated or not.

And as the Scriptures declare, when the choir in militant joy goes out as the advance guard of the army, then God's name is glorified, and His enemies are scattered. The worship is formal and exuberant.

Anthems of Conquest

And this brings us to the psalms. Psalms are a potent, world-changing force. Long neglected, the psalms are beginning to find their way back into the public worship of the Church.[10]

Now it is no secret that a debate over exclusive psalmody is ongoing in the Reformed world, but throughout the course of this standing debate, I am aware of no one who wants to maintain that Scripture *bans* the singing of psalms. And yet, despite this theoretical agreement, why, on a practical level, are the psalms virtually banned from the worship of the modern Church? We do not want to sing, "The shields of earth belong to God; He is exalted high."

Without getting into the issues involved with exclusive psalmody

---

[10] A wonderful encouragement to this can be found in James E.Adams, *War Psalms of the Prince of Peace* (Phillipsburg, NJ: Presbyterian and Reformed Publishing Company, 1991).

(yet), at the very least, we must say those interested in the reformation of the Church must also be actively promoting the singing and chanting of psalms. Without a restoration of the psalms to an honored place in worship, our musical worship of the Lord will continue to have the *gravitas* of a glad bag full of styrofoam packing peanuts. And this conflicts with the words of the psalms themselves — "All ends of earth, remembr'ing Him, shall turn themselves unto the Lord."

But we must be careful not to ruin the singing of psalms before we have even sung any of them. The Church should sing psalms because the Church loves to sing the psalms. Advocates of psalms must remember the vast difference which separates those who would create a controversy about the psalms and those who would create a love for the psalms themselves. The need of the hour is for saints who will promote the psalms, not a certain position *about* the psalms. This is because "the law of the Lord is perfect, converting the soul."

In one way, the debate over psalms has been unfortunate, because it has left more than a few believers thinking that psalm-singing is more a solemn duty than it is a joyful part of the privilege of *solempne*. Of course the privilege of worshipping God does not remove the fact that it is a duty. But the history of the Church has recorded more than a few who got hold of the wrong end of the stick. It is perilously easy to neglect the weightier matters of the law. At the same time, it is hard to do this when thinking about what you are singing. "From heav'n O praise the Lord, ye heights His glory raise."

Every congregation is different, and the situations vary. One group of activities cannot be translated without modification to another place. But in our church, it can honestly be said that God has restored psalm-singing among us in such a way that it is a great delight to us. As the Scripture puts it so pointedly, "Is any *merry*? Let him sing psalms" (Jas. 5:13).

Every Lord's Day evening, we have a men's forum for discussion which is prefaced with fifteen or twenty minutes of psalm-singing. Once a month, this men's forum is canceled, and the whole congregation is invited to gather together in order to sing psalms. We gather together, divide up and learn parts, learn new psalms, learn how to chant — in short, we learn to love the psalms. The harmonies are glorious, and the fellowship in the singing is better. The saints start to develop friendships with particular psalms. "Lift up your voice aloud to Him; sing psalms! Let joy resound!"

Generally, in our worship on the morning of the Lord's Day, we sing two hymns, not counting the doxology, and we sing three psalms. Call it dominant psalmody. One of the psalms is sung repeatedly over the course of a month so that we can all learn it. Simply put, the goal is for all the saints to learn how to sing all the psalter. And as much as we delight in what we have been given, we still have quite a bit to learn. And as we learn, the psalms themselves encourage us. "Advancing still from strength to strength, they go where other pilgrims trod, till each to Zion comes at length and stands before the face of God."

Chanting is a little odd, until you get used to it, not to mention through-composed psalms. The advantage of chanting or singing this way is that you do not have to rearrange the psalms into a convoluted meter in order to get them to fit. And it must be honestly admitted that our psalter does have some bizarre syntax here and there. "They utter shall abundantly"(?!)[11] Another blessing about chanting is that when it is done properly, a chanted psalm is simply lovely. "O let Thine ordinances help; my soul shall live and praise Thee yet."

When psalms are restored as a gift of God to His Church, the only right attitude in singing them is one of thoroughgoing gladness and joy. A reformation of the Church is not possible without a reformation of music. And a reformation of music is not going to be possible apart from the psalms. Part of this is the work of learning from the psalms what we should rejoice over. "Among the nations He shall judge; the slain shall fill His path."

When God is praised according to His Word, we may be confident in our praise. We are anchored to the text in our worship; we know that, as we sing, we are singing in the will of God. And the one undertaking this should be prepared — he may have been a Christian for thirty years, and if he starts singing psalms he will find himself singing things that have never occurred to him before. "All people that on earth do dwell, sing to the Lord with cheerful voice."

And when the joy of singing God's Word back to Him is restored, another great joy may be added as well. That is the joy of the spoken *amen*. At the conclusion of each hymn or psalm, the congregation says *amen* together, in one voice. In Scripture the amen is found as a solemn covenant oath, binding the people of God together in everlasting joy. So why not say it at every opportunity? Amen.

Why Not All Psalms?

Given this, is it necessary for Christians to limit their singing in public worship to nothing but psalms? Many sincere Reformed believers maintain just this position; they hold to what is called *exclusive psalmody*. Given what was argued above, that is, a high view of the psalms, exclusive psalmody is somehow thought to be required.

The passage in Colossians 3:16 obviously plays a central role in this debate. In the debate, particular emphasis is placed upon the phrase *psalms, hymns, and spiritual songs,* with the discussion centering on

---

[11] The culprit here is Psalm 145.

whether this phrase was given in reference to the Psalms (150 — no more, no less), or whether it had a broader reference, and could include the singing of uninspired songs.

Before turning to that question, it is important to notice what the passage says is the result of our singing. The apostle says that in the course of our singing we are *teaching* and *admonishing* one another. It is commonly assumed by many that the teaching ministry of the church is limited to the time during which someone occupies the pulpit. But this says the time of singing is also a very important time of *teaching.*

Therefore, the most basic questions to ask about singing in the church are these: Is it *scriptural?* Is it *true?* These are questions which cannot be answered apart from a careful reference to all of the Word of God. Moreover, it cannot be accomplished in our singing unless all the songs are carefully anchored in some way to the Word. This was not done in the last century, and there can be no doubt there was a very serious revolt against biblical doctrine and teaching in music, led by hymn writers such as Fanny Crosby. But was this the result of allowing uninspired hymns at all? Surprisingly to some, the answer is *no.* Rather, the problem was the singing of *erroneous hymns* – hymns that taught falsehood, or which taught truth out of balance.

A parallel can be seen in preaching. Since the death of the apostles, all preaching has been uninspired preaching. But God, in His inspired Word, *commands* uninspired men to teach His Word. Lack of inspiration means that error can creep in, and looking around at the modern Church, we see that a great deal has. Because of the possibility of erroneous preaching, we need some sort of check to keep fleshly imaginations from creeping into the pulpit. We also need a check to keep man-centered sentimentalism from wandering into the hymnbook — thus protecting us from the nuisance of having to come to the garden alone, while the dew is still on the roses.

Exclusive psalmodists are therefore greatly to be commended for calling the Church back to songs which are *anchored* to the mind of God revealed in a portion of Scripture. As mentioned earlier, if anyone questions the value of psalm-singing, but goes ahead and tries it, he will find himself singing truths he has never sung before in his life. This means that what he was singing before was clearly out of biblical balance.

But does Scripture require *nothing* but psalm-singing? No; at this point, unfortunately, exclusive psalmodists overstate the case.

The words found in the Colossians passage (*psalmois, humnois,* and *odais*) have in Scripture both a narrow usage and a broad usage, referring to inspired psalms, uninspired songs, and inspired songs outside the book of Psalms. Before restricting Paul's usage here to the book of Psalms, we need some sort of contextual *requirement* for doing so. The words themselves do not require it.

Secondly, the Old Testament does not require it. Hezekiah, upon recovering from his illness, writes a wonderful song which is not contained in Psalms. It is found in Isaiah 38, and concludes with this: "The LORD was ready to save me: therefore we will sing my songs to the stringed instruments all the days of our life in the house of the LORD" (Is. 38:20). Hezekiah refers to the singing of his songs (plural) in the house of the Lord. None of Hezekiah's songs were in the book of Psalms, and all but one were outside of Scripture. Yet they were sung in the house of God.

Third, restricting ourselves to the book of Psalms would mean that we could not sing the new song that believers sing in the presence of God. "And they sung as it were a new song before the throne, and before the four beasts, and the elders: and no man could learn that song but the hundred and forty and four thousand, which were redeemed from the earth" (Rev. 14:3). Why should we Christians, who are the 144,000, be unable to sing the heavenly song we have learned?

Fourth, the exclusive psalmodist has to make a case which can then be used against his own practice. Psalms put to meter in English, in order to fit a modern tune are, at best, a *paraphrase* of the psalms. The singing of the first seven verses of a psalm in four-part harmony is *not* what David did, and *not* what the Colossians did. Nevertheless, because such compositions are anchored to the text, they are *far better* than something composed by a rootless evangelical, wandering around in his emotions. If the standard is strict *psalming*, all modern psalters that I have seen fail the test. But if the standard is *expositorial and uninspired accuracy*, they are wonderful. The Psalms in my Bible don't rhyme.

If God grants reformation to our ailing church, it will be soon followed by an *explosion* of psalm-singing. But we fear that well-meaning friends of the psalms who claim more for psalming than Scripture warrants may unintentionally hinder that day.

Principles for Music

Thus far we have been very critical of contemporary pop-worship and the various monkeyshines that surround it. But criticism is one thing and articulating constructive principles for godly worship music is quite another. So at this point, we must change direction slightly.

God has given music to his people for His worship and praise throughout the history of his church.[12] From the temple worship under

---

[12] This section was originally a report from a committee on music, a report presented to the session of Christ Church. The committee was composed of Dr. Roy Atwood, Eddie Gray, and me. The bulk of scriptural support here was assembled and arranged by Roy, which I have subsequently written through, over, and around.

the Old Covenant to the new songs sung before the throne of the Lamb under the New Covenant, God calls us as much to faithfulness in our musical worship of Him as in our preaching and teaching of the Word (Col. 3:16).

As churches consider the music they offer to the Lord in worship, they should recognize the general principle first, before moving on to specific principles. The central general principle in determing worship music should be the glory of God. Everything we do in public worship should have this in view. The selection and use of music for public worship should always have as its primary motive the glory and honor of God (Rev. 4:8, 11; 1 Cor. 1:31). Our music should declare the glory of God in spirit and truth, and it is God alone who is to determine how this is best to be done.

This means, in turn, that we should look for specific principles from the Scriptures as we make specific judgments on particular kinds of music.

First, and obviously, the lyrics must be *biblical*. The words of our musical worship and praise should preserve, reflect, and declare the whole counsel of God, from Genesis to Revelation. "All thy works shall praise thee, O Lord; and thy saints shall bless thee" (Ps. 145:10).

God has provided a perfect example and expression of praise, confession, thanksgiving and supplication in the inspired words of the Psalms, the songbook of Israel. The Church must therefore give emphasis to the psalms in public worship (Eph. 5:19; Col. 3:16). One important way of keeping the music generally biblical is to have a constant anchor of singing directly from the Bible. Another way that music should reflect its biblical center is through being *Christ-centered*. The songs of the New Covenant people should direct worship to our New Covenant Head, that is, the Lord Jesus Christ (Rev. 5:12). In addition, our music must acknowledge our *covenantal* obligations and promises, and the blessings and curses sovereignly administered by our Lord (Ps. 72:5; Ps. 79:13). And last, the lyrics should proclaim the gospel; they should be *evangelical*. Christ, as our Lord and Redeemer, must be the only name we lift up under heaven whereby men may be saved (Rev. 5:9).

Secondly, the lyrics of public worship must have catholicity and balance. The range of our singing of psalms, hymn, and spiritual songs should reflect faithfully the whole counsel of God and avoid the temptation of limiting our music to only *some* truths, or to *some* favorite texts (Ps. 103:22). Music among the saints must not be denominational, sectarian, or partisan. Lyrics in public worship must not be limited only to some portions of the Word of God, but must reflect the fullness of God's infallible revelation (Ps. 145:10). Just as there is one Lord, one faith, one hope, and one baptism, so our music must reflect and encourage the true unity of all believers throughout the world and through all ages (Ps. 31:23; 89:7). Our music should reflect our unity with the people of God throughout all lands and all ages (Rev. 5:8). This is one important reason why our songs must not become too provincial — and whether the provincial thinking is chronologically bound or geographically bound is immaterial. Either way, it presents a threat to catholicity.

Third, the lyrics must be holy and reverent. Our songs must, in spirit and truth, embody the reverence and honor due to the Holy God, Creator and Redeemer, into whose presence we are unworthy to approach in our sinful condition apart from Christ (2 Chr. 20:20–21; Ps. 99; Ps. 48; Ps. 5:7).

Fourth, the lyrics should be creedal and doctrinal. The Church's music should state unambiguously the truths of the Christian faith and convictions expressed in our own statement of faith, as well as the ancient orthodox and Reformed creeds. Words which are creedally or doctrinally ambiguous on central concerns of the historic Christian faith should be avoided (Phil. 3:16).

Fifth, the lyrics should be pastoral. Of course, they should encourage and embody faithful worship in spirit and truth (Col. 3:16). In addition, they should provide occasion during the public worship for the congregation to meditate on the truths of the whole counsel of God (1 Cor. 14:15), to confess personal and corporate sins (Ps. 32:1), to receive comfort (Ps. 46), to find assurance of our faith and hope (Ps. 74; 77), to gain encouragement in times of trial and temptation (Acts 16:25; Ps. 102), to demonstrate the communion of the saints (Ps. 133:1–2), to remember God's great love and mercy to all generations (2 Chr. 20:21; Ps. 101), to express heartfelt joy and gratitude with reverence and respect (Ezra 3:10–11; Ps. 100), and to declare our personal and corporate faith in Jesus Christ as Lord and Savior (Phil. 2:10–11).

Sixth, the lyrics should be edifying. The apostle Paul requires that believers teach and admonish one another in their singing. This requires that the lyrics be suited to such a task — the lyrics must be *edifying* (Col. 3:16). They should be clear and understandable to the congregation (1 Cor. 14:16). They should be engaging, well-written and lively, avoiding either undue sobriety or frivolity (Ps. 33:3). They should be filled with the joy of our salvation, and yet avoid a joy tainted with emotionalism or romanticism (Jas. 5:13; Ps. 95:1; Ps. 81:1).

Seventh, the lyrics should be historical. All the lyrics should be set in the context of the historical outworking of God's purposes for human history. At the same time, songs may be topically isolated from historical events without being contextually isolated from the Church found in history (Ps. 80; Ps. 81:1). Specifically, this means that the lyrics should reflect the history of redemption — God's saving work from Genesis to Revelation (Ps. 44:1–8). They should reflect the history of God's preserving love and mercy to all generations of those who love him, and His judgment on those who are in rebellion against Him (Num. 21:17–18; Ps. 33). Lyrics should acknowledge the faith and examples of the saints who have gone before us, expressing the praise of God's people throughout *all* generations. And the lyrics should avoid mere individual spiritual experience, abstracted from God's saving work for his people in ages (Ps. 22:25–31; Ps. 18:49–50).

But, it must be said, lyrics are the easy part. What about the music itself? The first thing we must say is that the music used in public worship should serve the Word. Even with extraordinary gifts in the first century, the apostle Paul required that those who sang in the Spirit should sing with the mind also (1 Cor. 14:15). How much more should we be careful to submit our uninspired music to the authority of the Word as expressed in biblically-grounded lyrics.

Music should support the preaching of the Word in a musically appropriate manner. This means it should express true and spiritual worship, praise, confession, and assurance. Music should be drawn from faithful composers and congregations from throughout the history of the church, avoiding undue focus on one period or style of musical composition — the music should be catholic, just like the lyrics. In addition, the music should encourage a spirit of reverence and joy appropriate to the corporate worship of God by his covenant people.

Second, the music used in public worship should be conducive to *congregational* singing. The selection of tunes should facilitate the congregational singing, giving careful attention to the nature of the music and to the appropriateness of the tunes to the words and the occasion of their singing within the order of service. One issue is *singability*. This excludes some forms of "high" music which are outside the range of the ordinary congregation. All tunes should be conducive to robust, wholehearted singing after a reasonable period of familiarization and practice. However, tunes should not be limited only to those most familiar to the congregation. The people should be encouraged to practice and to improve their repertoire of songs appropriate for public worship (1 Chr. 25:7). Another consideration is *pitch*. A tune's range should match, as much as possible, the congregation's vocal ability, avoiding very high or very low ranges that will tend to exclude some from participation. The *melodies* should be appropriate to the words and occasion of singing within the order of public worship. The *tempo* should be appropriate to the words and occasion of their singing within the order of service, avoiding unduly fast or slow tempos which may exclude some from singing or participating, or make following the words and their meanings difficult. The *rhythm* should be appropriate to the words and occasion of their singing within the order of service, avoiding unduly complex or simplistic rhythms which may make congregational singing either too difficult, or terminally boring.

Third, the music used in public worship should be beautiful. In the lyrics as poetry, in the music as music, and in the combination of the two, laws of aesthetics, derived from a biblical worldview and understanding, should always be acknowledged (Ps. 33:3; 1 Chr. 25:1; Col. 3:16). Beautiful music can biblically be said objectively to exist, and consequently deciding whether a song is beautiful is *not* a matter of subjective personal taste. I have said this three or four times already, but given the pervasive relativism of our culture, this is woefully inadequate.

Fourth, related to the foregoing, those in the church who select the music should be equipped and trained to do so. This means those who are equipped to evaluate and make such determinations are mature (1 Chr. 23:3–5), musically talented and trained (1 Chr. 25:7–8), theologically astute (Heb. 5:14), and personally holy (Amos 5:23–24). Specifically, such judges should should take into account the importance of balance, unity, variety, harmony, design, rhythm, restraint, and fitness.

Our songs must always be offered by those who love and fear God. The congregation should be regularly exhorted to present their offering of song from hearts that have been filled with the Word of Christ (Col. 3:16) by the Holy Spirit (Eph. 5:18–20). Congregational singing is a duty and privilege; the singing of the congregation is an important time for the people of God to give full expression of their faith in God and love for one another. The song service should be approached with fear, joy, trembling, and peace (Ps. 81:1; 45:1; Is. 30:29; Eph. 5:19).

What about what is sometimes called "special music?" First, choir-singing as a distinct element of public worship is encouraged as a musical expression of praise and thanksgiving (1 Chr. 9:33; 15:16, 27; 25:5–7). However, any use of a choir must take care to avoid the denigration of congregational singing. In conjunction with the choir, soloists or small groups which sing on behalf of the congregation (1 Cor. 14:26) have a special obligation to avoid performing in the church to be seen by men (Mt. 6:5). They also should be trained and skilled in their music (1 Chr. 25:7). The best way to protect this important form of musical worship is to have the choir sing from the *back* of the church.

And what about instruments? Scripture encourages the use of a variety of instruments in the public worship of God (Ps. 98:6; 2 Sam. 6:5; Ps. 137:2; Is. 5:12; Gen. 4:21; Job 21:12; Ps. 150:3; 1 Sam. 10:5; Lev. 25:9; Ezra 3:10; Ps. 68:25). At the same time, the selection and use of instruments must be appropriate for the accompaniment of congregational singing and the enhancement of public worship. And, by this time, it should go without saying that those who play instruments during public worship should be trained and skilled in music (1 Chr. 25:7).

The overarching principle as we consider the issue of our musical service before God is that we are seeking to honor and glorify His name in *what* we sing and *how* we sing. We should want the lyrics to reflect biblical truth, and with a biblical emphasis and balance, in full accord with the doctrinal standards of the church. The lyrics should never allow us to forget our duty of holy reverence as we sing, and they should help to shepherd God's people as they sing. In the words they sing, the saints should be built up in their faith, together with all the saints throughout history. The music should always function as a servant to the Word. In addition, the music should be beautiful, fitting, and well-suited to congregational singing. And all who sing, or play instruments, should present themselves before the Lord in holiness, seeking to present an offering worthy of His name.

Public Prayer

Those who pray in the public worship of the Church have an important responsibility. Depending on the circumstances, the minister will pray, or the elders, or members of the congregation. But in all circumstances, it is important that the prayer fall within scriptural boundaries. And sometimes, those boundaries can be surprising.

For example, the Bible requires that public prayer be kept as *brief* as possible, given the duties and needs we have in prayer. As first glance, this seems counterintuitive, but it only seems this way because our carnal flesh is *very* religious. The Bible says that God is in heaven, and that we are on earth, and so therefore our words should be *few* (Eccl. 5:2). When Jesus taught us to pray, He gave us a prayer that was the very model of brevity (Mt. 6:9–13). Not only so, but He also went back and commented on this aspect of the prayer, chastizing those who think that God is somehow interested in a word count. They actually think, He said, that they will be heard because of their lengthy prayers. Within the church, we should be constantly on guard against the temptation to do a little showboating in the public prayer. Prayer offered up with one eye on the heavens and the other on the cheap seats, is not what we want.

This does not mean that public prayer should be offered for fifteen seconds. Our duties in public prayer are assigned to us, and if we discharge those duties it will take some time. The point being made here is merely that length is not to be valued as an end in itself. Given the time taken by the fixed nature of the prayers that must be offered up, our goal should be brevity, not length.

But brevity can be of two kinds. Someone can be brief because they have nothing to say, but there is a profound brevity as well. Many Christians assume that because they have a problem with the first kind of brevity in their personal prayers, that it therefore is necessary to make the prayers at church as long as possible. But this is a false assumption. Length is thought to be the opposite of ignorant brevity, but the problem is the ignorance.

Profound brevity requires preparation and training. This is an easy point for the garrulous to miss. If someone has been around in Christian circles for a while, and they know the jargon, it is very easy for them to go on in prayer for quite a while *without really saying anything*. Learning to pray through Scripture is one way to achieve a profound brevity.

In discussing the need for preparation and training, this raises the importance of learning how to write out prayers for public worship beforehand. This is likely to excite some prejudice, and so a few preliminary qualifiers are necessary. This not written against extemporaneous prayer at all, but it does assume that *biblical* extemporaneous prayer is far more difficult than a chatty people are likely to think.

When Jesus comments on the need for brevity in prayer, He tells us not to be like the Gentiles with their "vain repetition." The word *battalogeo*, refers to pious yammering. When we start talking about writing prayers down, this makes many evangelicals think of set prayers (as in the Book of Common Prayer), and they start getting more than a little nervous. The fear is that we are inching closer to this sin of vain repetition, and that if we keep this up we soon will be mumbling our way through prayers that we have not ever thought about.

The irony here is that this is the reverse of our actual temptations. If an anecdotal illustration may be permitted, I grew up in evangelical circles and knew the public prayer ropes. I could pray readily in public settings, particularly in church, and did so in accordance with the accepted canons for many years. When I finally began to write my prayers out before the service, I noticed something funny. I had *stopped* repeating myself. I found myself praying in new territory. In short, the previous situation had allowed me to pray predictable prayers that I had not really thought about. Composing prayers beforehand, sitting down and actually thinking through what I was going to say, brought in a whole new world of possibilities in prayer. Too many people, when they pray extemporaneously, pray in the same way they comb their hair. It is a habitual action that requires no thought.

Most forms of extemporaneous prayer may paddle about in new, little circles, but always stay close to the beach.[13] Thoughtful prayer, prepared prayer, sets out to sea. Consider this: "Heavenly Father, we thank you that we can gather here today to worship you . . ." Without preparation, I found myself praying some version of this over and over and over again. But the fact was invisible to me because it was never identical, never verbatim, to the previous prayers. I did not have memorized prayers, and did not play them note for note. But I was always improvising on the same basic melody. What broke this pattern up was the freedom brought by writing prayers down beforehand.

[13] Compare this type of prayer to those found in *Valley of Vision* (Carlisle, PA: Banner of Truth, 1975).

Many bad habits have grown up around our impromptu attempts to pad our prayers. As public prayer becomes more important in a congregation, and less given to rambling, these bad habits should be carefully rooted out.

When the people of God are praying to God, the one offering up prayers on their behalf should not start (or continue) preaching to the people.[14] If a pastor did not get his last point of the sermon in, he must not shoehorn it into the closing prayer. The one praying should never forget who is being addressed. When the prayer suffers a directional drift, the result is that the congregation is addressed in substance with a thin veneer of vocative references to God. "And dear Lord, You know that the Greek verb in verse seventeen is the aorist tense . . ."

Nor should prayer be filled up with pious substitutions for *um*. One favorite substitute is "just." "Lord, we just want to thank You, Lord, for just being our Lord, and we just come to You today to just . . ." And the same could be said, in the preceding example, for the name of God. His name is to be *hallowed*, and not used as a filler or a stop-gap.

Public prayer should not be sentimental and extremely personal. "Lord, Your name is so sweet and precious." The Church corporate is the bride and Christ is the bridegroom, but this should not be used as justification for romantic or syrupy prayers. This does not mean that prayer should be emotionless, but rather that the emotion should be fitting to a public and corporate setting. Here, as it often the case, our model should be the petitions in the psalms. The prayer has to be intimate without being too familiar in a chummy sort of way. We do pray to God as our Father, as Abba, but in the next breath the Lord requires us to *hallow* His name.

But sometimes when men seek to reverence God's name, they wind up on the top of what Samuel Miller called descriptive stilts. The problem is not that the language is reverent, but that it is artificially so. If we imitate the language, tone, and cadences of scriptural language, we will stay well away from this problem.

Writing prayers out beforehand helps to prevent the common problems of cliche-ridden language. Whether we are dealing with thrones of grace, bountiful mercies, or, while we are on the subject of mercies, traveling mercies, it is easy for Christians to develop a specialized prayer jargon. When prayers are written out, this is much easier to see. Writing prayers is also a preventative against rambling with no real direction or point to the prayer. This also helps those who hesitate over words or get otherwise stuck.

Sometimes staunch Calvinists (may their tribe increase) like to get more than a little worm theology into their prayers. What this prayer

[14] Samuel Miller, *Thoughts on Public Prayer* (Harrisonburg, VA: Sprinkle Publications, 1985).

time needs, the thinking seems to go, is about three feet of accumulated total depravity. Of course we are sinners, and of course we must acknowledge it in our prayers. But to wallow in our depravity simply displays it rather than confessing it humbly, receiving God's forgiveness, and moving on.

Also to be avoided would be attempts at wit, sarcasm or humor. In a public setting, it would be rare indeed for such an attempt to be anything other than an appeal to the human audience. But God is our audience. If the one praying thinks that He would think it funny, then there is no problem with offering it up to the Father who hears what we pray in secret.

Prayer can get far too detailed. It is one thing to pray that someone in the congregation would be healed of their sickness. It is another thing to work through their latest lab reports, and responses to various medications. On a related matter, the prayer requests can be too distant for the congregation to be able to say amen. This is the problem caused by a prayer request from someone in the congregation whose cousin in Chicago has a neighbor whose cat was hit by a car.

Sadly, this last problem area has to be addressed somehow. The subject matter should be decent. More than one congregation has been mortified to have to add their corporate *amen* to a plea for the healing of someone's hemorrhoids. While we perhaps have not gone as far as the Philistines and made gold replicas of them to set up in the foyer, we do talk about personal things in public worship far more than we should. Another appalling practice in this regard might be classed as gynecological prayer requests during childbirth. "Susan is now at eight centimeters, and we should all pray . . ." While we should all be concerned, in a *general* way, for the state of Susan's cervix, that's no reason to bring it up in the public prayers at church.

If the pastor offers up the public prayers in worship, he should keep these things in mind as he prepares his prayers and as he considers prayer requests. If the work of prayer is done by other men in the congregation, then the minister should see to it that some sort of pattern or set of guidelines are established so that those who pray can set themselves to mature in this area over time. And at the same time, the congregation is edified as they pray together with those who offer up prayer for the congregation.

Father God, Majestic Father, we come before You today as Your people, assembled together in the name of Jesus Christ. We appeal to Your kindness on that basis, and pray to You in His name, and amen. You created the heavens and the earth by a word, and when You spoke, all the galaxies sprang into being. You ordain how every river flows, and command the course of every breeze throughout the earth. Your Word established the mountains and Your

Word has summoned us here. We come before You, confessing our sins, knowing that apart from the righteousness of Jesus Christ, we could not stand before you at all. We thank You for the gift of His righteousness which enables us to serve You in holiness. Your blessings surround us on every hand. Every day we awake to a new series of gifts from Your hand, and we know that we do not thank You enough for them. Nonetheless, we are very grateful to You for the blessings You pour out constantly. We still require our daily bread, and so we ask You to continue to provide for us as You have done in the past. We depend upon You daily for our sustenance, our health, our finances, our happiness, and so we look to You again now. We ask You to remember us, Your people. In Jesus' name, amen.

A Defense of Liturgy

We like to think that there are liturgical churches and nonliturgical churches out there.[15] But actually what we have is a distinction between churches which are self-conscious about their liturgy and churches which like to pretend they don't have one. Regardless of how much informality is emphasized, over time concrete always sets. As my father once said, Southern Baptist churches like to think of themselves as nonliturgical, but if you go to a Southern Baptist church in Bangkok, you could easily think you were in Macon, Georgia. For another example, a lot of the praise and worship choruses that we like to think of as "contemporary" are not contemporary at all — they are twenty years old, and some folks have now been singing them long enough to be as attached to them as others used to be attached to the *Gloria Patri* and the *Nunc Dimittis*.

The word *liturgy* comes from the Greek *leitourgos*, which is found in numerous places of the New Testament. The word generally refers to *ministry*, whether angelic (Heb. 1:7), the general work of the church (Rom 15:16; Phil. 2:25), or even in the civil realm (Rom 13:6). But the context of the sanctuary in the heavenly Temple provides us with the highest example of it. "Now of the things which we have spoken this is the sum: We have such an high priest, who is set on the right hand of the throne of the Majesty in the heavens; *a minister of the sanctuary*, and of the true tabernacle, which the Lord pitched, and not man" (Heb. 8:1–2). As

---

[15]As with all inflammatory claims, background reading and references are important. See Terry L. Johnson, *Leading in Worship* (Oakridge, TN: The Covenant Foundation, 1996); Peter J. Leithart, *The Kingdom and the Power* (Phillipsburg, NJ: Presbyterian and Reformed, 1993); James Jordon, *Liturgical Nestorianism* (Niceville, FL: Transfiguration Press, 1994); James Jordon, *Theses on Worship* (Niceville, FL: Transfiguration Press, 1994, 1998); and Hughes Oliphant Old, *Worship* (Atlanta, GA: John Knox Press, 1984).

a minister of the sanctuary, the Lord Jesus performs His priestly work.

As a result, as it has developed in our language, liturgy refers to the order of worship in the church. But in popular usage, particularly among informal evangelicals, liturgy does not refer to those who have a set order of worship (which everyone does) but rather refers to those churches in which the order is formal and explicit. Thus we say that a liturgical church is one in which we are likely to find a formal call to worship, a reciting of the Apostles' Creed, a benediction, for some examples, and a nonliturgical church is one characterized by spontaneity, sharing, informality, and so forth. But in reality this is a difference *between* liturgies, not a difference *over* liturgy.

The issue therefore should be whether or not the elements of our liturgy can be defended from Scripture, and not whether we should have a liturgy. In fact, as we have seen, every church has a liturgy. Every church has an order of service. But those which deny they have a liturgy have the side "benefit" of not having to defend what they do scripturally. To take an example from each side of this thing, a minister of a church which recites the creeds will commonly be called up to defend the practice from Scripture (which can readily be done, but that is not the point here), while a pastor of a church which has a place in the liturgy for congregational "sharing" does not have to show scriptural warrant for the practice. In our day, the need to defend sharing is as invisible as air. But if we come to see it as an element of liturgy, we should want our liturgy to be biblical. Where does the Bible tell us to have sharing time? Or a skit? But because the skit is just "an idea," no one thinks that the practice should be defended from Scripture. But of course, all our worship should be scriptural.

One last comment in defense of open, identifiable, honest liturgy needs to be made to those who want to preserve such liturgy. A common mistake made about formal liturgy is that such worship is *necessarily* joyless, which is obviously unscriptural. Since our worship should be robust and joyful, many assume that we must reject formal liturgy. But this is a slander of liturgical worship, a slander, unfortunately, that is made by those on both sides of the debate. Those against liturgical worship will often caricature it as lifeless, cold, and dead. But too often the friends of open liturgy do everything they can to confirm the many prejudices. They mutter the creed, instead of wanting to shout it from the housetops. They mumble through psalms or hymns, rather than singing them the way they were written to be sung. The organist thinks her job description is to be a ball and chain attached to any hymn that threatens to get too robust. Instead of roaring *amen* at the conclusion of prayers, the corporate sentiment appears to be *huh*.

An essential part of the reformation of the modern Church will be a recovery of the excitement that goes with formal liturgy, biblically understood.

The Corporate Amen

Since the congregation is involved throughout the liturgy, it is important that their covenantal presence is acknowledged. One of the best ways to do this is through the corporate *amen*, a word which is probably the most universally-used and universally-recognized word throughout the world. Each of us probably uses it daily, and perhaps we understand it. But when we consider what it means, and consider how we usually say it, or respond to it, we may have to reevaluate. Jerome commented that in the early church, when visitors used to come, they were commonly frightened at the *amen* — it had the sound of thunder, said by people who understood it.

> Blessed be the Lord God of Israel from everlasting to everlasting: And let all the people say, Amen. Praise the Lord. (Ps. 106:48)

We begin with the name of God. In both Old and New Testaments, God identifies *Himself* with this word. In saying it, we must always remember this connection to His holy name and character. Speaking of the time of the New Covenant, Isaiah prophesies, "So that he who blesses himself in the earth shall bless himself in the God of truth [*lit.* "God of *Amen*"]; and he who swears in the earth shall swear by the God of truth [same]" (Is. 65:16).

And John the apostle records, "And to the angel of the church of the Laodiceans write, These things *says the Amen*, the Faithful and True Witness, the Beginning of the creation of God" (Rev. 3:14). And Paul teaches, "For all the promises of God in Him are Yes, *and in Him Amen*, to the glory of God through us" (2 Cor. 1:20).

Remembering this, we see three main uses of *amen* in Scripture. First, it is a covenant oath. This is a word which is taken in the context of affirming covenant obligations — recognizing both the blessings and the curses. We can see this in the law concerning a woman with a jealous husband (Num. 5:22). We have a whole chapter of it in Deuteronomy 27. When Nehemiah confronted the Jewish leaders about their oppression of their fellows, the covenant confrontation concluded with an *amen* (Neh.5:13).

The word *amen* therefore has the force of an oath, sealing an oath, and indicating the agreement of the speaker with the conditions of the covenant. This is far stronger than a simple, "Yes, I agree with that."

In addition, it can be used as a benediction, which is a blessing of the people of God. There are many examples in Scripture, and *amen* is usually a part of it. "Brethren, the grace of our Lord Jesus Christ be with your spirit. *Amen*" (Gal. 6:18). "The grace of our Lord Jesus Christ be with you all. *Amen*" (Phil. 4:23). "The Lord Jesus Christ be with your spirit. Grace be with you. *Amen*" (2 Tim. 4:22). The grace of our Lord Jesus Christ be with you all. *Amen*" (Rev. 22:21). When the people of God receive a blessing, it is right and proper to seal that blessing with an *amen*.

And *amen* also has a doxological use. Justified men have also been given the privilege of blessing *God*. And when men praise, honor, bless and glorify God, i.e., give a doxology, the Scriptures show us to conclude with *amen*—"the Creator, who is blessed forever. *Amen*" (Rom. 1:25). "Christ came, who is over all, the eternally blessed God. *Amen*" (Rom. 9:5); "to Him be glory in the church by Christ Jesus to all generations, forever and ever. *Amen*" (Eph. 3:21). "To Him be glory forever and ever. *Amen!*" (2 Tim. 4:18); "to whom be glory forever and ever. *Amen*" (Heb. 13:21). "To Him be the glory and the dominion forever and ever. *Amen*" (1 Pet. 5:11; cf. Jude 25 and Rev. 1:6). Whenever we say *amen* in this context, we are tasting eternity.

What is the application? In many of the places where Scripture records the use of this wonderful word, it is said by all God's people. This is not something restricted to religious professionals "up front." The whole congregation is involved in the worship of God, and the *amen* is one place where this involvement is most visible. Consider: "And *all the people* shall answer and say, Amen" (Deut. 27:15). "And *all the people* said, Amen, and praised the Lord" (1 Chr. 16:36). "And *all the assembly* said, Amen and praised the Lord" (Neh. 5:13). "Then *all the people* answered, Amen, Amen" (Neh. 8:6). "And let *all the people* say, Amen" (Ps. 106:48).

This may be a good place to note the problems with individualistic amen-ing, with particular congregants noting when and where and how the last point of the sermon struck them. We assemble as a congregation, and we should learn to worship together as a people. Individuals who respond to "can I get a witness" are not working toward this.

On this subject, we have the privilege of applying and obeying together. And so when should we say *amen* during our services? Whenever the Scriptures are read—God's covenant Word to us—we should respond together with *amen*. And when we receive God's blessing on us in the benediction, our grateful response must be *amen*—and *amen* together. And whenever we sing glory to Him in a psalm or hymn, we should conclude with a hearty *amen*. And we must remember the exclamation mark: *Amen!*

✝ CHAPTER VIII ✝

THE GOVERNMENT OF THE CHURCH

Authority and Membership

When we start to study the subject of church government, we are immediately confronted with a problem. One of the more common areas of conflict between nations is that of legitimate jurisdiction and territorial boundaries. It is the same with the church. What are the precise boundaries of the church? Where does the lawful authority of the elders of a church begin and end?

In the church, this question of jurisdiction can be brought to mind through the phrase "church membership." The elders of a church have no ecclesiastical jurisdiction over someone who is a reprobate pagan and outside the church. The duties of the church in such a situation are entirely evangelistic. "For what have I to do to judge them also that are without? do not ye judge them that are within? But them that are without God judgeth. Therefore put away from among yourselves that wicked person" (1 Cor. 5:12–13). The governmental authority of the church does not extend outside the church. In the same way, the civil authority of the United States does not extend beyond her borders. Because this is the case, we must know exactly where those borders and boundaries are.

The problem is, in the modern world, many Christians approach the matter of church membership in a somewhat cavalier fashion. They decide where to attend church in much the same way they do with grocery or department stores — and with the same lack of commitment and loyalty. The modern "no commitment" mentality is uncomfortable with the teaching about membership in Scripture. We should therefore remember the instructions given by the author of Hebrews.

> Remember them which have the rule over you, who have spoken unto you the word of God: whose faith follow, considering the end of their conversation. . . . Obey them that have the rule over you, and submit yourselves: for they watch for your souls, as they that must give account, that they may do it with joy, and not with grief: for that is unprofitable for you. (Heb. 13:7, 17)

These duties set forth for Christians can only be observed in submission to specific leaders in a specific local church. Such duties assigned to members exclude the sort of free-form approach to church membership that is so popular today. With regard to the elders who have the rule in a given church, the congregation of saints was expected to *remember* their rulers (Heb. 13:7), *hear* them teach the Word of God (13:7), *imitate* their lives over time (13:7), *consider* the outcome of their behavior (13:7), *obey* them (13:17), *submit* to them (13:17), and to be *mindful* of their responsibilities (13:17).

It should be obvious that such things simply cannot be done when someone is hopping from church to church, or is sitting in the back row of a mega-church. Church government and membership is both *personal* and *defined*. This personal contact is required in both directions. The elders should know the people in their charge (they must give an account); and, as the passages above make clear, the members must know their elders individually and by name. "And we beseech you, brethren, *to know them* which labour among you, and are over you in the Lord, and admonish you; and to esteem them very highly in love for their work's sake. And be at peace among yourselves" (1 Thes. 5:12–13).

Household Polity

We have already seen that the officers of the church are elected by the congregation. This requires that we must briefly address the question of ecclesiastical voting rights. Who votes in such elections, and why?

In our congregation we practice household voting, meaning that we vote by member households. This does not mean that we have restricted the vote to men only; it means that we have restricted the vote to the heads of member households, which in turn means that the voting is done mostly by men. But when a women is the head of her household, as Lydia was of hers (Acts 16:15), she represents her household and votes with the other heads.

This practice has to be defended on two sides. One criticism comes from those who say women should not vote at all, because this is an act of authority, and Paul says that in the church women should not exercise authority (1 Tim 2:12–15). But this is being overscrupulous with the text. Paul says that women should not teach men either, but in congregational singing, we all teach and admonish one another (Col. 3:16). If someone were to take this text as a prohibition of women participating in congregational singing, our response should be that their handling of the text is overspecifying, the error of making a text address more than it is actually addressing. The act of voting is not an act of authority in the sense that Paul prohibits it to women. Voting is not an exercise of democratic authority, but is rather a submissive representative delegation.

A woman "votes" for a man when she agrees to marry him, but this does not make her the head. It means that she is delegating the responsibilities of headship to him. In the same way, when a women votes in a congregational election, she is not exercising democratic authority any more than the male heads of households are.

On the other hand, the practice of household voting must be defended against critics who charge that this demeans women. In Christ, there is neither Jew nor Greek, slave nor free, male or female. The critic may want to take what was said in the previous paragraph and ask on what principle the vote is being denied to women at all. This should be answered by pointing out that the vote is also denied to *men*.

If we were maintaining that men should vote (because they are intelligent) and that women should not (because they are not), then this approach should indeed be opposed. Rather, this practice says that *households* vote. When a male head of household casts a vote he does so as a representative. He should only do so having been clearly instructed that he is doing so as the representative of his entire household. In particular, when he comes to the point of voting, he should have heard, understood, and thought through any concerns his wife has expressed to him. She already cast a very important vote when she married him, choosing him as her head and spokesman in the important issues of life. This approach simply acknowledges this within the church.

A host of thorny practical problems are solved by this approach as well. With household voting, there is no problem with what to do with baptized children. We simply say that their voice is heard through the head of their house. Churches which grant the vote to individual wives have a big problem when it comes to children—they must draw an arbitrary age line. We also remove the problem of democratic congregationalism. Representative (covenantal) thinking is very important to good order, and a lack of turmoil, in church government. This is not said because there is an assumption that women can't behave in a congregational meeting, but rather that men and women both need to be trained and instructed on the meaning of representation. The more this kind of thinking pervades a congregation, the more that congregation is characterized by mutual submission and charity. The congregation votes for the elders and deacons, but does not expect to vote on every issue that comes before the congregation. They have seen delegation work with their own homes, and so the whole congregation now delegates to the leadership of the church. This is a basis for sound and stable elder rule.

One last observation should be made here. Christian women are generally far more eager for their husbands to assume responsibility and lead than their husbands have been willing to lead. No woman wants to be bossed around, but Christian women usually delight in it when their husbands show interest in spiritual responsibility within the church, and when the husbands assume responsibility to represent their home. When we adopted this approach to household voting, it was implemented without controversy, and the women have delighted in how they have been represented. Without masculine responsibility, reformation in the Church is impossible, and this approach is an important means of inculcating such responsibility.

Biblical Church Discipline

Church discipline is rarely done in the modern Church, and, because it is rarely done, when it *is* done, it is rarely done well. As with everything, we have to turn to the Scriptures for guidance and protection.

> I wrote to you in my epistle not to keep company with sexually immoral people. Yet I certainly did not mean with the sexually immoral people of this world, or with the covetous, or extortioners, or idolaters, since then you would need to go out of the world. But now I have written to you not to keep company with anyone named a brother, who is sexually immoral, or covetous, or an idolater, or a reviler, or a drunkard, or an extortioner — not even to eat with such a person. For what have I to do with judging those also who are outside? Do you not judge those who are inside? But those who are outside God judges. Therefore put away from yourselves the evil person. (1 Cor. 5:9-13)

A moment's reflection shows the need for discipline. In a fallen world, sin will seek to corrupt anything of value. When sin begins to work, the one in a position to discipline has a choice to make. *Discipline is inescapable.* At that point, we will either discipline the sin, or we will discipline the righteous. But as long as the antithesis between the two exists (which is to say, throughout history) we must choose one way or the other.[1]

Scripture does not just command the discipline. We find in the Bible five basic reasons to practice church discipline. Not surprisingly, the practice of discipline generates many objections, but interestingly, these biblical reasons for disciplining usually anticipate and answer some of the more common objections.

First, we are to discipline to glorify God — our obedience in this matter glorifies God. We know that God intends discipline for His church (Mt. 18:15-19; Rom. 16:17; 1 Cor. 5; 1 Thes. 5:14; 2 Thes. 3:6-15; 1 Tim. 5:20; 6:3; Tit. 1:13; 2:15; 3:10; Rev. 2:2, 14-15, 20). God tells us what to do, and because we are His people we are called to do it. This answers the objection, "Who do you think you are?" We do not discipline in our own

---

[1] Jay E. Adams, *Handbook of Church Discipline* (Grand Rapids, MI: Zondervan Publishing House, 1986). See also James Durham, *Concerning Scandal* (Dallas, TX: Naphtali Press, 1990 [1680]).

name, or on our own authority. The Bible says that our good works (when defined by Scripture) glorify God (Mt. 5:16).

Second, we are to discipline in order to maintain the purity of the church. If we measure the "success" of discipline by whether or not the offender is restored, we will be forced to conclude that sometimes it "doesn't work." But if we see other things accomplished by means of discipline, our perspective changes. Conducted biblically, church discipline *always* purifies the church (1 Cor. 5:6–8). It also prevents the profanation of the Lord's Table (1 Cor. 11:27). This also answers the common objection against the faith — "too many hypocrites in church."

Third, we are to discipline to prevent God from setting Himself against the church. If we have a choice to distance ourselves from sin, and we choose rather to identify ourselves with it, then what will a holy God do? We see that God will come Himself and discipline a church which does not willingly follow Him in this (Rev. 2:14–25).

Fourth, we are to discipline in an attempt to restore the offender. We are not promised that the offender will be restored, but this end is nonetheless one of our goals. This rationale is clearly set forth in Scripture (Mt. 18:15; 1 Cor. 5:5; Gal. 6:1). This purpose answers the objection that "discipline is harsh and unloving." The goal is not to destroy the offender; the goal is a confrontation in which we formally protest the fact that the offender is destroying himself. Discipline is an act of love.

And fifth, we are to discipline to deter others from sin — The Bible teaches that consequences for sin deter others (Ecc. 8:11; 1 Tim. 5:20). The objection here is that "people sure wouldn't want to mention any of their spiritual problems around *those* elders!" But the issue is always impenitence, and if someone is intending to continue in sin impenitent, then he had better not mention it to any of the elders. But if he struggles against sin, as all of us do, then he will find nothing in church discipline except an aid in that struggle.

What does biblical discipline look like once it has been implemented? Many misunderstand what is actually being done in discipline. Discipline is not shunning or avoiding. It is rather avoiding company *on the other's terms.*

The most obvious result is that the one disciplined is refused access to the Lord's Supper, as well as the general communion which that Supper seals. But the offender is not being denied kindness, courtesy, opportunity to hear the Word preached, the duties owed to him by others, or anything else due him according to the law of love. He is merely denied one thing: the right to define the Christian faith.

But churches which still remember these principles, and which still practice discipline (and they are relatively few), tend to do so in a judicial manner. There are many admirable aspects to this, in that the principles we have discussed above have been for the most part preserved.

But at the same time, all is not well.

Every institution established by God maintains and protects itself through discipline. But at the same time, there is a vast difference between the civil magistrate, who is given the sword in order to take off the heads of malefactors, and a family, in which mother wields a rod over disobedient children. In the civil realm, we have attorneys, prosecutors, bailiffs, judges, and so forth. When a child disobeys, we have mom and dad. Now when churches discipline, especially presbyterian churches, the model that is usually followed is the civil judicial model.

It is often claimed that such a model is necessary to preserve the rights of the accused. And it is true that the "rules" are often structured that way, with a great noise made on behalf of the accused. But when rules and procedures multiply, students of history should see it as the manufacture of rope for possible judicial lynchings. Complexity in law is a friend to *lawyers*, not a friend to the accused. A certain kind of litigious mind gravitates to rules and procedures, and when that mind is sinful and clever, and the accused is not well-versed in the procedures, judicial mayhem is often in the air.

Put another way, we must beware of a too great reliance on a systematic reconstruction of the various references to discipline in the New Testament. Matthew 18 is not a paint-by-numbers kit, and we should not assume that when we get to "stage two" in a discipline process that we are at the second rung of a metal ladder. In the discipline cases I have observed, no two of them were alike. The attempt to have an *a priori* system set up that covers all contingencies is simply wrong-headed. Of course, certain principles should be publicly acknowledged, and elders should be publicly committed to them, but this is very different from the creation of a "legal system."

A church without discipline is a dying church, incapable of fighting off deadly infection. Throughout this book, the point has been made that the marks of the true Church are Word and sacrament, with both defended through discipline. Discipline is not essential to a church, but, in a fallen world, it is essential to the existence of a church *over time*. Without discipline, those things which are essential to a church, Word and sacrament, will both be corrupted. Church discipline is exercised against both heresy and moral corruption. Discipline protects the Word by disciplining heresy, while protecting the sacraments by discipling those whose lives are immoral.

But in order for this to occur, the discipline must be more than technically biblical. The protection of the church is to be found in wise, conscientious, and honest elders, not in an exhaustive Book of Church Order. Discipline must be biblical in tone, which means that wisdom governs, not procedures. It means that honesty prevails, not shrewdness. In Reformed churches generally, this is an area where continued reformation is greatly needed — the need to recover a more familial understanding of discipline, as opposed to the judicial model.

Denomination Blues

The relationship that should exist between the various local churches of Christ has long been a subject of debate among Christians. Of course, such debate does not necessarily mean that Scripture is silent on the important subject of broader Church government. Rather, it probably tells us more about the attitude of Christians toward such government than about the teaching of the Bible on church government.

Historically, three views have developed. Painting with a broad brush, the first relationship exists when local churches are bound together by means of a "top-down" hierarchy. This is called episcopacy, coming from the Greek word for bishop — *episkopos*. Churches governed in this fashion include the Methodist, Episcopal, Roman Catholic and others. Of course, it should go without saying that the use of a biblical word to describe a system does not necessarily mean it is a biblical system. That has to be determined by a careful study of the biblical requirements for church government.

The second relationship is that of no formal relationship between churches. In other words, each local church is governmentally independent of every other local church. Not surprisingly, this is called independency. Churches governed this way would include Baptist and Congregational churches. Each local congregation constitutes a separate, albeit small, denomination.

The third relationship is presbyterian. In this form of government, the churches are tied together through "bottom-up" representation. Each church, for example, sends several representative elders to a regional meeting, called a presbytery, or, in the continental tradition, a classis. There may be an intermediate level called a synod, and churches send representatives annually to a national gathering, usually called a general assembly. The "higher" gatherings are not necessarily higher at all — they may not originate or legislate any ecclesiastical bright ideas; they may only hear appeals or memorials brought to them by the local churches. Presbyterian and most Reformed churches are in some respect presbyterian.

In this discussion, one of the basic questions concerns how much continuity there is between the government of the Church in the Old Testament and the government of the Church in the New Testament. This is because the Old Testament governmental structure was so clearly "presbyterian" — with one of the key offices in that Church being that of the elder. For example, Numbers 11:16: "And the LORD said unto Moses, Gather unto me seventy men of the elders of Israel, whom thou knowest to be the elders of the people, and officers over them; and bring them unto the tabernacle of the congregation, that they may stand there with thee."

The straightforward use of the word *elder* in the government of the New Testament Church, without any redefinition, indicates continuity, as opposed to discontinuity. The Old Testament Church had elders in a presbyterian form of government (the Sanhedrin was their general assembly). The New Testament church uses the same term *elder* in a very natural way, with no attempt made to redefine how the word is being used. This should lead us to look for something which fits the description of a Christian Sanhedrin — which we do find in the Council at Jerusalem (Acts 15). At the very least, it appears the burden of proof should be upon the one who maintains that the same word is being used to describe an office in an entirely different kind of government.

Another issue in the debate concerns the meaning of the word *church*. If independency is correct, then the word church in the singular should never refer to a collection of local visible churches. But this is not what we find. For example, we should consider Acts 8:1. "Now Saul was consenting to his death. At that time a great persecution arose against the church which was at Jerusalem; and they were all scattered throughout the regions of Judea and Samaria, except the apostles." The Bible teaches us that there were many *thousands* of believers in the church at Jerusalem (Acts 21:20); because of architectural constraints, they certainly they did not all meet at the same location. Three thousand were converted in that city on the day of Pentecost alone, and many more were added subsequently. Nevertheless, they were part of one, regional (city-wide) *church*.

Third, in Acts 15:1-16:5, we see broad church government in action. As we read carefully through the passage, we should note certain particulars. First, a dispute with false teachers arose in a local church. The second point is that the dispute was not resolved in the church where it originated, even though an apostle was on the scene. Third, the matter was referred to a church council of apostles and elders at Jerusalem. Fourth, this council met publicly to deliberate. Fifth, they made a decision. Sixth, the churches of Antioch, Syria, and Cilicia yielded submission.

It is obvious that all the *details* of a presbyterian form of government are not to be found there. At the same time, we must not seek to evade the force of the passage. Governmental action, action by both elders and apostles, did take place, and the decision was applied to churches over an extended area. The authority of the council was not apostolic; otherwise they could have resolved the dispute with an apostolic decision in the church where it began. The elders, and the apostles *as elders*, delivered an authoritative decision to the churches. Probably the best way to understand this kind of extended church government is through the model of a representative, decentralized commonwealth. No permanent hierarchy is established, and yet there is true government which extends beyond the local church. That authority is representative, and, therefore, presbyterian.

Having gotten this straight, we must then factor in the problem of labels and bottle contents. In a perfect world, things would be what we called them — health food would be healthy, guaranteed savings would be, and so on. But this is a fallen world, and we can find, for example, both "independent" and "presbyterian" churches which are actually episcopal. Usually there are two culprits causing this mixup in labels. The first is the problem of a charismatic and influential leader. In an association of independent churches, the influence of a particular teacher may become very powerful. His teaching becomes the standard, and, like it or not, he becomes "the bishop." I recall a number of years ago our church was charged with not being "in submission" to another church. This would be a reasonable accusation if the one making it were advocating a form of episcopacy, but this was coming from someone who was staunchly in the independent tradition. Actually, he just *thought* he was staunchly in the independent tradition.

The second culprit is bureaucracy. This is the besetting sin of American presbyterianism. When an association of independent churches, or the representatives of presbyterian churches, makes the mistake of establishing a permanent headquarters somewhere (minimum requirements: one desk, one phone, one file cabinet), a certain type of bureaucratic mind is immediately attracted to the important task of getting the papers on the left side of the desk over to the right side of the desk. A person with this mindset soon learns where all the levers under the desk are located — what they can do, and how much they can control. Thus a bureaucratic bishopric is born, which soon dominates the representative meetings of the church — setting agendas, controlling missions, determining budgets, and so on.

As we consider these issues, we are not to determine which system is correct through looking at the choices made by godly men down through history. In the first place, each system of government has been adorned with numerous saintly men. Making a decision this way would be simply impossible. We must also remember that some men may have been providentially placed by God in their church, while entertaining serious doubts concerning the government of it. For example, the great theologian Jonathan Edwards, an independent minister, said that "as to the presbyterian government, I have long been perfectly out of conceit of our unsettled, independent, confused way of church government in this land, and the presbyterian way has ever appeared to me most agreeable to the word of God, and the reason and nature of things."[2] He was not presbyterian, but he was certainly sympathetic to that form of government.

In addition, although there are three basic governmental options, the line of demarcation between them is not always necessarily obvious. For example, the presbyterian James Bannerman once said that the independency articulated by John Owen was presbyterian enough for him. And as we go on to examine the details of church government, the anarcho-presbyterianism which will be advocated here will look like independency to some presbyterians, who may themselves be too close to episcopacy, in my opinion. Put another way, we must examine all the issues very carefully.

In the final analysis, we must resort to Scripture in order to address two basic questions. The first concerns whether Scripture reveals an authoritative pattern of church government at all. Perhaps God left this matter unaddressed, leaving it up to local circumstances and interpreted by a sanctified common sense. But if this first question is answered positively, it leads naturally to the second question. "Which pattern of church government is revealed through the Old and New Testaments?"

With a small p

We have identified the three basic options for the government of the broader Church. Those options, again, are no broad government — independency, top-down government — episcopacy, and representative government — presbyterianism.

The first question we must ask is whether the Bible has anything to say on this debate in the first place. Is this debate over church government comparable to a debate over which way the Bible requires us to arrange the chairs Sunday mornings? Or is a certain form of church government *jure divino*, divine law?[3] To answer, all who admit that the church is a divine institution, of which Christ is the Head, must also acknowledge it must therefore be governed according to His Word, and by His authority. Otherwise, we would have to say the governing of Christ's Church can be according to the inventions and whims of men. Clearly, in Bannerman's words, "the presumption is strongly against the notion that Church government is a matter of human arrangement and determination solely." But a key word here is *solely*. The broad outlines of church government can and should be derived from Scripture, but at the same time numerous details of church government have no divine warrant behind them.

---

[2] James Bannerman, *The Church of Christ* (Edmonton, AB: Still Waters Revival Books, 1991 [1869]).

[3] Sundry ministers of London, *Jus Divinum* (Dallas: Naphtali Press, 1995).

So our argument for a certain form of presbyterianism continues, but it is important to remember that the word presbyterian refers to a position, and not to a denominational affiliation. Indeed, being presbyterian in conviction excludes the possibility of joining many Presbyterian churches. We must be careful to set aside any confusion created by human sin or inconsistency on the part of others, or prejudice on our part. For biblical believers, the issue must always be "What does the Bible teach?"

Three basic arguments for presbyterian church government are presented below. Of course, no one argument addresses all the issues, but taken together, they do exclude the only alternatives.

The first thing to consider is the nature of covenantal continuity with the church of the Old Testament. The earliest Christian churches were synagogues (Jas. 2:2; 5:14), and the synagogue system was presbyterian in form. As the Christian Church expanded out into the Gentile world, it was not built *de novo*, from scratch. The establishment of episcopal or independent government would require a change from how God's people had been governed for centuries. The Lord certainly could have made such a change, but He would not have done so without informing His people of it. Nothing in the New Testament indicates a disruption of the system of church government, and in manifold instances we see the governmental continuity displayed in the transition from the Jewish Church to what we might call the International Church. Church officers are called by the same names (elders or *presbuteroi*); believing churches and synagogues were identified as one and the same; the first great controversy which troubled the Christian Church (which, incidentally, was over whether a non-Jew could even be a Christian) was settled in a Christian Sanhedrin, and so on. All these factors, taken together, exclude both principled episcopacy and independency. If the Lord had intended the time of transition to the New Covenant to be a time when the forms of government would also change, He would have revealed that change to us. What He does reveal to us is how the early Christians took over the basic forms of Jewish church government and adapted them, with minor and revealed variations, to their new situation. However, an important caveat must be mentioned here. The continuation of these Hebraic forms of government does not necessarily exclude the existence of "bishops," but it does exclude jure divino bishops, as well as prelatical bishops. There will be more on this in the pages to come.[4]

Secondly, the Bible excludes the possibility of independency by using the term *church*, in the singular, to refer to collections of local churches.

---

[4] Richard Hooker, *Of the Laws of Ecclesiastical Polity* (Grand Rapids, MI: Eerdmans, 1994).

Independency requires that the scriptural use of the word "church" refer only to a local assembly (1 Cor. 16:19), or to the universal, invisible company of the elect (Eph. 5:25). But the Bible clearly identifies historical local churches, taken together, as historically a church. The direct implication of this is that there must be some sort of governmental unity if we are to consider them a single church.

For example, in Acts 2:47, we are told that the Lord added to the Jerusalem church on a daily basis. But that church had at least three thousand members at Pentecost, and thousands more soon after. The Jerusalem church was evidently a church with multiple congregations (Acts 2:46), with a unified government (Acts 6:1-7; 11:30). The same thing is true elsewhere—Ephesus provides a good example of a city with multiple congregations (Acts 19:20) and unified government (Acts 20:17). One of the Ephesian congregations met in the home of Priscilla and Aquila (1 Cor. 16:8, 19). But if we have church government which extends beyond the walls of Priscilla and Aquila's home, this clearly excludes a principled independency. A glimpse of a developing episcopacy might be seen in the fact that Ephesus had multiple congregations, but only one "angel" of the church there. The angel is frequently taken by commentators (and rightly, I think) as a pastoral figure, which could mean that all the congregations in Ephesus had one pastor. This is a slender thread from which to hang a doctrine of jure divino episcopacy, but it is equally difficult to conceive of this shadowy figure as the stated clerk of presbytery.

This leads to the third point, which is the requirement of unity. Christ prayed that His disciples would have true love for one another, and that their unity would be obvious to the world. This unity certainly includes the warmth of Christian fellowship, and can be displayed when members of separate denominations can transcend their differences to fellowship together. But that which they have to transcend is some form of corporate sin. True Christian churches have no business keeping to themselves—our Lord forbade it. Unity includes a host of practical governmental details—e.g., receiving the baptism administered by other churches, communing with saints from other churches, and so on. Biblical unity in government is simply obedience.

Church Officers

Once we have seen the need for unity in church government, we must turn to consider those men responsible for guarding and maintaining that unity. But who are they?

The examination of the doctrines concerning church officers is one of the most rewarding and exciting doctrinal studies that a Christian can undertake. To be sure, for some, it may seem like one of those "dry" subjects, but only because the ramifications are not carefully considered. All churches are "active" on this subject. On this matter, it is impossible even to pretend neutrality. Every church functions in some governmental fashion. And this means that every church government will do what it does in one of two ways — with biblical understanding, or with an absence of biblical understanding.

Among churches which govern themselves according to a pattern not found in Scripture, usually one of two explanations is given. The first (and nobler) claim is to maintain that the practice in question is actually taught in (or permitted by) the Word of God. When such a claim is made, the question then becomes exegetical. Believers can open their Bibles together and study the matter out. But another attitude exists which does not want the question brought to the court of Scripture at all. Throughout history, many Christians have maintained that the various forms of church government are not really a matter of divine law (again, *jure divino*) at all, but rather that God has left us to work out the features of church government using Christian prudence and sanctified common sense. So the first kind of debate concerns what Scripture says on church government, and the second concerns whether Scripture says anything on the subject.

As the following arguments make clear, I believe the Bible does reveal a *general* pattern and obligatory form for church government, and therefore the Church today should conform herself to that pattern. This position acknowledges that every detail of governance is not revealed to us, and where it is not revealed, we *do* have the responsibility to use Christian prudence and sanctified common sense. But at the same time, where we have been given revelation, it simply means that out of the basic governmental options which confront us, the Bible is instructive and normative.

This should delight us. If God has revealed in Scripture how His Church is to be governed, then it is a great privilege for the leaders and members of churches to seek out His wisdom on the subject. And if we have been ignoring God-given instructions on the government of the church, we should not be surprised to see many problems in our churches vanish when we begin to behave in the way we were instructed.

The Church today is not in the same position as the first-century church. At that time, God was still moving in an extraordinary way as He established His apostles as foundation stones in the building of His Church. In the process, the Lord authenticated them in extraordinary ways, giving them a miraculous power. The genuine miracles in the Bible were performed in a way that makes it clear that some of the offices in the early Church were *not* intended to be perpetual.

For example, Paul mentions that the remarkable sign gifts were linked to a remarkable office. "Truly the signs of an apostle were wrought among you in all patience, in signs, and wonders, and mighty deeds" (2 Cor. 12:12). And the author of Hebrews says something similar. "How shall we escape, if we neglect so great salvation; which at the first began to be spoken by the Lord, and was confirmed unto us by them that heard him; God also bearing them witness, both with signs and wonders, and with divers miracles, and gifts of the Holy Ghost, according to his own will?" (Heb. 2:3-4). The fact that some offices are not perpetual must be kept in mind when we consider the government of the church in the first century. For example, the partial list of church offices given in Ephesians includes two, and possibly three, such extraordinary offices. "And He Himself gave some to be apostles, some prophets, some evangelists, and some pastors and teachers, for the equipping of the saints for the work of ministry, for the edifying of the body of Christ" (Eph. 4:11-12).

These extraordinary offices have ceased. The foundation of the apostles and prophets has been laid; it need not be laid again (Eph. 2:20). When building a house, no one pours the concrete over and over again. Foundation work ceases long before work on the building ceases. Consequently, church government today does not include living apostles and prophets. Nevertheless, the office of such men is continuous in the sense that we have their doctrines and teachings contained in the Scriptures, and the teaching of Scripture is normative for the Church. All church officers alive today are required by God to be in submission to these documents. While we do not continue to pour the foundation, we must build the building in line with the foundation that was poured.

Biblical scholars disagree over whether the office of evangelist is extraordinary or not. Those who hold that it is extraordinary believe it to have been the office of an apostolic emissary — something like the office Timothy and Titus held. Those who believe it to be an ordinary and perpetual office understand it as an office of church planting, mission work, and so forth.

All agree the office of pastor/teacher is ordinary and perpetual. Given what is taught in Scripture elsewhere, we can see that this pastoral office carries with it the office of elder. This does not necessarily mean that all elders are pastors, but it does require that all pastors be elders.

Three common biblical terms are used to describe men who lead in the Church. These three terms frequently refer to one man, holding one office. The first term is elder, and the Greek word is *presbuteros*. It is the word for "old man," as well as the word used by the Jews to describe their rulers, both elders in local congregations, and as with the national body of elders, called the Sanhedrin. These rulers need not have been elderly; the name came from the usual pattern, and not from a law. Our word *senator* has the same kind of history.

The second term is *bishop*, with the Greek word for this being *episkopos*. It means "overseer," which is how some translations render it. In the use of this word, we must be careful not to read the subsequent corruptions of church offices back into the first century. What we think of as a bishop today (mitred hat, long robe, etc.) is not the same as a bishop then. The third term is, of course, pastor. The Greek word for this is *poimenos*, and it means "shepherd."

Now how do we know that these different words can refer to men holding the same office? Our authority is Scripture, and we see the New Testament uses these words interchangeably. Consider Titus 1: 5-7: "For this cause left I thee in Crete, that thou shouldest set in order the things that are wanting, *and ordain elders* in every city, as I had appointed thee: If any be blameless, the husband of one wife, having faithful children not accused of riot or unruly. *For a bishop* must be blameless, as the steward of God; not selfwilled, not soon angry, not given to wine, no striker, not given to filthy lucre." We see the same interchangeable use of these words in Acts 20. Notice how Paul speaks to the elders of the church at Ephesus in verses 17 and 28. "And from Miletus he sent to Ephesus, and called *the elders* of the church . . . . Take heed therefore unto yourselves, and to all the flock, over the which the Holy Ghost hath made you *overseers* [bishops], to *feed* [pastor] the church of God, which he hath purchased with his own blood" (Acts 20:17, 28). Paul gathers the *elders* from the city of Ephesus, and during the course of his address to them, he calls them *overseers* or *bishops*. In the next breath, he tells them to *shepherd* or *pastor* the Church of God. We see that in the apostolic era, the city of Ephesus had multiple bishops, and not just one.[5]

The same kind of free interchange is seen in the instruction given by Peter. "The *elders* which are among you I exhort, who am also an *elder*, and a witness of the sufferings of Christ, and also a partaker of the glory that shall be revealed: *Feed* [pastor] the flock of God which is among you, *taking the oversight thereof* ["bishoping"], not by constraint, but willingly; not for filthy lucre, but of a ready mind; neither as being lords over God's heritage, but being ensamples to the flock. And when the chief *Shepherd* [pastor] shall appear, ye shall receive a crown of glory that fadeth not away" (1 Pet. 5:1-4). The Chief Shepherd here is Christ—the true senior Pastor. Under Him, lesser pastors serve. Under Him, these men are called *elders*; it is implied that they are *overseers*, and they are told to *shepherd* or *pastor* the flock. Peter, who held the extraordinary office of apostle, describes himself here as holding the ordinary and perpetual office of elder. John the apostle does something very similar, identifying himself as an elder (2 Jn. 1; 3 Jn. 1).

---

[5] This section is somewhat long and detailed and, depending on the time of day and your frame of mind, tedious. You might want to take a break and read P.G. Wodehouse, *Right Ho, Jeeves* (London: Penguin, 1934).

Of course, it is the responsibility of pastors and elders to constantly acknowledge that Christ is the final Head and only ultimate Pastor in the local church. In a well-ordered church, the headship of Christ will always be firmly and *practically* acknowledged. It is very easy, and very wrong, for a church to establish a head other than Christ. This may be done on a monstrous scale as it is in Roman Catholicism, where the pope is considered the vicar of Christ—Christ's substitute. This is an attempt to destroy the headship of Christ over the Church. Protestants do this on a smaller scale when the word of "the senior pastor" is given the place of the Word of God. It may be done politically, as in the Church of England, for there the Queen of England is the head of the church. In all cases it is wrong—Christ is the only head of His church. "And He is the head of the body, the church, who is the beginning, the firstborn from the dead, that in all things He may have the preeminence" (Col. 1:18).

At the same time, the congregation will be ruled and pastored by a session of elders with diverse gifts and callings. As discussed earlier, Scripture does not allow the natural (and very carnal) tendency to group men into an unbiblical hierarchy. Within the eldership, there is a division of gifts and functions, but this should not be understood as a basis for setting up a distinction of prelatical rank within the body of elders. Under Christ, the highest authority in the local church is the board of elders, or presbyters, in their corporate capacity. Individual elders are therefore responsible for those duties delegated to them by the body of elders, based upon their gifts, abilities, training, desires, and so on. In addition, this delegation should be based upon what the Bible teaches about the special work of those who labor in word and doctrine—pastors and teachers.

While all the elders are equally involved in ruling the church, some will be recognized by the church as especially given to the particular labor of preaching and teaching, word and doctrine. As *elders*, all elders share the same rank and authority without distinction. As *bishops*, all of them share the same general responsibility for oversight. As *pastors*, they are all generally responsible to see that the flock of God is fed and protected. Nevertheless, the church should gratefully acknowledge the variety of particular gifts and callings God gives to individual elders. The church should recognize that some of the elders, though equal in the matter of rule, are especially gifted and called to preach and teach the Word (1 Tim. 5:17-18). Some men are specially gifted in various aspects of the work which is the final responsibility of the whole session. They should be set apart to that work by the session of elders, not to supplant them, but rather to labor on their behalf, and as answerable to them.

Ultimately each local church has only one Pastor, one Bishop, one Elder—the Lord Jesus Christ. But as the Head of the Church, He has appointed a plurality of rulers in the local church, which has been deputized by Him to serve the congregation. And so each local church also has a corporate pastor, a corporate bishop, a corporate elder — the session of elders. But this session is *also* responsible before God to deputize. They do this in order to use the gifts distributed among them to the greatest effect as they labor for the edification of the saints. And so they set apart some individual elders as pastors or teachers. In this sense, an individual elder called as the minister may be considered the pastor, or shepherd, of a church. But if he remembers the pastoral authority of Christ and the pastoral responsibilities of the whole session of elders, he will not understand himself to be the *sole* shepherd of the flock. His role should be that of a well-trained border collie. There are shepherds above him.

With this in mind, we can consider the three distinct callings within the eldership that are found in Scripture.[6] The names used for these various callings within the eldership are descriptive; men must not grasp after them with any kind of lust for personal honor or glory (Mt. 23:8-10; 1 Thes. 2:6). They are to be used simply for the sake of maintaining clear governmental distinctions, and for the sake of honoring the offices Christ has established.

First, we have those elders who rule in the church. Secondly, we have elders who rule, but who also teach. And third, we have elders who rule, and who also teach and pastor. All elders rule, but not all elders are given to the work of teaching or pastoring.

In the first category, some are set apart for pastoral government and rule only. They can be called a *ruler* or *ruling elder* (1 Tim. 5:17; 1 Thes. 5:12-13; Heb. 13:7, 17; Rom. 12:8; 1 Cor. 12:28).[7] At the time of the Reformation (when this office was recovered), such ruling elders were called seniors. The ruling elders principally function in the pastoral government of the church. They are *not* a board of trustees; they are spiritual pastors who shepherd through their abilities in leading (Rom. 12:8) and administration (1 Cor. 12:28).[8] They also have the important role of making final decisions in discipline cases.

A second calling within the eldership is to a didactic ministry of the Word. Such an elder can be called a *teacher* or *doctor* (1 Cor. 12:28; Jas. 3:1; Rom. 12:7). These teachers share in the rule of the church (since all elders rule) and are also responsible for teaching and instruction from the

---

[6] For a contrary view, see B. M. Palmer, ed., *The Collected Writings of James Henley Thornwell,* (Edinburgh: The Banner of Truth Trust, 1974 [1875])and Alexander Strauch, *Biblical Eldership* (Littleton, CO; Lewis & Roth, 1986).

[7] Samuel Miller, *The Ruling Elder* (Dallas, TX: Presbyterian Heritage Publications, 1984 [1832]).

[8] In making this point, Strauch excels, *Biblical Eldership* (Littleton, CO: Lewis & Roth, 1986).

Word. The New Testament clearly distinguishes teaching from preaching, and it is to the former work that the teacher is called. In our parlance, a teacher is given to classroom instruction or catechism.

The third is called to a particular pastoral ministry of the Word; they can be called *teaching elders, ministers,* or *pastors* (Eph. 4:11-12; 1 Pet. 5:2-4; Jer. 3:15). This ministry is usually a pulpit ministry. Ministers share in the rule of the church with the other elders, and they may also share in the teaching load. In addition to this, they are also responsible for the preaching and proclamation of the Word.

The reason for distingushing these different types of elders is found in the usage of Scripture itself — for example, not all elders are given to teaching (1 Tim. 5:17), but there is a class of men in the New Testament called teachers (1 Cor. 12:28). The fact that all teachers are elders should not make us think that all elders are teachers. All spiritual responsibility for oversight belongs to the elders *collectively*; this does not mean that each aspect of such spiritual responsibility belongs to each elder individually. The elders together have pastoral oversight; therefore some of them must be pastors. The elders together have teaching responsibility; therefore some of them must be teachers. Now of course, any given elder should have enough spiritual maturity to teach and pastor individual members of the congregation as questions or concerns arise. But the constraints of time and training mean that the burden of teaching and pastoring a congregation should be delegated to individuals who are ordained to that office, and who serve under the authority and direction of the session of elders.[9]

So we see that the work of teaching and pastoring can be (to a certain extent) delegated. But the joint authority of ruling, however, cannot be delegated to some without destroying the scriptural requirement of plural leadership in the church. Leaders may delegate the responsibility for teaching and remain leaders; they cannot delegate the responsibility for rule and do so.

When Peter is warning Christian leaders against being ecclesiastical tyrants, he says they are not to be lords over those "entrusted" to them : "nor as being lords over those entrusted to you, but being examples to the flock" (1 Pet. 5:3). Literally, this phrase in the original reads nor as lording over "the lots." What is meant by the word *lots*? The various elders were assigned different spheres of work. This will be discussed in more detail when we come to the section which discusses the concept of parish. For the present, within each sphere, the elders

---

[9] I cannot leave this discussion without pointing out a wonderful definition of *monsignor*. "A high ecclesiastical title, of which the Founder of our religion overlooked the advantages." Ambrose Bierce, *The Devil's Dictionary* (New York: Dover Publications, Inc., 1958 [1911]).

were to serve and not dominate. This use of the word "lots" comes from the way the land of Canaan was divided up after the Israelites invaded and conquered it. They apportioned the land by lot. By implication, this means that each elder is to have an assigned task or area of work. When given that area of responsibility, he is commanded not to abuse it.

We should see therefore that government and rule in the church must be collegiate. In the New Testament, we do not see any approval of one-man government in the church. In all meetings of the session of presbyters, each elder has one vote. In their capacity as a session of elders, they oversee all the affairs of the church, including the labors of their fellow elders, the teachers and ministers. In order to see the scriptural basis for insisting upon the collegiate nature of the eldership, consider the following: "And when they had ordained them *elders in every church*, and had prayed with fasting, they commended them to the Lord, on whom they believed" (Acts 14:23). A little bit later, Luke also says, "And from Miletus he sent to Ephesus, and called *the elders of the church*" (Acts 20:17). At the beginning of Philippians, Paul notes, "Paul and Timotheus, the servants of Jesus Christ, to all the saints in Christ Jesus which are at Philippi, *with the bishops* and deacons" (Phil. 1:1).

We do not have one New Testament example of solitary rule or government in the church. On the one occasion that one-man preeminence is mentioned, it is soundly rebuked (3 Jn. 9). But the Diotrephesian spirit has not disappeared; many churches simply do not have genuine spiritual rule given to a college or session of elders. In many cases, the center of authority in a church rests with the senior pastor, an associate pastor, and a professional staff. If there are elders at all, they are often irrelevant in the actual oversight of the church.

In the New Testament, whenever we are given information about the number of men involved, there is always plurality, and it is a plurality at the top. The Hebraic precedent and the apostolic practice are clear. Although there is no express command that every church have multiple elders, we may be confident that to imitate the apostles here reflects the revealed mind of God on this subject. These elders, in their corporate authority, exercise oversight of the entire church, including the work of all individual elders — the "senior pastor" included.

Given the importance of knowing the precise boundaries within the government of the church, we see that church officers need to be set apart by ordination. At the same time, we must be careful with this mark of a well-ordered church because it has been much abused. Ordination is an act of *government*; it is not a charm, or a means by which power or some special apostolic authority is passed on to the recipient. As the passages concerning this demonstrate, ordination is performed by the existing government of the church, and it is solemnized through the laying on of hands. "And when they had ordained them elders in every church, and had prayed with fasting, they commended them to the Lord, on whom they believed" (Acts 14:23). And Paul says this: "Lay hands suddenly on no man, neither be partaker of other men's sins: keep thyself pure" (1 Tim. 5:22). In his vocabulary, to "lay hands" on someone meant to ordain that person.

We see this same responsible government through ordinations in the sending of missionaries (Acts 13:1-30), the appointment of the first deacons (Acts 6:6), and the commissioning of Timothy (1 Tim. 4:14). Such acts of government are especially important when we remember the duties of church members. The members of the church are required to recognize those who have the rule over them (Heb. 13:7, 17). This is not possible unless those who rule are set apart to that rule in an orderly way. This is discussed in more detail in our section of church membership.

Although new officers are ordained through the laying on of hands by the existing elders, they are chosen by the congregation. The Bible teaches that members of the congregation put the prospective elders or deacons forward, which is simply another way of saying that they elect them. After their election, they are subsequently ordained by the existing government of the church.

We see this procedure with special emissaries or representatives of the church in Corinth. "And we have sent with him the brother, whose praise is in the gospel throughout all the churches; And not that only, but who was also *chosen of the churches* to travel with us with this grace, which is administered by us to the glory of the same Lord, and declaration of your ready mind" (2 Cor. 8:18-19).

The verb translated here as "chosen" is *cheirotoneo*, which means "to elect by a show of hands." The same verb is used when we are told about the selection of elders in Acts 14:23. "So when they had appointed [chosen] elders in every church, and prayed with fasting, they commended them to the Lord in whom they had believed."

And of course, we should remember how the first deacons came to be selected. They were chosen in the same way by the "whole multitude." "And the saying pleased the whole multitude: and *they chose* Stephen, a man full of faith and of the Holy Ghost, and Philip, and Prochorus, and Nicanor, and Timon, and Parmenas, and Nicolas a proselyte of Antioch: Whom they set before the apostles: and when they had prayed, they laid their hands on them" (Acts 6:5-6).

Although the writings of early Christians are not finally authoritative for us in these matters, the following should nevertheless be of some historical interest. The post-apostolic book of *1 Clement* says this: "Our apostles also knew, through our Lord Jesus Christ . . . there would be strife on account of the office of the episcopate. For this reason, therefore, inasmuch as they had obtained a perfect fore-knowledge of this, they appointed those [ministers] already mentioned, and afterwards gave instructions, that when these should fall asleep, other approved men should succeed them in their ministry. We are of the opinion, therefore, that those appointed by them, or afterwards by other eminent men, *with the consent of the whole church*" (Chapter 44).

In a similar fashion, the early Christian document known as the *Didache* says, "*Appoint for yourselves*, then, bishops and deacons who are worthy of the Lord—men who are unassuming and not greedy, who are honest and have been proved." It is very clear that one of the features of government in the apostolic church is that the elders and deacons were elected by the people of the congregation.

Doctrinal Qualifications

In the modern world, ministry is often viewed as a profession, and someone is considered qualified to be a pastor as long as he has been certified by a religious graduate school. Further, *he* is supposed to be the trained professional, and the other elders simply bring along some business sense or other forms of practical experience. But this view is not found in the New Testament. If we are trying to follow the requirements of Scripture closely, what basic doctrinal qualifications should we look for in *all* men who are aspiring to the office of elder? Of course these qualifications should be met preeminently in those men who seek to be given to the labor of the Word and doctrine, but the qualifications are for all the elders.

As mentioned earlier, the elder should have a firm knowledge of the whole counsel of God, as contrasted with doctrinal ignorance. His approach to theology should not be a piecemeal one—a little here and a little there. Nor should it be a patchwork of pop-evangelical assumptions. An elder is one of the guardians of the faith in the local church, and he is required to *understand* the faith he is guarding. A bishop must "hold fast the faithful word as he has been taught, that he may be able, by sound doctrine, both to exhort and convict those who contradict" (Tit. 1:9). Paul exhorted Timothy to *hold fast the pattern of sound words* which he heard from Paul, in the "faith and love which are in Christ Jesus" (2 Tim. 1:13). Timothy, as a minister of Christ, had no authority to depart from the pattern of instruction which he had received.[10]

So the doctrinal qualifications of an elder require him to hold fast to the faithful word. He must not be swayed away from the gospel; he must hold to it firmly. In this, he is not to be an "original thinker"—he should

---

[10] The necessity to "not depart" is why an understanding of historical theology is so important. Louis Berkhof, *History of Christian Doctrines* (Carlisle, PA: Banner of Truth, 1937), and William Cunningham, *Historical Theology* (Edmonton, AB: Still Waters Revival Books, 1991 [1882]).

hold to the Word as he was taught. His grasp of doctrine must not be superficial. If he must be able to exhort and convict those who contradict by means of sound doctrine, then his understanding of the faithful Word must be thorough.[11]

Therefore an elder must have a firm understanding of the consequences of ideas. "Then they understood that He did not tell them to beware of the leaven of bread, but of the doctrine of the Pharisees and Sadducees" (Mt. 16:12). It is interesting that our Lord compared the teaching of the Pharisees and Sadducees to *leaven*. Leaven, or yeast, is not dormant. Leaven in a loaf of bread grows and works through the loaf until it pervades the whole. False teaching works in the same way. This means that an elder must be able to understand not only where a particular doctrine *is*, but also where it is *going*. Paul showed this kind of insight when he opposed the error of Peter at Antioch. The simple action of withdrawing table fellowship from Gentiles was seen by Paul (rightly) as something that, in principle, overthrew the gospel of grace. The rest of the church may not understand what all the fuss is about, but then again, the rest of the church is not called to the responsibility of eldership.

Elders must therefore have an ability to identify and grasp subtle error. "But I fear, lest somehow, as the serpent deceived Eve by his craftiness, so your minds may be corrupted from the simplicity that is in Christ" (2 Cor. 11:3). Notice the word *craftiness*. It is unlikely that someone is going to show up at a church member's door and say, "Hello, I'm a minion of Satan, and I am here to lead you astray." It doesn't happen that way.

Error is at its most dangerous when it seems most plausible. The Lord gave pastors and teachers to the church, men who are to build on the apostolic foundation—"so that we should no longer be children, tossed to and fro and carried about with every wind of doctrine, by the trickery of men, in the cunning craftiness of deceitful plotting." (Eph. 4:14). As the pastors give themselves to this work, they should be backed up by a session of elders who understand what they are doing and fully support it.

But the elders must not be content with a hostility toward false teaching. A church officer at Ephesus (that church's "angel" or messenger) is rebuked at this very point. He hated false apostles and was commended for it. But because he stopped there, having fallen from his first love, the Lord threatened to remove his lampstand.

Unto the angel of the church of Ephesus write; These things saith he that holdeth the seven stars in his right hand, who walketh in

---

[11] Harold O.J. Brown, *Heresies* (Grand Rapids, MI: Baker Book House, 1984).

the midst of the seven golden candlesticks; I know thy works, and thy labour, and thy patience, and how thou canst not bear them which are evil: and thou hast tried them which say they are apostles, and are not, and hast found them liars: And hast borne, and hast patience, and for my name's sake hast laboured, and hast not fainted. Nevertheless I have somewhat against thee, because thou hast left thy first love. Remember therefore from whence thou art fallen, and repent, and do the first works; or else I will come unto thee quickly, and will remove thy candlestick out of his place, except thou repent. But this thou hast, that thou hatest the deeds of the Nicolaitans, which I also hate. (Rev. 2:1-6)

As one of the guardians of the lampstand, an elder must therefore exhibit a love for Christ and a love for the truth of His gospel. This will, of course, result in collisions with those who do not love the truth (Acts 5:28). Still, the central teaching purpose of Christian elders is the declaration of truth to the saints, because that truth is *loved*, and not a mere zeal for the refutation of error. It is not enough to hate the deeds of the Nicolaitans.[12]

This obviously relates to the question of character in the eldership. We will address character qualifications for office in some more detail when we come to discuss the minister, but it is important to deal with it here as well.

An elder must have a godly and nonhypocritical lifestyle. "If you instruct the brethren in these things, you will be a good minister of Jesus Christ, nourished in the words of faith and of the good doctrine which you have carefully followed" (1 Tim. 4:6). In other words, Timothy was to teach sound doctrine, and he was to live in the same way he taught. As Timothy obeyed the doctrine which he was teaching others, the result was a good example for others.

Paul and Peter both put a heavy emphasis on the character of the prospective elder. "For this cause left I thee in Crete, that thou shouldest set in order the things that are wanting, and ordain elders in every city, as I had appointed thee: If any be blameless, the husband of one wife, having faithful children not accused of riot or unruly. For a bishop must be blameless, as the steward of God; not selfwilled, not soon angry, not given to wine, no striker, not given to filthy lucre; But a lover of hospitality, a lover of good men, sober, just, holy, temperate" (Tit. 1:5-8). Paul gives a very similar list elsewhere.

This is a true saying, If a man desire the office of a bishop, he desireth a good work. A bishop then must be blameless, the

---

[12] Francis Schaeffer, *The Complete Works of Francis A. Schaeffer, Vol. IV* (Westchester, IL: Crossway, 1982), p. 181ff.

husband of one wife, vigilant, sober, of good behaviour, given to hospitality, apt to teach; Not given to wine, no striker, not greedy of filthy lucre; but patient, not a brawler, not covetous; One that ruleth well his own house, having his children in subjection with all gravity; (For if a man know not how to rule his own house, how shall he take care of the church of God?) Not a novice, lest being lifted up with pride he fall into the condemnation of the devil. Moreover he must have a good report of them which are without; lest he fall into reproach and the snare of the devil. (1 Tim. 3:1-7)

Peter is also concerned about the character of the elders. He says, "Feed the flock of God which is among you, taking the oversight thereof, not by constraint, but willingly; not for filthy lucre, but of a ready mind; Neither as being lords over God's heritage, but being ensamples to the flock. And when the chief Shepherd shall appear, ye shall receive a crown of glory that fadeth not away" (1 Pet. 5:2-4).

So what does the Bible require, then, with regard to the character of elders? A man must be blameless. He must be a one-woman man, a faithful husband. He must feel the weight of the responsibilities of the office; he is to be a steward. He cannot be materialistic, greedy, or financially dishonest. He must be an eager, hard worker. He must not domineer over others. He cannot be violent and combative, self-willed, quick-tempered, or quarrelsome. He must not drink too much or take anything to excess. He must be dignified—sober-minded. He must be given to hospitality, one who loves to open his home to others. He must love good and do good. He should be a gentle man, holy and just. He cannot be a young scholar, vulnerable to the temptations of pride. His house must be managed well, and his children must be well-disciplined and faithful, not rebellious or dissolute. In all he must be conscious of setting an example of godly living for the saints. Those who are outside the church must respect him as well.

The Doctrinal Work of Elders

Modern Christians often overlook the importance of doctrine. In many ways, the modern Church is engaged in a headlong flight away from theology.[13] Because of this, many have difficulty appreciating the importance of the doctrinal work that is placed upon the eldership. In contrast, we should consider the value of doctrinal work in Paul's mind. "Let the elders that rule well be counted worthy of double honour, especially they who labour in the word and doctrine"(1 Tim. 5:17).

---

[13] And repentance means returning to the good work our fathers in the faith accomplished. William Cunningham, *The Reformation and Theology of Reformers* (Edinburgh: The Banner of Truth Trust, 1967, [1862]).

Elders who rule are to be honored. Those who rule well are to be counted worthy of double honor, *especially* those who labor in the word and doctrine. Doctrinal integrity within the Church was obviously a central concern to Paul.

The first doctrinal task of the elders is to see to it that the people are built up and established in the whole counsel of God. This is a positive task. In the following passage, the center of this counsel (the word of His grace) is not only the subject of the teaching, but also active *in* the teaching.

> And now, behold, I know that ye all, among whom I have gone preaching the kingdom of God, shall see my face no more. Wherefore I take you to record this day, that I am pure from the blood of all men. For I have not shunned *to declare unto you all the counsel of God*. Take heed therefore unto yourselves, and to all the flock, over the which the Holy Ghost hath made you overseers, to feed the church of God, which he hath purchased with his own blood. (Acts 20:25-28)

Paul was innocent of the blood of men precisely because he was a doctrinal minister. He shepherded the flock as a doctrinal minister. He valued the blood of Christ in redemption because he was a doctrinal minister.

A negative aspect to this responsibility exists as well. Doctrinal work involves a positive proclamation of the truth, and a guarding against falsehood. The task of a shepherd is to gather sheep and scatter wolves. A warning closely follows the earlier charge:

> For I know this, that after my departing shall grievous wolves enter in among you, not sparing the flock. Also of your own selves shall men arise, speaking perverse things, to draw away disciples after them. Therefore watch, and remember, that by the space of three years I ceased not to warn every one night and day with tears. And now, brethren, I commend you to God, and to the word of his grace, which is able to build you up, and to give you an inheritance among all them which are sanctified. (Acts 20:29-32)

We live in a fallen world. Sin manifests itself in false living and false teaching. To protect the flock against the encroachments of error is one of the basic responsibilities of the elders. It is so important that Paul includes an ability to debate theologically as one of the qualifications of an elder. "Holding fast the faithful word as he hath been taught, that he may be able by sound doctrine *both to exhort and to convince the gainsayers*. For there are many unruly and vain talkers and deceivers, specially they of the circumcision: *Whose mouths must be stopped*, who subvert whole houses, teaching things which they ought not, for filthy lucre's sake" (Titus 1:9-11).

The Intercessory Work of Elders

One of the central duties of the eldership is that of prayer for the congregation of the saints. This important truth is revealed to us through the
first crisis in the church at Jerusalem. The reason they appointed deacons to serve in that church is that they did not want to be taken from
their service of the church which they rendered through *prayer*. They
said, "We will give ourselves continually to prayer and to the ministry
of the word" (Acts 6:4). The truth is a very simple one; talking to men
about God must always be accompanied by talking to God about men.

When we consider the nature of pastoral prayer conducted by the
elders, one of the best things we can do is look at the examples of such
prayer given to us in the New Testament.

Pastoral humility is a necessity. True pastoral prayer does not exalt
those who are doing the praying. This is in contrast to the functioning of
a teaching ministry disconnected from prayer. If a man can teach, but
does not pray, the result will be an imbalanced adulation of a gifted
teacher. Pastoral prayer helps prevent this. "Now I pray to God that ye
do no evil; not that we should appear approved, but that ye should do
that which is honest, though we be as reprobates" (2 Cor. 13:7).

Ongoing pastoral prayer keeps an elder from thinking that he is the
"answer man." He should be praying in such a way that he does not
care who gets the credit for the fruit of the ministry. This cannot be done
apart from humble prayer before the Lord in the secret place.

As he prays, he should remember that it is in prayer that much of the
work of the ministry is really accomplished. "Confess your trespasses to
one another, and pray for one another, that you may be healed. The
effectual fervent prayer of a righteous man availeth much" (Jas. 5:16).
Prayer does not take the elders away from their ministry; it is one of the
principal tools given to them from God for the accomplishment of their
ministry.

Such prayer will include general prayer for the saints. We see this in
the examples of the New Testament. How was prayer offered for the
saints of the first-century church? "For we are glad, when we are weak,
and ye are strong: and this also we wish, even your perfection" (2 Cor.
13:9). Paul wants the saints to be completed in Christ. This is an aspect
of his prayer for them. For those elders who want to minister effectively
with their congregations, the same kind of prayer is needed.

We find another example in Philippians. "And this I pray, that your
love may abound yet more and more in knowledge and in all judgment"
(Phil. 1:9). Paul desires that their love to be abundant and intelligent.
But he does not just teach them that it should be so; he prays for them
this way. This also is seen in Colossians. "For this cause we also, since
the day we heard it, do not cease to pray for you, and to desire that ye

might be filled with the knowledge of his will in all wisdom and spiritual understanding" (Col. 1:9). Paul wants the saints to understand the will of God thoroughly. But this desire does not result in Paul explaining to them what he wants them to understand and then leaving it there. He *prays* for them that this would be done. The understanding of the saints is not accomplished through teaching alone. It is accomplished through the twin ministries of prayer and the teaching of the Word.

Paul prays for the Thessalonians as well. "Wherefore also we pray always for you, that our God would count you worthy of this calling, and fulfil all the good pleasure of his goodness, and the work of faith with power" (2 Thes. 1:11). The apostle wants the will of God to be worked out in the lives of these Christians. And for this, and for all these spiritual ends, he *prays*.

But pastoral prayer is not limited to such general spiritual requests. With the general requests, the same prayer is lifted up for all the saints. But the Christians of a particular congregation will also have specific needs. Consequently, the prayers of elders are not to be limited to "spiritual things" alone. God delights to hear all our requests, and if it is large enough to be a concern to us, it is large enough to be addressed in prayer. And sometimes the concern is great enough that the elders of the church should be involved in the concern through prayer. "Is any sick among you? let him call for the elders of the church; and let them pray over him, anointing him with oil in the name of the Lord" (Jas. 5:14). The same kind of prayer is offered by John. "Beloved, I wish above all things that thou mayest prosper and be in health, even as thy soul prospereth" (3 Jn. 1:2).

Once the elders begin praying for the congregation the way they ought to, it will soon be followed by prayer that recognizes how much work there is to do. When the elders begin truly praying, it will not be long before they are overwhelmed with how much still needs to be done. Oftentimes, we do not understand the magnitude of the task until we have undertaken it. And when that happens, elders will begin to pray the way our Lord instructed: "Pray ye therefore the Lord of the harvest, that he will send forth labourers into his harvest" (Mt. 9:38).

The Pastoral Work of Elders

As we have already seen, one of the tasks of the elders is that of pastoring, or shepherding. Because it is a function that can be abused, and has been, it is important for us to maintain our bearings on the nature of this sort of work. What is the biblical definition of pastoring?[14] First, whose responsibility is the work of shepherding, or pastoring? "The elders

[14] An essential book in pastoral work is by Jay E. Adams, *From Forgiven to Forgiving* (Amityville, NY: Calvary Press, 1994).

which are among you I exhort, who am also an elder, and a witness of the sufferings of Christ, and also a partaker of the glory that shall be revealed"(1 Pet. 5:1). What Peter is about to say in the subsequent verses, he addresses to the elders (plural) who are among the recipients of his letter. This is a work to which certain men are to be assigned. It is an identifiable field of labor, and they are to be identified and ordained laborers.

In this passage, Peter gives us a very clear explanation of what the pastoral obligation is and what it involves. In the course of his instruction, he also issues a very pointed warning. He first says, "Feed the flock of God." (5:2). The word translated feed here is the word for shepherding, or pastoring. We can see in the following verses that Peter is giving us the characteristics of godly shepherding or pastoring within the flock of God.

The responsibility assigned is pastoring the flock which is "among you." The responsibility to shepherd is limited to an identifiable flock. In Scripture, God never gives anyone undefined responsibilities. This is especially true of elders who are held strictly accountable for the work they do. Try to imagine a bookkeeper who had to give a financial accounting, but was not told how much money was involved, or to whom it belonged!

Part of the pastoral task is serving as overseers. An overseer has a general responsibility. A poor overseer micromanages on the one hand or abdicates on the other. One kind of man thinks he must exercise specific authority over every detail, and the other thinks it is enough for his name to be listed as one of the elders. The former type of elder can turn into a petty tyrant (which Peter warns against in this passage), and the other undermines the office of elder, turning it into a "figurehead" position.

An elder must not be browbeaten or forced into taking on this responsibility. He must serve not by compulsion but willingly. A man who does not want to shepherd is not qualified to shepherd. He will not have a pastor's heart if he comes to the task reluctantly. He also does not have a pastor's heart if he comes eagerly to the work for other reasons. He must not be in it for dishonest gain. An elder must not pastor or shepherd for the money. This is important because sheep, given their nature, can be sheared instead of fed.

Nor is he to be motivated by a hunger for power — nor as being lords. No ungodly domineering or power-seeking of any kind may be tolerated.

He is to be a godly elder over those entrusted to him. This phrase emphasizes the previous point about the importance of defined responsibilities. An elder, with those serving with him, has been entrusted the spiritual welfare of a defined group of people. It is therefore clearly important for him to know who those people are.

The next phrase provides clear teaching on how the sheep are to be pastored — by pastors who are examples to the flock. If the people are to learn how to be well-shepherded, then they must see the elders set the example of what it is to be well-shepherded. Submission certainly must be rendered to the elders, but it must first be taught through the godly example *of* the elders. Each elder must be a man who knows how to submit — to Christ, and to others. "For we do not preach ourselves, but Christ Jesus the Lord, and *ourselves your bondservants* for Jesus' sake" (2 Cor. 4:5). Those who preach the Lordship of Christ must always see that the message is preached by men who are bondslaves to the hearers for the Lord's sake. Those who want the members of the church to submit to them must have shown them through their own behavior what submission looks like.

All pastoral work is to be done before the Lord and in view of His judgment, and when the Chief Shepherd appears, the elders will receive the crown of glory that does not fade away. This shows us where all ultimate submission must be rendered. The Lord is the Chief Shepherd, the Senior Pastor. This means that in the final analysis, we are all sheep — shepherds and sheep both. The Lord is the only chief Pastor. Those elders who serve Him in shepherding the flock can consider themselves as faithful sheep dogs. The work is true service, and truly valuable, but there is no real room for boasting or putting on airs. Those who work faithfully will receive a glorious crown as a reward for their service.

The Role of the Diaconate

The second distinct office God has established in His church is that of the deacon. Paul, near the end of his life, includes the qualifications for deacons in his instruction to Timothy. This was an official practice that was intended to be continued in the church. Paul also, in writing to the Philippians, addressed the letter to the saints, along with two identified offices in the church — bishops and deacons. It is very clear that this is an office that we are meant to continue.

But the only place in Scripture where we have *any* indications about the nature of a deacon's job description is in Acts 6:1-7. And although the men selected in this passage are not expressly stated to have held the office of deacon, the description of the circumstances and their ordination makes it quite clear that this is the office they held.

First, why are deacons necessary? God had blessed the church in Jerusalem, and they had begun to experience the kind of problems which are associated with growth (v. 1).

When these deacons were ordained to their service, whom did the deacons relieve? The task they set out to perform brought relief to those responsible for the spiritual health of the church (vv. 2, 4). When the spiritual leaders of the church were being distracted from their primary duties through various mundane concerns, their response was to delegate the responsibility to spiritual men—men who would serve the church as deacons. The work of the deacons involved the serving of tables (v. 2), which was a physical concern of the church at Jerusalem.

As we saw earlier, the congregation was responsible for the selection of the men put forward (v. 3). When this was done, the ordination of the deacons was performed by the spiritual leaders of the church (vv. 2, 6). When this was done, the result was more sustained growth on the part of the church (v. 7). Rightly understood, the work of deacons is valuable indeed.

The Bible contains clear teaching on the qualification for this office as well. In 1 Timothy 3:8, we see that there is some comparison to be made between the character of elders and deacons. In the earlier part of the chapter, Paul had outlined the character of a godly elder. Then, in verse eight, he turns to discuss the qualifications for the deacons, and he begins with a *likewise*. The moral qualifications of deacon and elder are consequently very similar. We may therefore assume that our previous discussion of the qualifications for elder applies in large part to deacons as well.

Some notable differences, however, should be marked. First, the deacon is not required to be able to teach the doctrines of the faith, although he is required to understand and hold to them (3:8). He must be sound in the faith, although he may not be gifted in teaching. Another interesting difference is the requirement that deacons be tested before they assume the office (v. 10). They are to go through some sort of probationary period. Paul also gives a requirement for the wives of deacons, while there is no such requirement for the wives of elders (v. 11). Arguing by analogy, and on the strength of the *likewise*, we should expect the wives of elders to be like the wives of the deacons.

What all this means is that God wants His people to be well-governed. In Scripture, the people of Jesus Christ are not considered as an amorphous collection of worshippers. The Church of Christ is, among other things, a recognized institution with an established form of government. We know that the Lord will continue to establish His Church in the earth, and we also know that the day is coming when that Church will be presented to Him without any spot or blemish. We pray that a renewed study of the governmental issues involved in our corporate sanctification as the Church of Christ will be a part of what He uses to hasten that wonderful day.

✠ CHAPTER IX ✠

THE MINISTER'S CHARACTER

We have already seen how *all* the elders are involved in the work of pastoring, teaching, and ruling the Church of God. And they are all required to meet the qualifications for spiritual leadership that God sets forth in His Word. But at the same time, those elders who are ordained to the labor of Word and doctrine have, because of the prominence of their position, a special responsibility in this regard. For this reason, some of the more difficult aspects of the scriptural requirements will be discussed in the context of the life of the minister. Of course these requirements apply in a general way to all the elders, but they apply in a pointed way to those who are called to the ministry of the Word.

The Qualified Man

Jesus tells us that the hireling does not care for the sheep the way a good shepherd does. In saying this, the Lord was teaching in effect that the ministry cannot be allowed to become a profession. Despite this severe warning, the modern Church has steadily drifted into a compromise with what we might call ministerial professionalism. Pastors went to seminary the same way that doctors went to med school, and it is not long before they think of themselves as occupying the same social strata.

Seeing this problem, many Christians have reacted away from this in an egalitarian direction, thinking that if ministerial professionalism is the problem, then the solution must be to try to achieve a lack of professionalism.

Of course a minister of the Word must be competent, and well-trained. He must be fully-qualified to hold the office. These qualifications certainly include the kind of training that can be received in seminary — e.g., Hebrew and Greek. Paul requires that pastors be well-equipped to handle the Word of God, and nothing said here should be taken as a disparagement of requiring a learned ministry. "Meditate upon these things; *give thyself wholly to them*; that thy profitting may appear to all. Take heed unto thyself, *and unto the doctrine*; continue in them: for in doing this thou shalt both save thyself, and them that hear thee" (1 Tim. 4:15-16).

But with all this said, the basic qualifications which the Bible sets forth are character qualifications, both in the man's life and in his household. We should not consider a man for the office of minister unless he fully meets the description that Scriptures give us. Every ministerial candidate will be a sinner, and no one will achieve absolute perfection before God. But Paul and Peter describe a certain kind of man for a reason. Such men do exist, and the church should be governed by them.[1]

This is what a man must look like if he *aspires* to the office. If a man is disqualified on these grounds, or there is significant reason to think he may be disqualified, then he should not be ordained to office. Part of the reason it is so important to maintain high standards in this regard is that it is more difficult to remove an existing minister than it is to decline to ordain him. This is not just an observation we might make through observation of the natural world — the Bible requires us to make this distinction. There is a biblical difference in the standard for not ordaining and the standard for *removing*.

Suppose a minister has a teenager who falls into significant sin — sexual immorality or drunkenness, say. The sin has been confronted and repented of. Now what? I think we would be less than honest if we maintained that if these things occurred to a ministerial *candidate* they would somehow be irrelevant. In short, if a man were not a pastor, but simply a candidate, and his son's confessed involvement in such sin became public right before the election, any electors in the church who voted against him on the basis of these passages would be well within their rights to do so. Given this, are there not grounds for a charge of inconsistency if these men were to be retained in office?

This should be addressed by turning to Paul's instructions on the treatment of existing elders. Suppose something like this happens to someone who has been serving for some time as an elder. This brings another passage to bear:

> Against an elder receive not an accusation, but before two or three witnesses. Them that sin rebuke before all, that others also may fear. (1 Tim. 5:19-20)

---

[1] Uninspired books are not a means of grace, but they can be a tremendous encouragement to a minister in this regard. Donald S. Whitney, *Spiritual Disciplines for the Christian Life* (Colorado Springs, CO: NavPress Publishing Group, 1991); John Piper, *Future Grace* (Sisters, OR: Multnomah Publishers, Inc., 1995); Thomas Watson, *The Ten Commandments* (Edinburgh: The Banner of Truth Trust, 1959 [1692]); D. Martyn Lloyd-Jones, *Joy Unspeakable* (Wheaton, IL: Harold Shaw Publishers, 1984); Samuel Rutherford, *Letters of Samuel Rutherford* (Edinburgh: The Banner of Truth Trust, 1972, [1664]); and C. S. Lewis, *Four Loves* (New York: Harcourt Brace Jovanovich, 1960).

Two or three witnesses are necessary to bring an accusation against an elder. If this happens, and the charge is found to be true, then the elder is to be rebuked in the presence of all. This is done so that others will stand in fear. I believe it is significant that the only response mentioned in the text if the charge is found to be true is that of rebuke, and not removal. All serious charges that would bring removal would certainly include rebuke, but not every offense that would warrant rebuke includes removal.

So how do we make these distinctions? What criteria should we apply? I would suggest (at least) the following: the seriousness of the sin (scandalous or not?), the depth of the sin (longstanding or not?), the attitude toward the sin (repentant or not?), the extent of related sins (contained or extensive?), and level of responsibility (who committed the sin?).

It follows from all this that there are certain sins which are grievous enough to bring a rebuke to an elder, but which are not grievous enough to remove him from office. This addresses our earlier question about an elector's negative vote. A disqualification in the mind of an elector is very different than a disqualification in the mind of a judge. Any sin that is big enough to bring about a public rebuke would certainly be big enough to cause an elector not to vote for the man in the first place. And this *no* vote would certainly be legitimate and grounded in Scripture. At the same time, this passage also shows us the important distinction between someone aspiring to office and someone who already holds the office.

Put another way, the widespread neglect of elder qualifications certainly trivializes an office which the Bible says should be held in honor. But willingness to remove elders too quickly can have the same result. A young woman considering a suitor may legitimately decline his attentions for (comparatively) minor reasons. Those same reasons are not sufficient grounds for a divorce. To give them the same weight would be to diminish the office of husband. The point is not to equate the marriage and eldership, but rather to illustrate the fact that there is an important covenantal difference between getting into something and getting out of it. The bottom line here is this: it ought to be a bigger deal to remove an elder or deacon than to not install an elder or deacon.

Again, ironically, this is one of the reasons why high standards are so important to maintain. Elders have to make decisions in complicated situations, and so they must be wise, and they must be dedicated to preserving that wisdom on the board of elders.

Marriage Qualifications

The Bible describes clearly what an elder is to be like. Among other things, an elder must be "blameless." He must be "temperate" and of

"good behavior." He must not be a "covetous" man, or "quarrelsome."
He must have a good testimony with those who are outside the church.
The full descriptions of the biblical elder are found in 1 Timothy 3:1-7,
Titus 1:5-9, and 1 Peter 5:1-4.[2]

These passages describe required personal attributes and character—they are not a mechanical checklist. Paul and Peter require us to
find a certain kind of man. This is important for many reasons, but early
among them is that the elders are responsible to replenish their own
ranks, and in order to find a certain kind of man it is necessary for the
current elders to be certain kinds of men. In other words, when the elders
of a church are determining whether or not a new candidate is qualified
for the office, they must be the type of men who are mature in judgment.
They are discerning character, not counting rocks.

To take one example from Paul's list: an elder must be a "one-woman
man." These cryptic words require a judgment call. Does it mean no
polygamists? Does it exclude a man who has ever been divorced? A
man who has been married and divorced five times? Taking it further,
does Paul reject any man who has been with more than one woman
sexually at any time, with or without the marital paperwork? And what
about a man who has been married more than once because his first wife
has passed away? What Paul says is that an elder must be a one-woman
man. Clearly, when we come to apply God's absolute Word in a vari-
able world, the elders must be men of mature biblical judgment, because
they are called upon to make such judgments. To sin in making these
judgments is a grievous thing.

Two different attitudes interfere with mature judgment in such cases.
First is the sloppiness found in liberal and modern evangelical churches:
This attitude begins by decrying "legalism" and "perfectionism," moves
on to consider the biblical requirements as nothing more than mere "suggestions," then as a "noble ideal, but impossible to achieve in the real
world," and then, not surprisingly, disregarded entirely—dismissed from
consideration as "unrealistic." Countless churches have fallen from faithfulness to Christ into fuzzy-minded liberalism because they were faithless *first* in how they selected their leaders.

The second attitude is often a reaction to this modernist refusal to
take God's Word seriously. In this reaction, the list of attributes ceases to
be descriptive of a certain kind of man and hardens into a checklist. And
as with all "checklist" approaches to godliness, a clear arbitrariness
begins to creep in—no less humanistic even though it is thought to be
"strict" or "conservative." Countless churches have fallen away from
faithfulness to Christ into an unbiblical woodenness, because they were
faithless first in how they selected their leaders.

---

[2] Also see Richard Baxter, *The Reformed Pastor* (Edinburgh: The Banner of
Truth Trust, 1974, [1656]).

Thus a man who slept with twenty women before his conversion, but was enough of a jerk not to marry any of them, is thought to be qualified for eldership after his conversion, but a man who married one woman and was divorced from her before his conversion is thought to be automatically disqualified. This version of the "one-woman man" may have had any number of mistresses in his past, but no wife. Ironically, this "strict" approach can wind up approving men who have a glaring character deficiency with regard to women, and excluding a man who clearly does not. It is as though the elders insisted that a new pastor not be given to much wine, but oceans of beer are okay.

Now obviously the subject of marriage and divorce does relate very clearly to this qualification of the "one-woman man." A man most certainly can be excluded by the biblical requirements because of a divorce in his past. But wise elders will not exclude him out of hand; they will reject any attempt to reduce the evaluation of a man's character to a simple three-step process. The desire to have a handy-dandy checklist can easily be reduced to absurdity. An elder must not be given to much wine. Suppose he used to have a drinking problem thirty years ago? Now what? Suppose he used to have a drinking problem three weeks ago? The elders must use their heads as they apply God's descriptive standards.

The church cannot have leaders who are "blameless" by nature. By nature we are all objects of wrath. The blamelessness of the elders is by grace, and the task in considering a new elder is to determine whether the work of grace is real, lasting, and deep. This is not done by obtaining lip service to the requirements. ("Do you have any plans at this time to leave your wife?") With regard to this requirement, the fruit of a man's marriage over time must be evaluated. In other words, is he the kind of man who exhibits single-minded devotion to one woman, displaying for the congregation the characteristics of a biblical marriage? If yes, then he is a one-woman man. If no, then he should be excluded from office. If the question cannot be answered because there is not enough history to evaluate, then consideration of the candidate should be postponed.

Men of judicious character are rare, and the nature of such biblical requirements demonstrates how important it is to have them in the leadership of the church. "But strong meat belongeth to them that are of full age, even those who by reason of use have their senses exercised to discern both good and evil" (Heb. 5:14).

When the elders are examining a pastoral candidate, they should be asking whether that candidate meets the biblical description of an elder now, and, because we cannot see hearts, whether there has been a demonstrated pattern of God's grace at work over an extended period of time. Apart from God's grace, no one is qualified.

The Pastor's Kids

In these passages, Paul also gives several requirements regarding the children of elders. These are both discussed and disregarded with great regularity in the modern Church.

At the heart of the issue is whether the children of ministers and elders must be faithful Christians. In Titus, Paul says this of elders: "If any be blameless, the husband of one wife, *having faithful children* not accused of riot or unruly" (Tit. 1:6). In 1 Timothy, he requires that an elder must be one that "ruleth well his own house, having his children in subjection with all gravity" (3:4). He goes on to add that if a man does not know how to rule in his own house, then he will not take good care of the Church of God (v. 5).

When this discussion erupts, it is usually in the midst of a particular crisis—the unmarried daughter of the pastor is pregnant, the son of one of the ruling elders is in jail, etc. In that context, feelings usually run high and sometimes careful distinctions can be lost. So although these truths must be applied at some point, it would probably be best if we sought to work through them on the chalkboard first.

It is my purpose to argue here that the requirement Paul gives here should be taken at face value, and that if a man's children fall away from the faith (either doctrinally or morally), he is therefore disqualified from ordination to formal ministry in the church. Now Paul is talking about what kind of men to *appoint*; the issues surrounding post-ordination disqualification is admittedly not in the immediate context. But arguing from analogy requires that we relate the two situations somehow—otherwise no pastor could ever disqualify himself once ordained.

Of course, as already mentioned, the standards for removal are, by necessity, higher than the standards for admission. A woman might legitimately decline a suitor because he is not tall enough, but this could never be grounds for divorce. In a similar way, if an elector in the church saw the child of an elder candidate flipping out at the supermarket, he might decide not to vote for that candidate. But if the candidate were already ordained, the same incident would not necessarily constitute grounds for removal from office.

With all this acknowledged, we must confront the fact that Paul says that a man's qualification for office is tied up with the state of his children. In order to develop this, certain questions must be answered in order—exegetical, theological, and pastoral.

First, the exegetical question. Debate on this subject usually revolves around whether the phrase in Titus 1:6 should be translated "faithful children" or "believing children." Of course, if the proper translation is "believing children" then there is no debate anymore, at least among those who believe the Bible. If a minister must have believing children, then how could there be debate on whether he must have believing children?[3]

So for the sake of discussion, let us grant the translation "faithful children." It certainly is a legitimate translation, and in the last analysis I would like to argue that it doesn't really change anything. Faithful in *what*? Faithful to *whom*? When the translation "faithful children" is urged, it is generally with the thought that a child could be faithful and obedient in external matters, but still be unregenerate. In this thinking, a pastor should be required to run his household with good external discipline, but he cannot be expected to have any control over whether his children come to a saving knowledge of Christ.

But the word *pistos* is used frequently throughout the pastoral epistles, and while it is commonly translated as faithful, we never see this dichotomy between true heart condition and external conformity introduced (see 1 Tim. 1:12, 15; 3:11; 4:9; 6:2; 2 Tim. 2:2, 11, 13; Tit. 1:9; 3:8). In context, the word *faithful* means faithful down to the ground. If a son is obedient when his father tells him to take out the garbage, but disobeys when he is told to believe on the Lord Jesus Christ, in what *Pauline* sense can the son be described as faithful?

Nevertheless, a particular theological argument against this view has great force with many. The argument goes that the election of our children is in the hands of God, and not in the hands of parents. As Alexander Strauch has argued, "To say this passage means believing Christian children places an impossible standard upon a father. Salvation is a supernatural act of God. God, not good parents (although they are used of God), ultimately brings salvation."

Now I have argued elsewhere that parents are invited by God to believe that their children will inherit the promises of God. This is not attained by parental works in any way, but is rather a promise appropriated by faith.[4] But again, for the sake of discussion, let's grant this point. To place the salvation of a pastor's children outside his influence says nothing about this particular requirement. Suppose this to be the case, and God in His sovereignty has determined not to save one of the pastor's children. Unless we alter the wording or meaning of this passage, this would simply mean that the sovereign God has determined to reveal His desire to have the pastor step down from his ministerial responsibilities in this particular fashion.

The pastoral argument involves our understanding of what constitutes a good pastor. We still think in terms of qualifications from

[3] For a contrary view, see Alexander Strauch, *Biblical Eldership* (Littleton, CO: Lewis & Roth, 1994), p. 174.

[4] Douglas Wilson, *Standing on the Promises* (Moscow, ID: Canon Press, 1997). And for a wonderful book by a heretic on a similar subject, see Horace Bushnell, *Christian Nurture* (Cleveland, OH: The Pilgrim Press, 1994 [1861]).

graduate school and professional certification. The pastor cannot step down, we argue, because this is his livelihood. How could we expect him to abandon that? But the ministry is not a profession, and the men who hold office in the church do not hold that office as a matter of divine right.

This is why it is important for us to consider the reason Paul gives for placing this requirement on us (1 Tim. 3:5). We have every reason to believe that a man will shepherd the church in the same way he shepherds his family. This, incidentally, is another reason for believing that the work in the home concerns the fundamental spiritual issues, and not just external discipline. We are evaluating the same kind of work in different realms. A man is qualified for ministry through many instruments and means. But the spiritual condition of his children is right at the center of his qualifications.

Of course, many of these assertions can be (and have been) debated. But I trust that we can have a truce of sorts between all those who believe that the passages in question (1 Tim. 3:1–7; Tit. 1:5–9) mean *something*. The great problem of our time is that Paul teaches that a pastor's qualification for office are established in the home, but as far as the general leadership of the Christian church in our nation today is concerned, this text is a dead letter. But general agreement should be possible among those who exhibit submission to this text through an observable discipline of pastors and elders. Too often Reformed pastors want others to submit to them, but they themselves submit to nothing or no one.

Second, in our discussion in the earlier section of another pastoral qualification (that an elder should be a one-woman-man), we noted that we are evaluating character, not counting rocks. The world is a messy place, and this is frequently hard on perfectionists. Thus, all questions flowing from weird circumstances not addressed in the text should be acknowledged to be anomalous and dealt with on a case-by-case basis. What about a pastor who adopts his fifteen-year-old nephew whose parents just died, and that nephew never comes to faith? What about a child fathered out of wedlock ten years before the father was converted and married? The man's six legitimate children are all faithful Christians. My point is not that we should apply Paul's requirements in a wooden manner, with our eyes tight shut, but rather that if we are careful to obey him in those areas which are *clearly* addressed in the text, we will have the wisdom necessary when we come to the difficult cases.

Third, we should distinguish the *loci* of decision-making on this issue, which vary according to the circumstance. In short, we should be fully convinced in our own minds concerning those conditions in our own families which would cause us voluntarily to step down, and those conditions in the life and household of another that would justify a fight at presbytery. Whatever we understand Paul to be saying, our standards of application should be tighter for ourselves and more charitable for others. For example, a man might decide (and, I think, *should* decide) to step down if one of his six children denies the faith. But if another pastor in his presbytery in the same situation does not decide to do so, and his other five children are saintly, only a crank would express his disagreement through a big church fight. But say another pastor has six hellions, and how all this happened is a grand mystery to him questions about his fitness for office should be raised and pursued.

With those qualifiers, we can turn to some of the more formidable objections. One objection is that this whole discussion distracts attention from the issue Paul raises in this passage, namely, the character traits of the man who would be an elder. In other words, why are we talking about his *kids'* character instead of his? The answer is that children frequently make excellent mirrors; they reflect more than we usually want to have reflected. We commonly turn away from gaining a knowledge of a pastor's character because we refuse to follow the trail of clues. The clues would lead us directly to that man's arrogant and harsh demeanor around the dinner table. Finally, when one of the kids has had his fill of the hypocrisy, he leaves the faith, but we don't ask any questions because the pastor is so saintly in the pulpit. However many men find it far easier to act saintly *there* than they do in conversation with their wife and children.

A second objection is that this standard runs contrary to the words of warning Christ gave His apostles in Matthew 10. "And the brother shall deliver up the brother to death, and the father the child: and the children shall rise up against their parents, and cause them to be put to death" (10:21). Doesn't this presuppose that certain godly fathers will have their children turn on them for the sake of the gospel? And if they are godly fathers, then why could they not be elders? Two responses can be made to this. The first is that Christ is telling his apostles what will happen to them, as indicated by the pronoun *you* used throughout the discourse. In verse 21, He shifts to the third person, and then goes back to *you,* in v. 22. The apostles were not going to be doing the work of ministry all by themselves; they were going to be working with congregations, and many of the families in those congregations were going to be divided, as we know was the case at Corinth. The second response is that this situation could contribute to the occasional anomalous situation referred to earlier. Suppose a father brings his children up in a false religion, but when they are grown, he is then converted. His family turns on him, but he remains faithful. The point of division is the *gospel* here, and not twenty years of ladling reformational arrogance and conceit over the tops of the childrens' heads.

A final caution: Children learn far more unspoken theology than we tend to think. Suppose parents have operated with the doctrinal assumption that the kids might or might not turn out, who knows? Why should the children have any confidence about it? Unbelief is the constant, unspoken *option*. And one day, the option is spoken out loud. But it was always there, hidden away in the hearts of the parents, who always hoped for their childrens' faith, but never believed for it.

We have all seen various examples of this problem. A popular new evangelical pastor at a metropolitan church has a teenage son with hair down his back, a nose ring, 3 tattoos, and a bad attitude. When asked about his son's spiritual condition, the pastor just shakes his head. "You do everything you can," he says. The questioners nod sympathetically.

Our willingness to tolerate a lack of pastoral leadership in the home has had profound ramifications. The Industrial Revolution gave us far more than machinery and cheap textiles. One of the results of coming into a "scientific age" was the birth of the notion that "experts" were now needed everywhere. Everything became fair game for centralizers and planners, including the work of the home.

The problem, however, was that the experts in the area of child rearing and development were not qualified to teach according to Scripture, and their teaching consequently was not grounded at all in Scripture. They were self-appointed "experts" nonetheless, and their inane observations about children began to fill the country. And whether it was in response to Dr. Spock discouraging the spanking of disobedient children in the home, or Horace Mann and John Dewey building the Great Kidnapping Machine that we still call "public schools," parents began to acquiesce, feeling as though they were not equipped to bring up the children God gave them. After all, they were not experts. But the central problem was not that others offered to take over the rearing of children. The central problem was that parents in disobedience to God let it happen. And because Christian parents abdicated, for a number of generations, their children have been covenantally molested.

Outside the church, critics have observed the mess the family is in, and so they have begun to argue for a necessary abandonment of the "traditional family." Single-parent homes, sodomite parents, child divorce, and day-care centers are all offered as legitimate options among many. But of course such perversity is not really an abandonment of the traditional home; the traditional home disappeared a long time ago. Modernity is merely attacking the vestiges. All this is merely the logical outcome of a disobedience that began a long time ago, in the last century, and is bearing bitter fruit now.

Within the Church, we have countless youth ministries that have no idea that they are simply mimicking the world. Hedonism is thought to be an acceptable worldview for Christians if they are under eighteen; it only becomes false doctrine later in life. A glance at the ads for Christian colleges demonstrates beyond all question that the Christian Church has generally accepted the Fun Imperative.

When Christians fight for the family at all, they fight a defensive rear-guard action, fighting the more egregious symptoms (like child porn), and not the lies and distortions that brought this crisis about.

We must not heal the wound of the people lightly. We must not say peace, when there is no peace. In our reformation, and in our repentance, we must go to the root of the matter. Children must be brought up according to the Word of God and according to nothing else. But who will show us how this is to be done?

Reformation must first come in the requirements that churches place upon their elders and deacons. As we have discussed, the Scripture requires that church officers manage their homes well and requires that the children of church officers be faithful.

The officers of the church are placed by God in a position to be an example to the congregation. The members of the church are commanded to *imitate* them, carefully considering the outcome of their way of life (Heb. 13:7, 17). This way of life includes the very important matter of how they bring up their children. There will be no reformation among us until those pastors who do not meet the child-rearing qualifications of their office step down, in repentance, from their office. Men who have a household in disarray are just as unqualified for church office as an unbeliever. The time has passed for conservative Christians to cease being outraged with the disobedience of others. Why do we remove the beam from their radical eye, when we have a telephone pole in our conservative eye?

Since the Church routinely permits disqualified ministers, then it is not surprising that the households of the membership are in shambles as well. Such disobedience cannot produce good fruit. We are guilty of such disobedience, and we must not be astonished at the results. Christians, of course, need to address other areas of child-rearing as well. But unless this happens within the *leadership* of the church, all other efforts are futile. And when it happens, as it will, all other reforms will follow.

Honorific Titles

But temptations in the household are not the only ethical issues that affect a minister's qualifications. Another one of the temptations common to religious leaders is that of showboating. Our Lord's words are worth quoting at length.

> But all their works they do to be seen by men. They make their phylacteries broad and enlarge the borders of their garments. They love the best places at feasts, the best seats in the synagogues, greetings in the marketplaces, and to be called by men, "Rabbi, Rabbi." But you, do not be called "Rabbi," for one is your Teacher,

the Christ, and you are all brethren. Do not call anyone on earth your father; for one is your Father, He who is in heaven. But be not ye called Rabbi: for one is your Master, even Christ; and all ye are brethren. And call no man your father upon the earth: for one is your Father, which is in heaven. Neither be ye called masters: for one is your Master, even Christ. But he that is greatest among you shall be your servant. And whosoever shall exalt himself shall be abased; and he that shall humble himself shall be exalted. (Mt. 23:5–12)

On some issues, it is astonishing how easy it is for us to miss the plain meaning of Scripture. In this passage, Christ forbids the love of honorific titles within His Church. He knew the temptation to self-exaltation and personal ambition was going to be strong in the Church. From the history of the Church, we can see how important this prohibition was, and how much it has been disregarded. The Christian Church has managed to avoid the use of the term *rabbi*, but in all other respects, Christ's requirement is ignored. He forbade titles of spiritual respect for the leaders of the church; so we are not in the clear if we hunger to be called *reverend* instead of *rabbi*.

There are of course two errors that must be avoided with regard to this. The first is the error of ecclesiastical pride — the error Christ is addressing here. Honorific titles are often a symptom indicating that the governmental structure of the church is not biblical, with the structure being conducive to arrogance. But Christ was insistent that the leadership of the Church must never pursue honor through the use of titles. The leaders of the Church are to be distinguished and set apart, but this is to happen through service and self-sacrifice. Pastors have to avoid the common sin of wanting to be *known* as a servant without being *treated* as a servant.

But the second error is one of spiritual egalitarianism. Christ established a government in His Church; the leadership provided by the elders of a church is very real, and their authority is genuine (Heb. 13:7, 17). God requires the members of a church to *obey* their leaders. While God has not established a proud elite within the Church, neither has He established a democracy. There is true authority vested in the eldership.

There are several protections God has set forth in His word to keep this required obedience from becoming a yoke of bondage. One protection is that when the leadership in the church is following the pattern of the New Testament, meaning that the leadership consists of a plurality of elders. We have no example in the New Testament of a church governed by a solitary pastor. Each church was governed by a group of men called bishops (Phil. 1:1) or elders (Acts 14:23). Multiple elders help to check the growth of overweening pride.

The second protection is Christ's prohibition of a love for titles in this passage. Men who are hungry for power and prestige will generally not be content to forego the distinction of such titles. Certainly there will be some who embrace the sin and suppress the symptom, but they will be rare. There will occasionally be a church run by a Diotrephes, who loves to have preeminence (3 Jn. 9), but which avoids such titles. Like a communist tyrant, who goes by a simple "comrade," it is possible for a dictator in a church to be simply called "brother." But over time, the lust for preeminence will result in a verbal acknowledgement of that preeminence.

This does *not* mean that every leader in a church who uses such titles is guilty of the gross sin of selfish ambition. Great and good men have allowed themselves to be addressed in this manner. But for whatever reason, whenever this becomes the norm, the purity of the church is at least endangered.

In the Scottish Reformation, Andrew Melville addressed this question: "All [ministers] should take their titles and names only (lest they be exalted and puffed up in themselves) which the Scriptures give them as those which import labor, travel and work, and are names of offices and service, and not of idleness, dignity nor worldly honor or preeminence, which by Christ our Master is expressly reproven and forbidden."

For too many the ministry is an indoor job with small amounts of heavy lifting. Our Lord refused to give His blessing to such hirelings; ministers are forbidden by the Lord to be "in it" for the money (Jn. 10:12; 1 Pet. 5:2). But we must remember that money is not the only lousy motivation. The Bible also teaches that vainglory is a great and dangerous snare for those in the ministry. For example, in one passage Christ lampoons the clerical stuffed shirts of His day by making fun of their clothes (Mk. 12:38). Apparently some of the scribes thought that ecclesiastical poobahs should look more like circus horses. As we have already noted, Christ thought differently: "Beware of the scribes, who desire to go around in long robes, love greetings in the marketplace." Now of course, Christ was not requiring rabbis to wear trousers (everyone wore robes) any more than He was requiring them to be cranky and sullen in the marketplaces, refusing to return greetings. As mentioned above, the point of His warning was the common temptation to have an undue love of such things. But He was identifying a sin which has been common to the ministry in all eras,—practicing religion and spiritual leadership for an audience of men—vainglory.

Christ describes numerous examples of the basic sin—that of looking for applause from the cheap seats and not seeking the approval of God. But in different eras, the inhabitants of the cheap seats have applauded different things. We must be very careful here. We no longer care how broad someone's phylactery is, but we do comment on how underlined his Bible is. We no longer cheer when he calls himself *rabbi*, we just nod approvingly when he calls himself a *brother*. Way to be humble, bro. If he keeps it up, we could start calling him the Rev. Bro. The problem is ecclesiastical grandstanding, and the raw material for this is always available at hand. Christ's teaching is violated whenever one finds out what is respected in His Church (and there is always something) and then maneuvers to gain the applause of men by displaying that particular thing front and center.

The question of whether Christ was absolutely prohibiting the use of any ecclesiastical titles shows the importance of understanding the context of the first-century synagogue. The prideful abuses of the rabbis in Christ's day were simply unbelievable. Edersheim relates one story of a discussion in Heaven between God and the heavenly Academy about purity. Because they were at an impasse, a certain Rabbi was summoned from earth to decide the point! Christ was condemning a rampant sin in His day, and which, of course, also afflicts any minister filled with balloon juice in any era. He did not say the synagogue was wrong for having best seats; He simply said that people who were driven to sit in them had a spiritual problem.

This means pastors should not worry about it if they are in a church where they are addressed by others with such names—provided the focus is on the work, and there is no idolatrous adulation. And men who are indignant and greatly put out if they are addressed "improperly" should never have been entrusted with such titles, still less with the care of souls. Further, ministers of any church should not suffer guilt attacks when they receive mail from someone trying to be nice, addressing them as the Rev.

The absence of the titles does not mean the absence of vainglory. Comrade Stalin and Citizen Robespierre come to mind. For this reason brother Smith needs to take care that he does not become the biggest blowfish in his little ecclesiastical pond, title or no title. The second thing to remember is that there is no biblical requirement or reason to adopt our more common cultural titles like Rev. But one can appropriately decline such a title without insisting that others who have not declined are guilty of the sin Christ proscribed here. That depends on what they love—it is not what goes on a mailing label that defiles a man.

Honest Subscription

At first glance, we might think that a discussion of confessional subscription should be located elsewhere in this volume. But we are still addressing a minister's character; doctrinal issues are frequently *character* issues as well. Confessional integrity has been destroyed far more frequently by old-fashioned dishonesty than by any other thing, including the quality of seminary education.

Hermeneutics, the art and science of interpretation, sounds to many like a horribly dusty affair. And of course, some have handled the subject along these lines. This is not how it should be; when the question of how a text is to be interpreted arises, we should feel a leaden weight in the gut, and adreneline in the veins, as men feel before a battle. Of course we need to pay sound attention to our texts — but not as the scribes.

How we handle the Word of God has eternal consequences. If we trifle with the text, we are risking our own eternal salvation. Peter spoke of hermenuetics as a life and death issue; he noted that ignorant and unstable people twist the Scriptures, and that they do so to their own destruction. The word he used to describe the twisting is a word out of ancient torture chambers. The plain meaning of the text is put to the rack, and bizarre confessions are coerced from it. And unfortunately, to this day, when many self-appointed interpreters turn to their text, torture and mayhem are in the air.

But despite this beginning, the interpretation of the *Scriptures* is not my subject. My point is somewhat downstream from this important issue, but still directly related, as all downstream issues are. The adoption of a disobedient hermeneutic with regard to Scripture — or even the toleration of one — has broad cultural ramifications as well. How we interpret our most sacred text will have a profound impact on the respect we show, or refuse to show, to lesser texts. For example, in American history, we see the Church's disrespect for the text of Scripture followed, imitatively, by disrespect in our culture at large for lesser documents. We as Christians are the people of the Word, and how we treat the *Word* will affect how we and others respect the meaning of *words*.

This explains how we came to handle the Constitution of the United States the way that we do. The prevailing sentiment in our courts today is that the Constitution is a "living document" and that we should not attempt to tie it down to the "original intent" of the framers. But if we are not to be bound by the intent of the framers, then why not dispense with the framers entirely, and with the very idea of a written constitution? If all we wanted was a blank screen on which to project our current desires, then it would seem that all those curious, old-fashioned words just get in the way.

The reason we do this is that we want to have it both ways. Suppose we had judges who delivered their skewed rulings and, when pressed, said that they did this because it seemed like a good idea at the time. They had too much anchovy pizza the night before, and this ruling came to them in a dream. The general public would be upset, and the game would be over. But, in contrast, if they limited themselves to the plain meaning of the Constitution, *their* party would be over. And so the Constitution must be kept around to provide the smell of a hoary antiquity, and a relativistic hermeneutic is slapped on top of the whole operation to provide them with the untrammeled liberty of doing what-ever they want.

But these exegetical monkeyshines were not invented by Supreme Court justices. They were not developed by secular humanists trying to overthrow our fair Republic. In her better days, the Christian Church had given to our civil republic the idea of limiting and defining the role of government by means of a written constitution. Just as the faithful had creeds and confessions, so the civil government could have a writ-ten civil order. And in her days of decline, the Christian Church then showed our civil authorities what to do when these written documents get to be a little too stifling. How does one honor a document one is trying to circumvent?

Often a liberal is far more honest in handling the text than is an evangelical. This is because the evangelical is stuck with the results of his exegesis. The liberal can say that the apostle Paul taught the headship of the man in marriage, and wasn't that silly? The evangelical, trying to keep up with current trends, and also trying to keep the Bible, has to try to make Paul into a contemporary sensitive male, which is frankly not very easy. In the same way, a disinterested observer is often more honest in telling us what the Westminster Confession says, for example, than a fellow who has sworn to uphold it, but doesn't want to. The issue is not strict or loose subscription, but rather honest subscription.

Jesus taught us to pray, asking the Father to treat us in just the same way that we treat our enemies. The principle can be extended to other areas. Over the last century or so, the Christian church in our nation has mishandled the Bible in remarkable ways, and has reinterpreted her own creeds and confessions in a fashion that can only be described as entirely dishonest. By this we were asking God to give us civil rulers who would behave in exactly the same way with our civil texts. We now see He has granted our request and sent leanness to our souls.

How then, does honest subscription work? A candidate for office would specify any exceptions to the confession of faith that he might have, and the body responsible for examining him would make the de-termination whether or not the exception was acceptable. If the excep-tion is to the doctrine of the Trinity, or Scripture, then the candidate is down the road. The process ends at that point. But if the exceptions are minor and are allowed, and the candidate is ordained, then he has a *moral* obligation to remain faithful to the spirit and letter of the rest of the confession, and to any restrictions placed on him with regard to his exceptions. If his convictions at any point change, he has, again, a *moral* responsibility to bring that fact to the appropriate authority. Failure to do any of this does not indicate doctrinal problems primarily but rather shows a failure of character. Heterodox men do present a problem to the Church, but the central problem is their very common dishonesty.

Ministers in Skirts

Another common pastoral character problem is that of functional effeminacy. In the modern Church, masculinity in ministry is rare. And behind this is a somewhat complicated history.[5]

Believers very rarely fight strategic battles. When provoked, they sometimes fight effectively and well in tactical skirmishes, but they do not do well outside their tactical radius. Then, when some outrage can no longer be ignored, battle may be joined and the outrage attacked. But scarcely any believers see a pattern in the general mayhem. Very few generals can stand on a hill and consider all the movements of all the troops.

In our cultural wars, this is why the issue of women in the pulpit, or on the elder board, has been handled the way it has been — which is to say, ineffectively. Many good folks have dedicated themselves to fighting this thing as though it were a tactical issue. But it is not. In the current climate of unbelief, the proper exegesis of the Pauline teaching on the role of women in the Church will never settle anything.

The words seem plain enough. "Let the woman learn in silence with all subjection. But I suffer not a woman to teach, nor to usurp authority over the man, but to be in silence. For Adam was first formed, then Eve. And Adam was not deceived, but the woman being deceived was in the transgression. Not withstanding she shall be saved in childbearing, if they continue in faith and charity and holiness with sobriety" (1 Tim. 2:11–15). But here is the catch: the words are plain only to those who are willing for them to be plain. For those reckoned among the unwilling, the passage is full of mysteries.

Because woman is the glory of man, a wife should go to the local congregation with a covering of hair, a humble woman's glory. And why is this? "For the man is not of the woman; but the woman of the man. Neither was the man created for the woman; but the woman for the man" (1 Cor. 11:8–9). It may fill all us moderns with regret, but such teaching cannot in any way be reconciled with feminism of any kind. But for those in the Church who want to conduct some kind of dialogue with feminism, the words present an exegetical obstacle course. How can we keep this wording, and thus remain evangelical, and at the same

---

[5] George Gilder, *Men and Marriage* (Gretna, LA: Pelican Publishing Company, Inc., 1986); James B. Hurley, *Man and Woman in Biblical Perspective* (Grand Rapids, MI: Zondervan Publishing House, 1981); Ann Douglas, *The Feminization of American Culture* (New York: Alfred A. Knopf, Inc., 1977); C. S. Lewis, *Allegory of Love* (Oxford: Oxford University Press, 1936); Leon J. Podles, *The Church Impotent* (Dallas, TX: Spence Publishing Company, 1999); Greg L. Bahnsen, *Homosexuality — A Biblical View* (Grand Rapids, MI: Baker Book House, 1978); and C. S. Lewis, *God in the Dock* (Grand Rapids, MI: Eerdmans, 1970), p. 234ff.

time get around what it says, and thus be theologically trendy? We need to look at the original Greek!

But the existence of debate within the Church tells us far more about the muddiness of our hearts than it does about the obscurity of any text. Those Christians who do see what these passages say will frequently be sucked into a tactical debate because they foolishly believe that their opponents have accepted the authority of the text. But this is not the case at all. Evangelical feminists have not accepted the (patriarchal) authority of the text; they are simply at that early stage of subversion where open defiance would be counterproductive of their purposes.

So what is our strategic position? How has this debate gotten a foothold? Why is there such an interest, in evangelical circles, to admit women into the leadership of the church? The answer is that we do not want feminine leadership; we want more feminine leadership. The men in our pulpits for many years have been simply jury-rigged women; when the request comes to bring in the real thing, on what principle will the request be denied? We cannot say that we must have masculinity in the pulpit because we do not have that *now*.

For well over a century in the American church, the norms of spirituality have been the standards set by a saccharine Victorian feminism. As Ann Douglas cogently argued, in the early part of the nineteenth century, like two mobs converging on a quiet crossroads, two revolutions merged to produce this effect, and we have not yet recovered any understanding of what life in the Church was like before this happened to us.[6]

The first was the rise of a sentimental and domestic feminism. Prior to the industrial revolution, the role of women in America was at the center of the economy. Women managed the home, manufactured the cloth, processed the food, fed the entire family, and so forth. But with the rise of industrialized wealth, the role of women shifted from producing to consuming. The women were, in effect, disestablished—and became decorative. Middle class women became a new leisure class, with money to spend and time to fill. And one of the things they began to do was to write and read sappy novels.

The second factor was the sentimental revolt of ministers against the strictures of theological Calvinism. The older Calvinist establishment was perceived as austere and harsh (and in the Yankee culture of New England, it frequently was). This revolt had manifestations on both the right-wing and the left-wing. The left-wing anti-Calvinists were the Unitarians, who captured Harvard in 1805.[7] The right-wing anti-

[6] Ann Douglas, *The Feminization of American Culture* (New York: Alfred A. Knopf, Inc., 1977).
[7] Samuel Blumenfeld, *NEA: Trojan Horse in American Education* (Boise, ID: The Paradigm Company, 1984), p. 8.

Calvinists were the revivalists, typified by leaders such as Charles Finney, who were greatly swelled with a humanistic, democratic spirit which they all thought was the Holy Ghost.[8]

All this occurred while the churches of New England were in the process of being disestablished, no longer receiving funding from tax revenues. More important than the loss of tax money, however, was the fact that these Congregational clergymen, long accustomed to their role as a central part of the Establishment, found themselves outsiders, now having to compete for parishioners, just like the lowly Baptists and frontier Methodists.

The women with time on their hands provided a ready audience for these ministers, and the anti-Calvinist ministers provided a suitably sentimental gospel for the women accustomed to their feminized literary entertainment. So an alliance was formed between the clergymen and the women, and a new spiritual norm was established within the Church.

All these developments, centered largely in New England, were not followed for the most part by the more conservative and agrarian South. But the new regime of feminization came to the Southern church as well. The War Between the States decimated the strong masculine leadership of the South for all intents and purposes. The men were no longer leading because the men were dead. Since that time (exaggerating only slightly) southern churches have been run by three women and the pastor.

The literature of the nineteenth century was not reticent in propagating this new sentimental view of the gospel. In these stories, we see an iron regime of domesticity — feminine tastes and values are set up as the standard of godliness and as a genuine regenerative influence. The unregenerate man in the stories was, of course, worldly wise, and something of a rake, unless was converted to — what? Until he was converted to see it her way, and came around to bask in the gospel of the feminine aura.

We are so besotted, that current "traditional values" Christians are actually reprinting and circulating this nineteenth-century treacle as though it represented a biblical view of the world. But Elsie Dinsmore represents nothing of the kind. She simply stands for an early form of feminism, and conservatives who hail her piety are revealing that they do not know what has happened to the Church. Another example is the ancestor of our moronic WWJD bracelet — that book entitled *In His Steps*. The book was in many ways typical of the genre; the divine influence is mediated through a woman. Men can be converted by listening to a

---

[8] Iain Murray, *Revival and Revivalism* (Edinburgh: The Banner of Truth Trust, 1994).

pretty voice. It reminds me of a time in boot camp when we were all entertained at chapel by a visiting singing group of lovely women. When the altar call was given, one poor sailor, thoroughly revived, went forward over the tops of the pews.

As a result of all these factors, a standard of feminine piety has been accepted as normative in the Church as the standard for all the saints, both men and women. Clergymen, trying to live up to their reputation as the third sex, have labored mightily to be what they need to be in order to maintain this standard. But try as they might, men are no good at being women. However hard they try, their attempts ring hollow. The pressure is therefore on to make room for those who can be feminine in leadership more convincingly: women. When the standards of Christian leadership are all feminine, the individuals most obviously qualified to be Christian leaders will be women. And so this poses a dilemma — why should we exclude women from leadership when they are so obviously qualified for what we call leadership? At that point we divide, with some calling for them to be included, with other reluctant conservatives admitting that women could do as good a job, or better, but still, we have to submit to this arbitrary pronouncement of Paul. For now.

When the background is understood, it explains many things about the contemporary Church. It explains why Promise Keepers, a masculine renewal movement, was so easily diverted into a maudlin and weepy sentimentality.[9] It explains why ministers cannot teach on certain subjects from the pulpit. It explains why Christians cannot articulate why women in combat is an abomination. It explains why the masculine virtues of courage, initiative, responsibility, and strength are in such short supply. We cannot resist the demand to let pretty women lead us for the simple reason that we are currently being led by pretty men.

So a skirmish here or there about women's role in the Church will never settle anything. This is why this particular debate, or that particular controversy, will always end, once again, in a stalemate, with the cause of the feminists slightly advanced. The pattern will repeat itself, again and again, until the conservatives finally cave in. They must cave, because the feminist opposition is consistently able to appeal to shared assumptions and presuppositions. Until that changes, nothing significant will change. And when it changes, we will see a strategic battle joined.

We have not failed because our exegetical skills are rusty. We have failed because we have forgotten what masculine piety even looks like. When it occasionally appears among us, we are entirely flumoxed by it. But God gave the pattern of feminine piety to complement, not to rule.

---

[9] Hagopian and Wilson, *Beyond Promises* (Moscow, ID: Canon Press, 1996).

Headship has been given to men. When such headship is challenged, everything is out of joint, and nothing but repentance can put things right.

For a final example, in more ways than one, consider the recent evangelical attempts to sandpaper the Bible to a finer and more delicate texture. The reader may recall the situation was an attempt by the folks responsible for the NIV to alter the language of Scripture — fixing some of those pesky and troublesome gender spots. When the plan became public, there was a dust-up and howls of protest from all over. And the tactical skirmish was won by the good guys — for the present.

But with regard to the underlying issues, nothing changed. With regard to the contributing cultural pressures, nothing changed. With regard to the state of the Church, nothing changed. So when we consider all this, and the condition of the modern Church, there is really no reason to object to any such modifications in the NIV. There is really no reason to object to women in the pulpit of evangelical churches.

This is because modern evangelicalism has been covenantally castrated for well over a hundred years. It is high time they got some ministers, and a Bible, to match their effeminate condition.

Hollow Men

I mentioned earlier the fact that Herman Melville once compared the pulpit to the prow of a ship, setting the direction and course of a society. We may protest, saying that this might have been true in his day, but in ours, the pulpit does not set any cultural direction whatever. This is quite true, but beside the point, because it is also true that our culture *has* no direction whatever. Politicians may talk glibly of setting a course for the twenty-first century, but this has about as much directional content as determining to fall down when dropped. All our scholars, statesmen, politicians, bureaucrats, philosophers, musicians, painters, and anchormen haven't a clue. The bugle blows indistinctly, and we all think it is a new form of jazz.

We are continuing our discussion of the character of the minister, and one place where moral failure has been most apparent is in the area of courageous moral leadership. Our cultural malaise began in the pulpits of America and is maintained by the pulpits of America. Every Lord's Day, thousands of temporizing (let us call them) preachers assume their place and begin to speak. But they are not preachers, for the simple reason that they do not *preach*. They share, and chat, and tell anecdotes, and relate stories from the heart which warm the heart.

A judgment of profound spiritual stupor rests upon our people — but this deep sleep must be understood for what it is. "For the Lord hath poured out upon you the spirit of deep sleep, and hath closed your eyes: the prophets and your rulers, the seers hath he covered" (Is. 29:10). In righteous indignation and wrath, the Lord determined to drive our nation into a covenantal stupor, and His instrument for doing this was to cover the eyes of the Church, the prophets and seers. The Church is asleep because the pulpit is asleep.

Who has given us all these pseudo-men, who caper so prettily on the stage for the televangelistic cameras? The Lord is clearly angry with us. Who was it that decided that churches should start having Super Bowl parties instead of the Word and sacraments? This is nothing less than the hand of God upon us. The Lord did promise us that when we ask for bread, He will not give us stones. But what happens when we ask for stones? "They soon forgat his works; they waited not for his counsel: but lusted exceedingly in the wilderness, and tempted God in the desert. And he gave them their request; but sent leanness into their soul" (Ps. 106:13–15). Our fists are full of what we wanted, and we have just this kind of leanness of soul. The Lord has done it—He is the one who made the determination that we would be so emaciated, while happily feasting on our own conceits.

God decided to inflict upon us the wasteland that is the American pulpit today. The Lord has brought us into this wilderness. Some might say this is all right because wandering aimlessly in the desert could be called an activity that is seeker friendly. But not all are enamoured with the new foolishness. We still have plenty of traditionalist opponents of all this who would lead us back to the ancient paths by preaching through their noses. God has done all of it, and may God deliver us.

This kind of language has far more hard and sharp edges than we like. We have heard too many smooth sermons from too many pretty boys to tolerate this kind of thing. "Oh," we say, "God would never do that kind of thing to His people. All our low self-esteem in the pulpit, for that is what this problem really amounts to, just breaks His heart"—as though the Lord were up in heaven wringing his hands over what He could possibly do about those stinkers we preach.

Confronted with the hard evidence of the judicially-imposed stupidity that stands in the pulpit today, we broaden the extent of that stupidity by refusing to honor the Lord who has brought us to this point. We either think the problem is not a problem, and sing another chorus, or we think that the problem is just happening for no particular reason. Our stupor amounts to a rejection of God and His attributes. We are in love with our own notions of what God has to be like instead of loving Him as He has revealed Himself. This idol would be very nice if he existed.

To acknowledge that this is from the Lord is not to accuse Him. When God's people are hard-hearted their sin does not disappear simply because the Lord wields absolute control over it. "O Lord, why hast thou made us to err from thy ways, and hardened our heart from thy fear? Return for thy servants' sake, the tribes of thine inheritance" (Is. 63:17). The Bible makes it as plain as words can say that God remains God regardless of the circumstances, and that when the Church is drifting from one disaster to another, God is not standing helplessly by.

Oysters always whistle out of tune,[10] and we should not be surprised when men cannot accomplish their own salvation. We should not marvel that men cannot restore and reform the Church. How could they? We look to see if a man is asleep by looking to see if his eyes are closed. As we look to see if the Church is asleep, we should do the same. The eyes of the Church are the pulpit and the eyes of the Church are sightless because the Lord has brought this spirit of moronic stupor upon us. The pulpit today is the central problem in the midst of that *fin de siecle* disaster that we like to call our culture. With our indistinct mutterings, we have "preached" our way into a culture that we deserve. Because we are the problem, we cannot be the solution. "For the Lord is our judge, the Lord is our lawgiver, the Lord is our king; he will save us" (Is. 33:22).

But when the Lord turns to deliver us, He will do so according to His Word, which means that He will raise up men, men courageous enough to preach the Word in season and out of season, whether the people want to hear it or not.

Books and Men

These things cannot be accomplished by men who will not or cannot read. This is more than a practical point; it is a theological one. It is unfortunate, but there are many Christians who believe in the supremacy of Scripture, but who do not believe in the fruitfulness of Scripture. For example, if a pastor is reading a work of systematic theology, some well-meaning soul will gently admonish him to put aside the works of men, and devote himself to the study of Scripture alone. Such an admonition, although quite well-intentioned, is actually dishonoring to the Scriptures.

For suppose someone does devote himself to the study of Scripture alone. He pours over it, and he is saturated in its teaching. It can be said of him what Spurgeon said of John Bunyan — prick him anywhere and his blood would run bibline. Will such a brother learn anything? The answer is obvious — he will learn a tremendous amount. Look at Bunyan!

But having learned so much, is it permissible for him to share anything that he has learned with other Christians? May he teach? Or must we interrupt any such conversation to admonish listeners not to listen to the words of a mere man?

Whenever the Book has been honored and studied, the result has always been countless multitudes of books — the inevitable fruit of that

[10] As Spurgeon said somewhere.

study. Those who fear the Lord speak often with one another, and one of the natural ways to do this is through the publication of books. This is because the Bible tells us how the saints are to be instructed, and it is clear then that it is not through private time reading the Bible alone. The writing and reading of God-honoring books is not a substitute for Bible-reading; it is the *result* of Bible-reading.

But we have still been told to go the Bible alone — let us do so: "And he gave some, apostles; and some, prophets; and some, evangelists; and some, pastors and teachers; For the perfecting of the saints, for the work of the ministry, for the edifying of the body of Christ" (Eph. 4:11–12). "Also Jeshua, and Bani, and Sherebiah, Jamin, Akkub, Shabbethai, Hodijah, Maaseiah, Kelita, Azariah, Jozabad, Hanan, Pelaiah, and the Levites, caused the people to understand the law: and the people stood in their place. So they read in the book in the law of God distinctly, and gave the sense, and caused them to understand the reading" (Neh. 8:7–8).

The teaching of Scripture on this point is very clear. God requires uninspired teachers to exposit His Word and apply it to the lives of God's people. The Bible does not say that worship services should consist of Scripture reading only — with no interpretive voice inflections. On the contrary, the Bible tells us that we are to receive much of our religious instruction from uninspired sources — parents (Deut. 6:6–9), husbands (Eph. 5:25–27), elders (Heb. 13:7), and fellow Christians (Heb. 10:25).

And if some of the believers are tempted to give too much wide-eyed credence to their fallible teachers, then their teachers should warn them about that, just as they warn them of other sins. And because all human teachers are fallible, it is very important for them to stick as close to the text as they are able. Those who refuse to listen to such teachers (and who refuse to read books by them) may do so in the name of honoring Scripture, but they are really kicking against the requirement of Scripture. They say, in effect, that the Bible should be honored — so long as it is kept barren and produces no teachers, and no books. And incidentally, it must also be remembered that although they maintain that they sit at the feet of no man, there is at least one kind of human teaching they do think highly of — whatever has been forged in their own brain.

But someone may protest that there really is a genuine problem when people pay attention to the words of men rather than the words of God. Of course it is a problem! But how did our brother warn us of this danger? Through his own words — the words of a man. Should we therefore dismiss his warning? Not at all. It is a biblical warning. But in heeding this admonition, we are not at liberty to set aside what the Bible elsewhere tells us to do, which is to heed and honor our uninspired teachers.

And even though this is a genuine problem, how is it solved through avoidance of publication? So long as Christians speak with one another, as long as there are teachers and preachers in the body of Christ, there will be some who find it easier to follow men than to follow Christ. We cannot remove this temptation from the church; this is part of how God made the world. A man who has a problem with lust should not beseech God to solve his problem by removing all women from the planet. Nor should we seek to solve the problem of hero-worship by removing the teachers. Rather, when there is a problem, we should address it the same way we address other problems in the church — through God-centered and biblical *teaching*.

So all attempts to banish scholarship and published learning will only result in a theological know-nothingism. If we succeeded in getting the saints to avoid listening to scholars and godly men, we would only discover that they now line up at the cash registers to buy the books of ignoramuses and mountebanks. The only way to avoid this is to require every Christian to be his own teacher, and place us all under a vow of perpetual silence — which, as a solution, would have the disadvantage of being disobedient to Scripture. And besides, who is going to teach us this requirement of silence? Not a human teacher, surely?

Nevertheless, we may still learn from this misguided attempt to empty the libraries and minds of Christians. Although we cannot agree that uninspired books necessarily supplant Scripture, we may and must insist upon books which uphold the primacy of Scripture.

If someone is reading God-honoring Christian books (as opposed to the theological treacle which most Christian bookstores specialize in today), those books will admonish, advise, teach, and instruct. But above all, they will do what all godly teaching does — drive their readers back to the Scriptures. And that will result in more books.

All this means that ministers should glory in their books. They should of course be immersed in the Scriptures, but in addition to this, they should surround themselves with commentaries, works of theology, and history. As they participate in this process of reading, submitting themselves to the learning of others, they may come to the point where they feel they can contribute to the discussion, and write some books of their own.

Too many pastors feel like they read all they had to read in seminary, and after entering the ministry they do not have any time for real reading. Further, they have been fully trained, haven't they? Why read any more? This attitude is a real dereliction of duty. Because it relates to what a minister knows, it could be considered a mere academic issue. But because it frequently proceeds from laziness, it has to be considered a moral disqualification as well.

In order to be a godly minister, a man must love God and His Word.

He is a shepherd of souls, and so he must also love those among whom he ministers. But if he understands well, he will also love his library. "The cloak that I left at Troas with Carpus, when thou comest, bring with thee, and the books, but especially the parchments" (2 Tim. 4:13).

A Call to the Ministry

The ministry is an indoor job with no heavy lifting, and so it attracts some who are not called to the work. Couple this with the fact that many foolish things have been perpetrated within evangelical Christianity about "determining the will of God," and you have a recipe for problems.

It is a common assumption among evangelical Christians that the "will of God" should be determined before major decisions, and once His will has been established, it is our responsibility to go and do that thing. This is assumed among many pious individuals for all sorts of important decisions (marriage, major in college, moving, etc.), and *a fortiori* the same kind of assumptions drive these same pious individuals when they are contemplating the ministry.

But God never tells us to find out the specific will He has for us so that we may then go do it.[11] Nor does He tell us to make an arbitrary distinction between important decisions and unimportant ones. Put simply, our responsibility is to live in the will of God, which is quite different from determining it beforehand.

Apart from the gift of prophetic utterance, we do not know what will happen tomorrow. Our lives, James informs us, are a mist, and so we ought not talk long and loud about tomorrow. The fact that I am in the ministry now, and in the will of God being in the ministry today, does not mean that I know the will of God concerning my ministry tomorrow. My life is a mist. I might be dead tomorrow, and entirely relieved of my responsibilities for sermon prep. I am married now, but have no idea whether or not it is God's will for me to be married tomorrow. How would a mist know something like that? This is why James tells people not to boast, saying that they will go here and there, making big bucks as they go. He says that they ought to say, "*If* the Lord wills . . ."

He does not say that they ought to pray all night, and then pronounce that God has told them to go here and there, making the big money. If it is arrogant to commit the former error, to place "the will of God" upon the declarations of a bragging fog in the latter instance is far worse.

And those who insist on a preprinted agenda from the Lord before big decisions are in the difficult position of trying to decide which are

[11] Gary R. Friesen, et al,. *Decision Making and the Will of God* (Sisters, OR: Multnomah Publishers, Inc., 1983).

the big decisions. Because we are eternal creatures, and our births and deaths are all suspended, a moment's reflection shows that there are no little decisions. Every son of Adam was at one point a fertilized egg. The moment before millions of sperm were vying to be the one. During the course of that day, how many actions affected the outcome of this most fascinating race? *This* sperm results in *this* individual (along with the many thousands of *this* individual's descendants), and all because that day dad scratched his head, stopped to tie his shoe, let the other fellow go ahead of him in line, and so on. No such thing as a little decision.

Up ahead on the freeway is an accident waiting to happen. As the driver of an automobile, a pious Christian, is driving toward that point, and every tap on the brakes, every lane change, every head check, affects whether or not they will be at that point, at that point in time. No such thing as a little decision.

But if a man stops to get the will of God in tying his shoe, or on making a lane change, he will soon be experiencing what might be called piety paralysis. God governs the world; we are not competent. Our lives are a mist.

This does not mean we are to throw up our hands and abdicate all responsibility in decision-making. It simply means that God is God and we are not, and He wants us to make responsible decisions (according to our best light), not because He needs our help running the world, but because He is shaping us into the kind of creatures He has called us to be. We think we are making the world, when actually God is using the world to make us.

Now how does this relate to a decision to seek the ministry? It is a decision to be made the same way all decisions should be made.

The first thing to ask concerns God's general will for all believers. Does the pursuit of the ministry contradict God's revealed will at any point? For example, this question would stop a woman from seeking the pastorate, or a man who does not meet the scriptural qualifications for office.

If this standard is met, and it is lawful for the individual to aspire to ministry, then three additional considerations should be weighed in order to make a wise decision. But when we get to this point, under no circumstances should an aspiring minister appeal to dreams, visions, promptings, whisperings, or voices in the night. The candidate should ask himself, and those around him who know him best, how he measures up according to three criteria: *What are his abilities? What are his opportunities? What are his desires?*

He may speak most authoritatively about his desire, but others have more authority on the question of his abilities and opportunities. This is why counsel from others is so important. He may have the desire because God is calling him—nothing is wrong with the desire. "If a man desire the office of bishop, he desireth a good work" (1 Tim. 3:1). But while the desire may be a godly one, it could also be prompted by ambition, envy, incompetent piety, or greed. Others should be able to vouch for his character, and for his ability. They should be able to answer the question whether he has the ability to be a godly minister, and they should be able to recommend him without question. This recommendation would best come from the young man's pastor and elders.

The question of opportunity is open and shut. If no one accepts the candidate for ministerial training, or if no one will listen to him preach, or if no church calls an individual, this falls under the heading of opportunity (and also may have something to say about ability).

So a young man may feel "called," but this internal call has no mystic authority over others. It may (and should) prompt the candidate to pursue these options, but this motivation would fall under the heading of his desires.

This means that someone is called to the ministry when they have decided to pursue the training for it in wisdom, they have been trained, and the Church of Christ has authenticated the call by inviting him to minister to them. This man is called. Is he called to be a minister tomorrow? Maybe.

Ministerial Training

The idea of formal seminary education dies hard.[12] We have trained so many generations of ministers in this fashion that we can scarcely credit any other way of doing it. We also hear, from time to time, of churches which take pride in having an *uneducated* ministry, and we want nothing to do with that sort of know-nothingism. So we easily slip into the fallacy of thinking that the only alternative to formal, professional seminary training for the ministry is that of informal and unprofessional *lack* of preparation.

Whenever a false dilemma is presented to us, and this is one of them, we must be careful to avoid being rushed into choosing. Is the only choice really between *no* education on the one hand, and *graduate* school education on the other?

Some of the positions taken here, either directly or by implication, may strike some as unnecessarily rigid or perhaps even severe. This is not the intention at all. It is freely admitted that various seminaries in the course of their histories have served the cause of Christ ably and well, and that many graduates of seminaries have been among the Church's brightest lights. Princeton had a glorious history, for example.

---

[12] An unabridged form of this section appeared in *The Paideia of God* (Moscow, ID: Canon Press, 1999). The outline of the argument appears here for obvious reasons.

But an unbiblical system, however well-intentioned, will not bear biblical fruit over the course of generations.

The fact remains that, for the most part, seminary education in the United States has become the realm of parachurch organizations (this is even generally true of denominational seminaries as well), governed more by the rules of the academy and various secular accrediting agencies than by the rules of the Church, which someone once said was the pillar and ground of the truth. No one should dispute that parachurch organizations have done good, and in some instances, have done much good. But Christ is the head of the *Church,* and He did not leave the evangelization and discipleship of the world to freewheeling parachurch ministries. The fact that good has been done is a testimony to the goodness and mercy of God, and not a basis for us to continue with a system of ministerial education for the Church which is not conducted within the Church, or effectively overseen by the Church.

A system of ordination has developed where seminaries provide the rigorous "graduate school" education, while the local churches are supposed to determine a candidate's fitness for ministry. The elders of a local church, for their part, assume that if a student made it through an approved seminary, he must be a fit candidate. The result is that many have found their way into ministry because they have shown a great aptitude for graduate level study and test-taking. Human nature being what it is, we may continue to expect much more of the same kind of thing if we continue on the same course. The disease has so far progressed that we now tend to assume that graduate school honors are the qualifications we should look for in a ministerial candidate. Paul's requirements for a godly ministry are set aside, and we think that it is all right to do this because the man whose marriage and family is a stretcher case (and got that way while he was working his guts out in seminary) nevertheless *has professional certification.*

What is the biblical pattern for ministerial training? The pastoral epistles have that name for a reason. Because Christians are accustomed to treat the entire Bible as a book of inspirational quotes, we sometimes miss specific instructions which are addressed to particular officers. For example, in the famous passage about the inspiration of the Word of God, Paul says that the Bible builds up the "man of God" so that he may be complete, "equipped for every good work" (2 Tim. 3:17). This is not addressed to every Christian (although it may be extended to them by analogy). It is addressed to *the man of God,* the minister — one who is responsible before the Lord for the spiritual well-being of others. This one needs to be able to rebuke, admonish, exhort, etc.

In 2 Timothy, Paul also teaches us how the leadership of the church is to reproduce itself. He says:

> You therefore, my son, be strong in the grace that is in Christ Jesus. And the things that you have heard from me among many witnesses, commit these to faithful men who will be able to teach others also. (2 Tim. 2:1–2)

This is not a requirement that every Christian should disciple others in such a way that they are able in turn to disciple others. When this does happen in an informal way, we are all grateful for it. The Bible does encourage this sort of instruction—for example, the older women are told to teach and instruct the younger women (Tit. 2:3–5).

But the charge to Timothy *here* refers to the duty of church leadership to reproduce itself. What Timothy had heard from the apostle Paul, he was to pass on to faithful men. These faithful men in turn were to teach and instruct others. This clearly occurs within the context of the work of the Church. This is how Paul trained Timothy in evangelistic and pastoral work, and he here tells Timothy to go and do the same.

In a similar way, the Great Commission was given to the apostles, but in a way which ensures the commission is self-perpetuating. Christ told the apostles to teach obedience to *everything* which Christ had commanded (Mt. 28:18–20). This would, of course, include His last command, that the nations be discipled. This means that the apostles who received the initial commission were to pass it on to the next generation, and the next generation was to do the same. But this commission is given to the *Church*, not to every individual Christian. This means that the leadership of the Church is to receive the commission, and the leadership of the Church is to pass on the commission.

As we return to a more biblical pattern of training future elders and ministers, we do not expect a transformation overnight. The current system has a tremendous amount of inertia behind it. As we present an alternative to seminary education, we do not expect seminaries or seminarians to go away—and we are very happy to cooperate with those seminaries which remain faithful to the Word of God. In presenting what we believe to be a more biblical approach, we do not want to inculcate a perfectionistic attitude which demands everything be reformed immediately. That would only ensure that nothing substantive will ever change.

Nevertheless, a local church which takes its mission of evangelism and discipleship seriously should be able to fully train leaders for service in the local church. *Any calling which is incapable of reproducing itself is incompetent in that calling.*

This training is for her own leaders in the years to come. A thriving church can easily assume that they "have it covered" because their current elders are doing a fine job, and their current pastor preaches well and looks healthy. Everyone has trouble imagining what the church will look like in fifty years when none of the current leaders is alive. No one even thinks about it. But Charles deGaulle put it well when he said that the graveyards are full of indispensable men. That day will come whether we want it to or not. A church which does not think of establishing continuity with the future generations of that same church is, in principle, a church populated by short term and anti-covenantal thinkers.

When a pastor retires or dies, the usual tendency is to scramble, form a pastoral search committee and — you know the rest of the drill. An outsider, someone who is not in touch with the local and organic life of that particular congregation is called, and he steps into the pastorate. His paper qualifications were impressive, and his pulpit delivery while he was "candidating" was good, but the fact remains that churches which get a pastor this way are basically getting a mail-order bride.

The church, which will be the beneficiary of the training, should be involved in the decision to train someone for the ministry. Men should not be preparing for the ministry unless there is good reason to believe that they have the gifts and calling for that ministry. This understanding should be shared by others in the church, and particularly by the leaders of the church. Far too many pious young men, zealous for ministry, have been misled into thinking that intense desire for ministry is an adequate substitute for ability and call.

The church which provides the training should testify that she believes a young man is called to the work of ministry by paying for the costs of instruction. If a church has sent someone to be trained at another church, then that sending church can add her testimony by paying for books, or helping with living expenses. Obviously this will not be done unless the churches in question have a good understanding of the student's character and ability.

It is a truism that if you don't name it, someone else will. In our situation we have called this course of training *a ministerial hall*. Graduates of this hall do *not* receive a professional degree, or anything that sounds like a professional degree. The bureaucratic system which governs the granting of all such degrees is well-entrenched, and any attempt to compete with them while using their terminology is not likely to be blessed. A ministerial hall avoids the assumptions that govern the running of graduate schools. As a hall for study, there is no pretense of "professionalism."

At the same time, the phrase *ministerial hall* does indicate a rigorous preparation for the ministry. An informal, casual, and undefined system of education simply will not do. If an apprentice for the ministry were simply to hang around the leadership of a church for several years, he would no doubt learn many valuable things, but mostly he would simply learn "how things are done around here."

Those prospective ministers who are graduated from this hall should receive a letter of commendation, stating that they have performed their work ably and well, and that the instructors and elders overseeing the training of this man have learned enough about him to be able to say he is qualified for the Christian ministry, in his character, history, and gifts.

✠ CHAPTER X ✠

THE LIFE OF THE CHURCH

A Multitude of Counselors

I am not trying to be offensive, but it appears to us that the evangelical church in America has turned into a vast army of dedicated whiners— so dedicated we are willing to pay *another* vast army to listen to us.

As with all movements that are not grounded on Scripture, the modern counseling revolution has been, and will continue to be, truly destructive. There are many objectionable things about it; in what follows I want to identify some of the more basic problems. But the real disaster lies in the fact that the mentality of this counseling revolution has invaded the Church, and has altered our approach to pastoral counsel.[1]

The first problem is that counseling has become a profession rather than a ministry. Now it is perfectly acceptable for a dentist, architect, doctor, or lawyer to charge for his time. But when someone has a spiritual problem, the solution is always efficacious *grace*. And the ministers of this grace must proclaim it to the needy without money and without price. To charge the spiritually hurting for listening to a message of grace is an abomination. (And if the message given is not the biblical message of grace, then that is a worse problem.)

Jesus was blunt about this sort of thing—he who is a hireling and not the shepherd does not care about the sheep (Jn. 10:12–13). It is of course true that ministers have to eat, and, if the ministry is a true one, the Bible is clear that the church should support them. But the Church does this to enable ministers of grace to give themselves away, and the Church should only support the kind of men who are willing to give themselves away.

There is a correlative problem associated with this sort of pastoral prostitution. When someone goes into business—say, that of selling

---

[1] For a shrewd and biblical approach, see D. Martyn Lloyd-Jones, *Spiritual Depression* (Grand Rapids, MI: William B. Eerdman's Publishing Company, 1965).

shoes — one of his first tasks is to convince the buying public of their need for his product. In some cases, as with grocers, this is not a hard sell. But when the product is not an essential one, a shrewd businessman will seek to create a demand for his product. Given this quite natural tendency, it is no great mystery why the wellness-mongers have found that America has somehow sunk into a veritable swamp of codependency — reliable figures place our current number of codependents at around three kabillion. And if we buy their book or check into their treatment facility, they will help us to start draining the swamp (for a fee).

Another problem of pandemic proportions is the important matter of verifying the truth. The Bible teaches that every matter is to be established through two or three witnesses. A very high standard is set for those who would accuse anyone. But in this brave new world of counseling, no one has to prove anything. Suppose a woman comes in and tells her counselor that she was abused as a child. The first question in a pastor's mind should be, "Is this true?" In other words, he must make a decision about whether he is teaching a true victim of real abuse (the kind of abuse a policeman could tell you about), or whether he is talking to a liar, or perhaps someone who has spent too much time in the wrong section of a Christian bookstore.

I have done enough marriage counseling to know that the picture I get from one partner is not at all the entire picture — even if that one is trying to be honest. The first one to plead his cause seems right, until his neighbor comes and examines him (Prov. 18:17).

As with many counseling situations, it is extremely difficult to reconstruct an objective account of what happened thirty years ago. So instead of attempting this, many modern counselors simply accept at face value whatever story comes through their door. Instead of pastoral ministry, which seeks even-handedness for all concerned (whether they are present or absent) and reconciliation between them when possible, we are seeing more and more professional service which places the counselor in the position of an attorney. The difference is between a counselor who takes money from a client, and who then finds it very easy to represent the interests of that client, and a pastor, who is supported by the Church in order that he may represent the interests of Christ, as represented in His Word.

As a result, how many counselors have tolerated, without a challenge of any kind, slander of individuals they have never met? This mentality can even lead the counselor to tempt his client into such slander. The counselor seeks to break down the "denial" of "abuse" he knows must be there, and then when some horror story comes gushing out, he simply assumes it to be true. This foolish assumption is seen in counseling sessions all over the country. It is seen because the counselor is simply hearing what he already believed and assumed to be true. And he believes it because he is paid to believe it.

This is not a denial that true abuse exists. But we should call it by its biblical names (which are sin and rebellion) and seek to establish the facts of the case through diligent application of biblical guidelines. And if the fact of such sin is established, then it should be followed by godly confrontation, which in turn will be followed either by repentance or church discipline. It should not be followed by everyone concerned and their cousin's dog getting into a support group (Wife-beaters Anonymous, Adult Grandchildren of Wife-beaters On Their Mother's Side Anonymous, etc.). I once saw in a major city (and I am not making this one up) a store front that was called something like the Center for the Empowerment of Deaf Alcoholics. A lot of this foolishness is simply abundant evidence that Americans have too much money and time on their hands.

The last point to make in this regard is that the counseling industry, as a spiritual lie, has been successful for no other reason than that the Church has not been proclaiming the spiritual truth. If the cross of Jesus Christ does not save drunkards, liars, thieves, cheats, and philanderers, then the ministers of the gospel should go out and get a useful job down at Wendy's.

But some may object that the modern Church does talk about Jesus and His love. Yes, but the Church at large long ago gave up talking about the Lord Jesus Christ, His efficacious death, His conquering cross, and His glorious triumph over death, grave, and sin, as well as over our miserable and filthy little rag-tag band of self-justifying *isms* — alcoholism, sexaholism, rageaholism, and can't-be-nice-to-my-wife-a-hol-ism.

Those who have seen their sin for what it is through the wonderful life-giving and effectual call of the Holy Spirit are truly justified. They have begun the life-long task of restraining and subduing forgiven sin. But for those who insist upon thinking of sin as a disease—he who is filthy, let him be filthy still. In the meantime, the Church should be engaged in the only ministry capable of addressing all such problems. That ministry is the Word of grace.

Youth Ministry

At the outset, we have to distinguish ministry to youth and the particular industry that has grown up in the last generation that we call youth ministry. When Paul turns to the children of Ephesus and speaks to them (Eph. 6:1–3), he is ministering to young people with a particular set of needs. John does something similar when he addresses the young men (1 Jn 2:13).

So there is no problem whatever in sponsoring or encouraging Bible studies among young people. In our congregation, we have several Bible studies geared to teenagers, and numerous studies for our college students. On the Lord's Day, we have several catechism classes through which the children of our church are memorizing the Shorter Catechism, and when they are done, they will move on to the Heidelberg.

In addition, the parents in our church provide a Christian education for their children, either through homeschooling, our local Christian school, Christian tutorials, or a combination of these. Among these hundreds of children, none of them are being educated in the government schools. Our children are disciples of the Lord Jesus Christ, along with us, and they need to be instructed and brought along in that discipleship. But many on the contemporary scene would look at all this and say that we have no youth ministry. And, considering what they may mean by it, they are quite right.

But how is this possible? How could a group of saints so focused on teaching their children, *ministering* to them, be accused of not having a youth ministry? This is because the phrase *youth ministry* refers to a particular *cultural* phenomenon in the American church today, and not to actual ministry, biblically defined.

A young man, who never really wanted to graduate from high school himself, gets hired as a youth minister. His task is to put together a wild and crazy time down at the church, with perhaps a little inspirational message attached. The driving assumption is that young people today will not tolerate serious instruction and discipleship, and so we must give them large amounts of what they do want, which is "fun, fun, fun, till her daddy takes the T-bird away." The problem here is not that the kids in the high school group get together, but rather that we have assumed that their time together should consist largely of froth and vanity. As these children grow up, we find that they are unaccustomed to any kind of serious, sustained worship, and so the pressure mounts to make the worship service more and more like the youth group used to be. Because we have tolerated and encouraged the dumbing down of the faith among young people, we discover over time, as they grow up, that it *stays* dumbed down.

Another element of this cultural phenomenon of youth ministry is what we might call *radical* division between various age groups. I emphasize the word radical because some, in reaction to our modern approach to educating children, have begun to oppose all forms of age segregation. This is clearly an overreaction; children do grow naturally through various stages, and it is the part of wisdom to teach thirteen-year-olds differently than six-year-olds. At the same time, modernity has a mania for age segregation and is not open to any kind of mixed multitude. This is seen in many churches where little ones are actually prohibited from remaining through the worship service.

The modern Church has been atomized, with singles here, teens there, young marrieds across the hall, and so forth. This is the end result of analytic paradigm, which wants to break everything down to its constituent parts. Of course there is a place for analysis, just as there is a place for taking teenage boys aside to instruct them in areas which are of importance to them. But as we do this, we must never forget that Abraham was promised that through him the *families* of the earth would be blessed (Acts 3:25). We should therefore see that if an age-segregated approach begins to compete with the possibility of a man being able to appear before the Lord with his wife and little ones, then that approach is an idolatrous rival to the true worship of God.

Whenever children are taken aside for any kind of instruction, in order to be biblical, the instruction must be equipping them for the time when they come back together with their families. But instruction which feeds and nurtures youthful discontent, and which encourages the young people to continue their pilgrimage away from those who do not really understand them, should be rejected. For these reasons, churches which have such a "youth ministry" should undertake the important reform of getting rid of it.[2]

As churches move away from this concept of youth ministry, the pastor must take care to instruct parents carefully on their responsibilities. The instruction undertaken by the church must supplement, help, and aid the parents as they teach their children, and should not seek to replace it. For example, our catechism classes depend upon parents working with the kids throughout the week on memorizing the answers to the questions. The church provides direction and accountability but does not shove the parents off to the side.

Another important area where this is necessary is that of maintaining order in the worship service. Young children may be kept through the service or put in the nursery. Older children should be instructed and trained by their parents on how to pay attention reverently throughout the service. If children misbehave or otherwise become a distraction to others, they should be removed in order to be taught or disciplined. Sometimes churches have adopted a "no Sunday school or nursery for us" kind of mentality without simultaneously inculcating a culture of discipline so that the children are being trained up to join their parents and older brothers and sisters, as soon as possible, in the orderly worship of God. This naturally gives an advantage to those who argue that children are not ready for this worship. In order to refute this claim, more is necessary than to simply require the physical presence of the children. They are to be with us in order to be able to participate. From the lips of nursing infants and the junior high group God has ordained praise.

---

[2] And a good place to start is through getting a copy of Chris Schlect, *Critique of Modern Youth Ministry* (Moscow, ID: Canon Press, 1995).

The Parish

In his lectures, George Grant has been highlighting the remarkable work of Thomas Chalmers, the great Scottish theologian and preacher of the last century.[3] At the center of that work was the concept of "parish."

We frequently start our discussions at the wrong end. Say, for example, that we bring up the issue of the relation of the Church to the world. In doing this, we think first about the whole Church and the abstract world. We rarely bring our thoughts down to the level of particular congregations and particular communities surrounding them. The result of this mistake is that we find ourselves trafficking in abstractions.

The church is not the parish, and the parish is not the church. At the same time, the church thrives at the center of the parish, informing and discipling those who live their lives in the parish. Life in the church involves Word and sacraments, while life in the parish involves auto mechanics, farming, retail shops, and schools, along with all the other stuff men and women do.

But the denominational system, as it has developed in America, has greatly undermined our capacity even to think in terms of parish. This in turn means that we have lost even the concept of true community. The closest approximation we have to it is found in good churches where the members of the congregation worship together, love each other, and share the occasional potluck or picnic. This is good as far as it goes, but it must be acknowledged in all honesty that it does not go very far. We have first truncated our churches and then have detached them from the soil. We will drive by thirty churches in order to attend the one we like. Whatever advantages this has (and there *are* some significant ones), it still means that churches are selected in a way that is inconsistent with the formation of true community. In an average town of modest size, the Christians in that town will arise on the Lord's Day, and then as they make their way in scores of different directions to multiple churches, they perform an ecclesiastical version of a Chinese fire drill.

But in the older parish system, the members of the congregation would certainly worship together on the Lord's Day, just as we do. But for the rest of the week, they would labor together in the fields, fish together on the seas, work in the same shops, go to war together in the same regiment. Their lives were intertwined—but these intertwined lives were also ordered. They had a hierarchy of values, and the centerpiece of their lives was the worship of God.

All this affects how we think about the Great Commission. Too often we are too quick to dash off to an evangelistic field which is exciting,

---

[3] An audio tape on this is available from Canon Press.

fruitful, *distant*. How many churches think seriously of their duty to fulfill the Great Commission in their neighborhoods? And even when we think "locally," it is too easy to think about establishing a "ministry" in a town with a sufficient population to provide the new church with its "market share." Thus we are selective in our local ministry. In order for this system to work we cater to our market niche. The church functions on exactly the same principles as a new department store. This also mitigates against true community. Community will never arise from groups with "special interests," whether those interests include ham radio, square dancing, or the five points of Calvinism.

The problem is deep and systemic, and there are no quick fixes. But one place to begin is to think seriously about where we live. At least two criteria should be considered — living near the church, and living near one another. Christians should love one another, not just on the Lord's Day, and loving one another involves wanting to be together. This involves wanting to create opportunities for our children to play together, for our men to work together in various "barn raising" tasks, for the women to be involved in one another's lives on a daily basis.

Before all this is dismissed as being both agrarian *and* utopian, unfit for the demands of modern urban living, it should be noted that Thomas Chalmers was successful in establishing coherent parish communities in urban centers. The foundational issues here do not really concern what is possible, but rather what we want. For all our longing for "community," when it comes down to the point, we sometimes discover that we still prefer our institutionalized loneliness.

And we also must remember that to whatever extent we decide to pursue the parish ideal, the modernity system will know how to defend itself. When people start loving one another and seeking to live close to one another, they clearly belong to a "cult," and will probably end up drinking funny-tasting Kool Aid. A cult mentality is "obviously" exhibited by anyone who does not want to live in the prescribed atomistic and detached way — one who does not want to be just another loose ball bearing rattling around in modernity's machine. The contemporary standards will beckon with a siren call — *any* kind of weirdness is accepted by us, as long as it is not the weirdness of normality and sanity. You may dye your hair purple if you like, and you are just trying to get in touch with yourself, but if you express a desire to live close to your friends, you obviously have a deep problem. So it is long overdue for Christians to think about turning away from the insanity which modernity has labeled as normal and sane.

The modern world is a big place and will not be transformed in any fifteen-minute processes. But if we are thinking about our grandchildren, a good place to start is with the idea of parish. Now much of what we have said up to this point is biblically self-evident — of course we should love each other and seek to be involved in one another's lives. But we too often interpret this as an ethereal call to "universal love for mankind." Like Linus, we love mankind—its people we can't stand.

In this, we reverse the meaning of the parable of the Good Samaritan. Jesus told that story to teach us that our neighbor is anyone we may happen to meet along the road. This is quite true, but He did not intend for us to start ignoring our neighbors next door. In the ancient world, it took some explaining to show that, in the command to love our neighbor, a despised alien fell under the biblical definition of neighbor. But in the modern world, it takes some explaining to show that our neighbors are our neighbors.

In addition to these problems, many Protestants may feel nervous about using the term *parish*, because they are accustomed to hearing it used in a particular Roman Catholic or Anglican sense—that is, an administrative part of a diocese containing its own church.[4] But there are other definitions—definitions which lie right at the heart of what it means to be a biblical church. As I am using it here, *parish* refers to a community of saints tied together by covenant in two ways. The first is their common membership in the church, and the second is their geographical connection to one another.

While biblical Greek is not in view, the word is descended from a Greek word *paroikios*, which means *neighboring*. The word literally means "alongside the house." This turned into the Latin *parochia*, which meant diocese, and then grew into the old French *parroche*. From here it was taken over into Middle English as *parish*. During all these changes, the word never really lost part of the meaning central to it, that of *neighboring*.

And this is where we start—we start where we are. When Paul addresses the saints at Colosse for example, he locates them in two ways.

Paul, an apostle of Jesus Christ by the will of God, and Timotheus our brother, to the saints and faithful brethren *in Christ* which are *at Colosse:* Grace be unto you, and peace, from God our Father and the Lord Jesus Christ. (Col. 1:1-2)

The believers here are in Christ and they are in Colosse. As moderns, we must realize how much our mobility has skewed our understanding of what the premodern Church had to have been like. Parish made a lot more sense when most people had to walk to church. But in the modern world we have overcome such physical limitations, little realizing that we are destroying more than minor inconveniences relating to distance. Our ability to drive an hour to get to church has more often than not

---

[4] An interesting reformational application of the concept of parish can be found in Ronald S. Wallace, *Calvin, Geneva, and the Reformation* (Eugene, OR: Wipf & Stock Publishers, 1998), p. 125.

created distance from our next door neighbors, and it has done this without really creating closeness to those we worship with when we are done with our drive. For various reasons, we do more driving *away* than driving *to*.

And so this is the mentality we are seeking to overcome as we are rebuilding the concept of parish life. What we are arguing here is that the saints are not just to be geographically identified, they should be geographically pastored. And this is what we mean by parish.

In many larger modern churches, we see a modern synthetic substitute for parish in "cell groups," or "zip code zones," or "prayer chain lists." In any congregation of appreciable size (over two or three hundred), many of the pastoral needs simply cannot be met in that larger setting and so the congregation is broken up into smaller groups. But even here, though it is better than nothing, what we have at the end is a list of names and phone numbers. We do not yet have *neighbors*; we are not yet parishoners.

Not surprisingly, the Bible tells us what to do about this problem in certain requirements given to the elders of the church.

> Feed the flock of God which is among you, taking the oversight thereof, not by constraint, but willingly; not for filthy lucre, but of a ready mind; neither as being lords over God's heritage, but being ensamples to the flock. (1 Pet. 5:2–3)

The elders here are told to shepherd, or pastor, the flock of God, which is "among" them. The elders are told to live in such a way that they are *examples* to the flock, which cannot happen if the flock does not know the names of the elders who are pastoring them. The elders cannot be mere names in the front of the church directory. This lines up with the author of Hebrews when he says that the saints should be able to consider the outcome of their rulers' way of life (Heb. 13:7, 17).

Of particular interest in the passage from 1 Peter is the word translated *heritage*. The word is *kleros*, and it literally means "lots". It is the word used in all four gospels in describing the activities of the soldiers who cast lots in order to keep from tearing Christ's robe. So how did it come to mean *inheritance*, or *heritage*?

When the people of God invaded the promised land as described in the book of Joshua, the land was apportioned by lot. Each tribe received a different region of Canaan by lot (Josh. 13:6). The inheritance was divided up by lot, and so the inheritance came to be known as "the lots." What was being divided was territory.

The fact that Jesus chose twelve apostles was no accident. They were clearly chosen as the foundation stones for a new Israel, the Christian church. And just as the people of Israel had received their lot, so the apostles did also. In Acts 1:17, we see that one of these apostles was

MOTHER KIRK

guilty of apostasy and fell away from his portion, his allotment. The text says, "For he was numbered with us, and obtained part of this minis-try." The word translated *part* here is *kleros*. A moment later, in verse 25, it is not an insignificant detail that the apostles chose Matthias to re-place him through the casting of lots. They were filling an allotment; of course they cast lots. Judas fell from his lot, and so they replaced him by lot. Just as Joshua did before the tabernacle of the Lord, when the land of Canaan was being divided up (Josh. 13:6–7), so the apostles did in the presence of the Lord.

> And they prayed, and said, Thou, Lord, which knowest the hearts of all men, shew whether of these two thou hast chosen, that he may take part [kleros] of this ministry and apostleship, from which Judas by transgression fell, that he might go to his own place. And they gave forth their lots [kleros]; and the lot [kleros] fell upon Matthias; and he was numbered with the eleven apostles. (Acts 1:24–26)

Some years later, Simon Magus tried to buy his way into an allot-ment. Peter rebuked him and said he had neither part nor lot in the matter (Acts 8:20–21). This settled apportionment of apostolic responsi-bilities explains, for example, Paul's concern about building on another man's foundation (Rom. 15:20).

Now in the new covenant the land of Canaan is no longer being divided up. But this is not because the Church is now a spiritual, ethe-real institution. What this means is that we now are to divide up the world. Abraham and his seed were promised the world. The meek will inherit the earth. We are told to pray that God's kingdom will come, and that His will be done on earth as it is in heaven. And this is why each local church has an identity in Christ and an identity in its neighbor-hood. Our first identity in Christ is our spiritual inheritance, our spiri-tual allotment.

> To open their eyes, and to turn them from darkness to light, and from the power of Satan unto God, that they may receive forgive-ness of sins, and inheritance [kleros] among them which are sanctified by faith that is in me. (Acts 26:18; cf. Col. 1:12)

But not only are the saints of God to receive the inheritance, in an-other sense they are the inheritance. They are "the land" which is to be divided. And this is what brings us back to Peter's admonition to elders on how they were to treat the saints under their charge. Peter tells the elders to be examples to a specific group of people, and tells them not to lord it over those people. In order for this to happen in the way the Bible requires, they must not only know one another's names, they must know one another's lives. Overstating the case just a little, this will not happen unless they are borrowing one another's lawn mowers because they live next door.

So what does all this have to do with the concept of parish? In a church that is effectively shepherded by the elders, each elder will have a certain amount of pastoral responsibility. He will have a subgroup within the congregation that he will check up on, pray for, and so forth. The parish concept simply means that these names are assigned to individual elders with neighborhoods in mind.

In our church, most of the people who attend live in identifiable "clusters." Rather than have one elder be responsible for ten families from six different "clusters," the point is to have one or two elders take responsibility for pastoring in their neighborhoods. When this happens, we are dealing with real people and real lives. Too often the artificial distance we experience at church is the result of real distance elsewhere.

With this understanding, a small church will have one small parish. A larger church will have multiple parishes. This creates an opportunity for the saints in each parish to get to know one another on a genuine level. The church would continue to have church-wide fellowship events, but the possibilities for closeness are much expanded. The various parishes can have get-togethers, fellowship meals, and so on. Another important part of all this is the work of evangelism in the parishes. Nonbelievers will gradually come to realize that they are living in a part of town that has been *named* by the church.

And this means the Church can recover something precious that modernity has mangled. Who is my neighbor? My neighbor is my neighbor.

Building the Kirk

But before the Church can be at the center of the neighborhood, it has to be built there. And before we can build it there, we must have a theology of building.

In ancient Israel, when the people drifted away from faithfulness to God, this was regularly manifested through their worship on the "high places." It was unbelief that drove them from the place God had assigned to establish His name—but at least they knew that religious worship required height, groves, blood, and a cultivated sense of the numinous. They sought out their false religions, but at least, damning them with faint praise, they were religions.

We are just as disobedient in our worship as they were but are too lazy even to create a false religion. So we just make up something that fits in with the zoning regulations and call it good. Because modernity is also driven by unbelief, just like the ancient apostasies, an alternative to the right worship of God must be found. But because we are modern, that alternative ends up being about as numinous as the parking lot at Safeway. In short, for modern evangelicals, worship must be boring and grubby, just like us. And after a time, the vestigial forms of our worship trickle down to join the puddle made by our sorry little secular lives, not distinguished from those lives in any significant way.

Not surprisingly, our architecture, like the rest of our lives, will reflect the gods we worship. If we worship the living God in truth, that will of course be reflected, as we discuss elsewhere in this issue. But if we worship the local baals, then our houses of assembly will soon resemble them in all their splendor. Splendor, aye.

We build temples to the gods of commerce, and this is why the modern church looks like a shopping mall, sprawling and flat, plenty of parking, Visa and MasterCard accepted. In one city, a church mailed out hundreds of thousands of brochures hawking their wares. Come to our church, they said, and we'll give you higher job satisfaction and a better sex life. Just like Alice's restaurant, you can get anything you want. Churches now have weight rooms, they have food courts, they have Christian book stores. In the old days, this last item would not have been a matter of shame, but in the old days, Christian book stores had Christian books in them. (I have not heard of any church that has a Victoria's Secret outlet, but this is probably because I don't get around much.)

We hustle and sell because we think we need the customers. We market the Church because we think the gospel is a product. Because we think the gospel is a product, we measure our success by counting the dollars that flow in. If the stream slows down, we do what all enterprising entrepreneurs do — modify the product until it is more to the customers' liking. The customer, as the fellow said, is always right. But Jesus said that you cannot serve God and mammon. And because the modern evangelical church is clearly hot in the pursuit of mammon, it cannot be serving God. Christ cleansed the Temple because the avaricious had made it into a den of thieves. We have thought to do them one better and have tried to turn a den of thieves into a Temple. We build structures that make people think they are expected to buy something, again, just like they do at the mall. And this is why our churches look the way they do.

Another American baal is the god of pragmatism. This ugly little god is why modern Christians gravitate to the multipurpose building. Over the years I have been in many conversations with many Christians about the prospect of building church facilities, and one thing that comes up with metranome-like regularity is the strong desire that the building be "used more than just one day a week." The strange thing is that these comments are never made as a request for divine services on a daily basis. The desire expressed is not for a daily exposition of the Word, or for more opportunities to sing psalms.

The assumption is always that the facility has to be usable by us for the majority of the week. The thing is like a time-share condominium for God, where He gets the use of the place for a couple hours on Sunday morning. The rest of the time, all that square footage needs to be available for our little occupations—basketball games and concerts, just to mention a few. And thus it comes about that the sermon is preached underneath a backboard and hoop, not as a temporary and regrettable necessity, but as a monument to pragmatic efficiency.

The third compromise we make has to do with our willingness for our worship to be captured by gravity. Our contemporary gods, like us, are earthbound. So we worship in long, low, flat rooms, with the acoustic tile ceiling shutting us in tight. What is above our heads doesn't really matter to us, because we are far more concerned with relationships down here. Our religion is no longer vertical. Besides, in all those old drafty churches, the empty space up in the vault was not very heat-efficient, and God wants us to be good stewards. And so we make our worship centers (gakkk!) very much like a living room, with carpet, padded chairs, curtains, and cushions. Our worship (of one another, apparently) must be cozy.

We have a lot of thinking to do, and after that, a lot of work. Our English word church descends from the Greek kuriakos—house of the Lord. It would be nice to be able to invite one another, as each week drew to a close, to come, worship the Lord in such places. But first we have to build a few.

Facilities and Debt

Of course, after we have decided what we shall build, we must also consider how we will do so. And one of the first questions to arise in matters of church building is the matter of debt.[5] As the Word is ministered faithfully, churches grow in numbers. And as they grow, especially if they grow rapidly, one of the first and great needs is a facility—an adequate place for everyone to meet. How should a church respond when far more people attend than can be accommodated in one service? When the deacons start checking around, they soon discover that everything is quite expensive, and that the church will not be able to purchase or build a building without significant debt service. And so the building drive begins—the death knell of many once-thriving ministries. But when this matter is debated in the church, unfortunately, the wrong question is often the one debated.

The central issue to be presented to such a church is tithing, not borrowing. Now my purpose here is not to defend the ongoing

[5] Jeff Berg and Jim Burgess, *The Debt Free Church* (Chicago: Moody Press, 1996).

legitimacy of the tithe. That has been done effectively elsewhere. Suffice it to say that the ministry of the gospel is to be funded in the same way as was the Levitical ministry (1 Cor. 9:13–14). And that means the tithe.

Assuming this to be the case, we should ask a question with regard to borrowing money in order to finance a new church building. The question is not, "Should a church borrow money to build or buy a structure?" The question rather breaks into two questions. The first is, "Does a tithing church need to borrow money?" The second is, "Should a nontithing church even try to borrow money?"

> With regard to the first, consider one fruit of the great reformation at the time of Hezekiah. "And as soon as the commandment came abroad, the children of Israel brought in *abundance* the firstfruits of corn, wine, and oil, and honey, and of all the increase of the field; and the tithe of all things brought they in *abundantly*. And concerning the children of Israel and Judah, that dwelt in the cities of Judah, they also brought in the tithe of oxen and sheep, and the tithe of holy things which were consecrated unto the LORD their God, *and laid them by heaps*. In the third month they began to lay the foundation of the heaps, and finished them in the seventh month. And when Hezekiah and the princes came and saw the heaps, they blessed the LORD, and his people Israel. Then Hezekiah questioned with the priests and the Levites concerning the heaps. And Azariah the chief priest of the house of Zadok answered him, and said, Since the people began to bring the offerings into the house of the LORD, we have had enough to eat, and have left plenty: for the LORD hath blessed his people; *and that which is left is this great store*" (2 Chr. 31:5–10).

An average church which practices tithing, and which manages its money biblically, should have no problem meeting all its needs. Just to illustrate, imagine a congregation of one hundred households with an average income of $25,000 annually. Such a church (if tithing) could support two full-time staff members and one missionary family at a very reasonable wage and still be able to save $750,000 in five years. Having done so, then such a church is qualified to debate the issue of debt. But if they do so, someone in the back row is sure to ask, "Why do we need to borrow? We have the money right here."

Those churches which need to borrow the money need to do some other things first. The church must never attempt to use debt as an instrument to escape the necessary consequences of disregarding God's assigned means of funding the work of His kingdom. The complaint in response to this is understandable to all of us — "But we need the building." This is quite true, but such a church most certainly should not have a building.

Consequently, the duty of the pastor in such a church is to lead and teach the people on the subject of tithing. Of course this has to be done with great discretion — the saints are not to be coerced into giving, with the church leadership giving the example on "how to take." God loves a cheerful giver — and the saints love to give to those who love to give. The congregation should learn to tithe so that the church will be in a position to give with great liberality. We must learn to give, not as the divine money-maker for ourselves, but rather we must learn to give in order to receive, in order that we may give again. And the attitude exhibited by the households of the congregation should also be exhibited by the church at large.

If the situation is so delicate that the subject cannot even be mentioned, then the elders should simply pray until the church is willing to learn to tithe. But until the elders have good reason to believe that the congregation as a whole is under God's financial blessing in response to the obedience of tithing, they should not even consider borrowing money in order to finance a church building.

Giving money is not the cause of reformation. As in Hezekiah's case, the outpouring of the tithe is the fruit of reformation. Our response therefore should be to pray and preach and teach accordingly. But until we have received the fruit of that blessing from God, we ought not to spend money as though we have.

We must look forward to another problem. Our problem should be where to locate all the heaps and how to express our gratitude to the God who has so richly blessed us — at that time we will turn to "bless the Lord and His people Israel."

The Tithe

One of the odd things about the tithe is that even many antinominan churches are in favor of it. The sabbath? Old Testament. Covenant thinking about children? More Old Testament. But with the tithe, we have something with direct relevance to the church's monthly budget, and so the tithe must be preserved!

But there is a more charitable take on the subject. It is difficult to argue with how God made the world. Whether we believe in a sabbath or not, it will keep surfacing somehow. Whether we like gravity or not, we keep sticking to the ground. And whether or not we hold to the continuing obligation of the tithe, the work of the kingdom must still be funded. So even if we reject it formally, we must still find a substitute for it. And many have found the simplest solution in not rejecting it formally, even if other aspects of their theological approach would seem to call for it.

But the tithe, like the sabbath, and like circumcision, belongs to the promise, not the law. We see clearly that the tithe belongs to Melchizedek, a type of the Christ to come, and was operative long before the law of Moses. How is it possible for us to argue that ten percent went to the shadow, but that nothing need go to the reality?

> For this Melchizedec, king of Salem, priest of the most high God, who met Abraham returning from the slaughter of the kings, and blessed him; to whom also Abraham gave a tenth part of all; first being by interpretation King of righteousness, and after that also King of Salem, which is, King of peace; without father, without mother, without descent, having neither beginning of days, nor end of life; but made like unto the Son of God; abideth a priest continually. Now consider how great this man *was*, unto whom even the patriarch Abraham gave the tenth of the spoils. (Heb. 7:1–4)

The shadow of Christ in Melchizedek received the tithes of Abraham; how have we come to argue that the sons of Abraham need not tithe to Christ Himself?

We may divide the law of the Old Testament into two basic categories, those of creation law and redemptive law. Creation law is that which looks the same throughout the history of the world. The definition of marriage and adultery did not change in the transition between the old and new covenants. Theft looked the same in 700 B.C. as it looks today. Redemption law is law to which obedience may vary in appearance drastically. Keeping the Passover before Christ involved a sacrificial paschal lamb and the removal of all physical leaven from the house (Exod. 12:15), while today we sit down at the Lord's Supper, removing the leaven of malice and wickedness (1 Cor. 5:7–8). The transition between the covenants has dramatically altered the appearance of obedience.

In this context, we see that the tithe falls under the heading of creation law. In the first place, we have no indications in Scripture that the tithe was typological in any way. Thus it does not fall under the heading of other typological laws which pointed to Christ in a figure. Such laws would include the dietary laws, the sacrificial laws, and so forth.

Secondly, in the New Testament, we have clear teaching that the *principles* involved in the tithe are fully operative. Money remains seed, and it remains true that the one who sows sparingly will reap sparingly. "But this *I say*, He which soweth sparingly shall reap also sparingly; and he which soweth bountifully shall reap also bountifully" (2 Cor. 9:6). The New Testament contains many references to the fact that this is the way the world *is*. A man reaps what he sows (Gal. 6:6–8).

> Who goeth a warfare any time at his own charges? who planteth a vineyard, and eateth not of the fruit thereof? or who feedeth a flock, and eateth not of the milk of the flock? Say I these things as

THE LIFE OF THE CHURCH

a man? or saith not the law the same also? For it is written in the law of Moses, Thou shalt not muzzle the mouth of the ox that treadeth out the corn. Doth God take care for oxen? Or saith he it altogether for our sakes? For our sakes, no doubt, this is written: that he that ploweth should plow in hope; and that he that thresheth in hope should be partaker of his hope. If we have sown unto you spiritual things, is it a great thing if we shall reap your carnal things? (1 Cor. 9:7–11)

And third, we have a pointed reference to the continuation of the *tithe* supporting the Christian ministry. This answers the concerns of those who agree that the principles surrounding giving are still operative, but that we have no New Testament grounds for continuing the required ten percent.

If others be partakers of this power over you, are not we rather? Nevertheless we have not used this power; but suffer all things, lest we should hinder the gospel of Christ. Do ye not know that they which minister about holy things live of the things of the temple? and they which wait at the altar are partakers with the altar? Even so hath the Lord ordained that they which preach the gospel should live of the gospel. (1 Cor. 9:12–14)

Paul here argues that Christian ministers, those who labor in the gospel, should receive their support *in the same way* that Levitical ministers received their support. The phrase he uses translated here as *even so* is *houto kai*, which should be understood as "even thus" or "in the same way." Levitical teachers and ministers were supported by the tithe, and so Christian ministers should be supported the same way.

What is the tithe for? As the church receives the gifts from members, the elders should keep in mind the three basic functions of the tithe; The tithe would support the ministers of the gospel, the relief of the poor, and celebration before the Lord. We have already seen Paul's requirement of the first category. Christian ministers are heirs of the Levites, and so the tithe can be given to them (Is. 66:21).

But the tithe also supports the work of the diaconate. This work of relieving the poor begins within the household of faith (Acts 6:1–2), but as the church grows in maturity and wealth, thought should immediately turn to the relief of those who do not know Christ, as a divinely appointed means of bringing them in (Lk. 16:9).

And last, a wonderful boon to uptight modern Christians, the tithe should be used to buy beer for the great ecclesiastical Thanksgiving bash.

Thou shalt truly tithe all the increase of thy seed, that the field bringeth forth year by year. And thou shalt eat before the LORD thy

God, in the place which he shall choose to place his name there, the tithe of thy corn, of thy wine, and of thine oil, and the firstlings of thy herds and of thy flocks; that thou mayest learn to fear the LORD thy God always. And if the way be too long for thee, so that thou art not able to carry it; or if the place be too far from thee, which the LORD thy God shall choose to set his name there, when the LORD thy God hath blessed thee: Then shalt thou turn it into money, and bind up the money in thine hand, and shalt go unto the place which the LORD thy God shall choose: And thou shalt bestow that money for whatsoever thy soul lusteth after, for oxen, or for sheep, or for wine, or for strong drink, or for whatsoever thy soul desireth: and thou shalt eat there before the LORD thy God, and thou shalt rejoice, thou, and thine household. (Deut. 14:22–26)

This celebration should be in the presence of the Lord, and as with every exercise of Christian liberty, it should be characterized by discipline, restraint, joy, drinking, eating, laughing, and deep satisfaction in the kindness and mercy of God. One good way for a church to fulfill this function of the tithe would be through an annual ecclesiastical celebration of Thanksgiving — over the course of two or three days, with dancing, singing psalms, feasting, and communal joy. Done right, it would be the talk of the community, as we try to put the fun back into fundamentalism.

And in this mountain shall the LORD of hosts make unto all people a feast of fat things, a feast of wines on the lees, of fat things full of marrow, of wines on the lees well refined. (Is. 25:6)

Grateful Consumers

But tithing (among other things) contributes to prosperity, and that brings problems. Cotton Mather once commented that the faithfulness of the people begat prosperity, but the daughter devoured the mother. In some ways this irony is a perpetual one. When a man comes to Christ, and begins to obey Him, this means working with his hands and living quiet life in all diligence. One of the consequences of this behavior is that the cocaine bill goes way down.

The man is no longer sinning his money away and begins to live within his means. He begins to tithe, which the Bible describes as putting seed corn in the ground. Soon, in spite of himself, he finds himself not only a believer in Jesus Christ, but one in possession of a substantial amount of material goods.

All this can be considered as fruit of sanctification. They are truly God's blessings, but these blessings will always bring with them the temptations of the blessed. When a man enrolls in a math class, we hope he is not surprised when he soon encounters math problems. When a man is living under the blessings of God, his temptation will of course come from those blessings.

Now one of our central temptations, according to Scripture, is to forget God and develop an undue fondness for our stuff — "And thou say in thine heart, My power and the might of mine hand hath gotten me this wealth. But thou shalt remember the LORD thy God: for it is he that giveth thee power to get wealth, that he may establish his covenant which he sware unto thy fathers, as it is this day" (Deut. 8:17–18). Periodically this man under blessing, with his first love many years behind him now, will hear a message on materialism which begins to convict him. He begins to worry about it until someone reassures him. "God doesn't mind his people having money. He minds money having his people." The conscience is thus dabbed with true words, instead of being pierced with the truth, and the man goes back to raking it in. Now it is quite true that a wealthy man can be saved — look at Abraham — but it is equally true that the Bible is filled with stern warnings about the seductions of wealth. Modern Americans are among the wealthiest people ever to have lived. So surely, when we consider the warnings of Scripture, more is warranted than mere head nodding. If we do not turn to a biblical examination of our blessings, we will soon become the prey of those who seek to manipulate our guilty consciences. This is very commonly done with biblical terminology draped around some socialist foolishness or other. "The Bible says to share. This is why we need minimum wage laws."

But the biblical instructions on this go to the heart of the matter, which, not surprisingly, is the heart. For example, Paul tells Timothy in 1 Timothy 6:17–19 how he should instruct those who are rich in this present world. If Timothy were with us today (and in an important sense, he is), these instructions would be passed on to American Christians with a great deal of urgency.

The first instruction is that we should not be haughty or proud of our wealth. One of the silliest things we do is elevate the nose to the same altitude as our bank account. Second, we are told not to set our hopes on riches, which are as unstable as a house of Federal Reserve notes. Who wants to worship a god subject to interest rates? The third is to acknowledge that God gives to us while intending us to enjoy His gifts. The writer of Ecclesiastes notes that this can only happen by the grace of God. "Every man also to whom God hath given riches and wealth, and hath given him power to eat thereof, and to take his portion, and to rejoice in his labour; this is the gift of God" (Ecc. 5:19). By grace are ye enabled to enjoy the wealth — lest any man should boast. This principle of enjoyment is alien to many who are concerned about the problems of consumerism. But it is part of the necessary foundation for any successful rejection of the worship of wealth.

So the last principle is to have richness of wealth be matched by a richness of good works. We are not to give to others because we have been infected with wealth, and we, the guilty, want to pass on the cooties. We are to give from a sense of enjoyment and gratitude. A man plagued with guilt will give only enough to bring down the level of guilt to acceptable levels. A man giving from gratitude will always give far more.

Consumerism is an ideology — an idolatrous ideology. But we are not to forget who we are. As men and women, we must all be consumers. Not to belabor the obvious, this is because God made us with mouths. And here, as grateful consumers, we may exhibit our gratitude and thanksgiving for all the stuff. "Thou crownest the year with thy goodness; and thy paths drop fatness" (Ps. 65:11).

Pastoring Masculinity

A number of years ago, a visitor to our church commented on something which struck him as uncommon, or at least more rare than it should be. "The men *pray*," he said. Too often the picture of men at church is that of the hapless drone, maneuvered through the doors by a pious wife. He is not exactly spiritual, but he is docile, and that is reckoned to be close enough.[6]

In recent years, the church has consequently placed a great deal of emphasis upon recovering the concept of biblical masculinity within the church. Much of the discussion has been good and helpful, but an important element has still been lacking. We *do* need to talk about ministry to individual men, and encourage them to serve God as men, and so forth. We may be thankful that such teaching has sought to equip men to function as individual members of their families. At the same time, we must be careful that this focus on individual men does not backfire, and we find ourselves ministering to men as just another special subgrouping of the church, with their own special needs. We have a youth group, we have college and career, and, off in the corner, we have — the men.

We have not yet begun to teach and encourage men as representatives of their families — or, to use the biblical phrase, as heads of households. For example, the biblical pattern of evangelism was not at all like our modern method of picking off the devil's stragglers, but rather a pattern of bringing the good news to household after household.

Crispus provides just one of many examples. "And Crispus, the

---

[6] One of the reasons we have trouble with this is that we have forgotten the point of our worship — God the Father. See Thomas A. Smail, *The Forgotten Father* (Grand Rapids, MI: Eerdmans, 1980).

chief ruler of the synagogue, believed on the Lord with all his house; and many of the Corinthians hearing believed, and were baptized" (Acts 18:8). Not surprisingly, the heads of these households held a key role in that household coming to the faith in the first place. Why should this change *after* a household has come into the church?

This is an issue which has direct bearing on the health of every church. We are frequently conscious of the fact that large modern churches are too often "impersonal," and so we try to restore that personal element through various programs of undershepherds or cell groups, etc. But God has already established a primary system of "undershepherds." They are called fathers and husbands. Ministry which treats fathers and husbands as "just another group" of people in the church is doomed, trying unsuccessfully to shepherd a disconnected crowd of individualists, loners, egalitarians, and democrats. And such is the American church.

Pastors must therefore find a way to encourage and equip men, as the heads of their respective households, to function in a pastoral way in their homes. The duties of a Christian father are clear in Scripture, and they are *pastoral* in nature. This does not mean setting up a pulpit in the living room or administering the sacraments around the dinner table. But a father *is* to bring up his children in the nurture and admonition of the Lord. A husband *is* to nourish and cherish his wife, loving her as Christ loved the Church. These duties cannot be performed by anyone else in the church, and their performance (or lack of performance) directly relates to the health of the church. Sound households are the key to a sound church.

Of course if a man is not being encouraged by his pastor to take this role seriously, he is not therefore exempt from his duties. A man is responsible for this pastoral oversight in the home whether or not others around him are being helpful. At the same time, if the minister of a congregation takes his task seriously, he can be a tremendous help to those men who want to be responsible leaders in the governments of their families. In turn, this provides a great blessing to the church because it is constituted in line with the Word.

There are different ways a pastor can encourage this mindset. The first is to teach the congregation, clearly and forcefully, what the Bible says about the subject. There may be some commotion as a result, but cowardice in the pulpit has never been anointed by God. Secondly, the elders of a church can discipline themselves to think differently by changing a few expressions. We need to learn to count by fours. "How many go to your church?" "We are grateful—the Lord has given us about 100 households." And when the men of the church gather (i.e., at the meeting, at the conference, or whatever), they should be seen, recognized, and addressed as *representing* the church. Individualism is pervasive in the modern Church, which is why we react to such suggestions as though they sought to exclude women and children, rather than a biblical attempt to include households.

Pastors need to ask themselves hard questions — "What role, if any, do households *as households* perform in the life of our church?" Until the question can be answered clearly, the men of the church will not assume the role to which God has called them. In the meantime, they can still play softball at the church picnics.

Men's Forum

In order for men to assume responsibility, they have to be encouraged and trained to do so. One of ways we have undertaken to do this is through what we call our men's forum. Our church does not have a Sunday evening service, and in place of it we have a two-hour meeting open to the men of the church.

For the first twenty minutes or so, we sing psalms. As we are trying to learn new psalms as a congregation, we have frequently introduced them at the men's forum. This enables men to exercise leadership in their homes, as they are learning the psalms first. Also related is the blessing of men learning that singing is not inconsistent with masculinity. The singing is robust and a great blessing.

When the singing is over, we pray and begin our discussion. The remaining time is not strictly speaking a Bible or book study. We usually have some assigned reading to guide our discussion, but this is not strictly bounded. Tangents and diversions are fine, and the whole thing would probably best be described as a free discussion around an assigned center.

At this time of writing, we are currently reading through Calvin's *Institutes* together, a section at a time. Discussion questions are circulated ahead of time. In a previous exercise, we spent two years going through Thomas Vincent's commentary on the Westminster Shorter Catechism. If our progress there was a reliable indicator, we will probably spend a good decade in the *Institutes*. There are worse ways to spend your time.

Attendance is good, ranging from twenty to forty men. The fellowship is also good, and the theological foundations for godly living in the home are consistently and regularly reinforced. A significant part of what is accomplished is the formal and public recognition that men are important to the life of the church. Moreover, it is understood that men who are not training to be church officers are important to the life of the church. Theological discussion and application are not topics for religious "professionals" only; they are topics which address how we are to live our lives.

The fact that men can get together with other men in an ongoing and regular way is a great encouragement to them. The time spent away from families is more than paid back in how they are equipped to minister within their families.

Another blessing that comes from this is the result of men bringing their sons with them to listen to the discussion, and at times to join in or ask questions. The effect is similar to what happens in many churches with father/son retreats, but instead of an annual experience, it is weekly — ongoing.

This weekly discussion is doctrinal and practical. Once a month we have a heads of households meeting, in which the elders and deacons get feedback from the heads of households, and reports of the various church ministries are delivered to the heads of households of the congregation. This is what might be called a business meeting. It is important also, but the weekly forum provides the foundational structure for what we do.

Women's Ministry

In the modern Church, men are generally neglected, and the women are the recipients, not of too much ministry, but of too much of the wrong kind of ministry. As the reformation of the Church is established, it is important that an overreaction not set in, with women's ministries disbanded or neglected. But in many cases, they should be redirected.

With women's ministry, an important consideration concerns what the church does not do. At the very center of what should not be done is the all too common practice of teaching women how their husbands are failing to meet their needs, and how they need to compensate.

Nor should women be thrown together in settings which could encourage a lack of care with regard to the tongue. One woman's "prayer request" can look to another woman an awful lot like disrespect of her husband. It is important that when women gather together they be encouraged to stay on an edifying track.

In our congregation, our women's ministry consists of a monthly women's fellowship, where the women gather to sing psalms, hear a missionary report, hear a talk on how to set an attractive table, and so forth. In this, the older women are doing what Paul requires in Titus when he says that the older women should instruct the younger women in domesticity (Tit. 2:3–5).

The other regular form of women's ministry is Bible and book studies. The usual book of choice would be practical Puritan writers, like Jeremiah Burrough's *Rare Jewel of Christian Contentment*, or Thomas Watson's *All Things for Good*.

The direction of the women's ministries is to encourage them to pursue their duties. They do not need to be reminded to remind their husbands to do their duty, because the ministry we seek to have to the men does this constantly. And we have found that while men do not listen to their wives on this subject (however regrettable this might be), they do listen to other men.

We do not teach the men to love their wives if their wives do thus and such. And we do not teach the wives to respect their husbands if the husbands get respectable. The emphasis is to teach the men what the Bible gives to men, and teach women what the Bible gives to women.

And not surprisingly, solid doctrinal teaching is the foundation for both.

Involvement in Politics

As they say, politics makes strange bedfellows. Over the last several decades, many evangelical believers have found themselves working together in various political crusades with members of other faiths. The point of the political cooperation has been to address some of the more egregious crimes against our republic — abortion, infanticide, feminism, egalitarianism, sodomy, and so on. In some cases, the political goal has been met, and in other cases not. But in all cases, a problem has presented itself. How are evangelical Christians to relate to members of other religious communities as they work together in the civil realm? The problem has left more than one Christian concerned that the political work was resulting in the blurring of some important doctrinal issues. In turn, this has led some Christians to make the charge that all such political work will lead inevitably to such compromise — and that politics should therefore be avoided.

In the Second World War, the United States and Great Britain were on the same side and were fighting against Nazi Germany from the same general framework. In the true sense of the word, the two nations were allies. Later, the Soviet Union happened to be fighting against Germany also, but only because Hitler had double-crossed Stalin in the middle of the war. At the beginning, the two had been allies, and because both were secularist scoundrels of the first rank, they had much in common. Unfortunately for Stalin, one of the things they had in common was treachery, so consequently, part way into the hostilities, Hitler attacked Stalin. As a result, in the second part of that war, the United States and the Soviet Union were co-belligerents — they happened to be fighting against a common enemy at the same time, but they were doing so for completely different reasons.[7]

Our world is such that this often happens: two groups with very little in common find they have common cause, for a time, against something else. If this is understood in a clear-headed way, there is usually

---

[7] Marvin Olasky, *Fighting for Liberty and Virtue* (Wheaton, IL: Crossway Books, 1995).

not a problem with it. But problems arise whenever there is a failure to maintain the important distinction between allies and co-belligerents .

For example, we may be grateful to God that Roman Catholics and Eastern Orthodox oppose the atrocity of abortion. We may lawfully join together with them in protest against a government which tolerates and encourages such slaughter. If someone erects a banner which says "Citizens United for Life," we as Reformed evangelicals should be glad to march under that banner to remonstrate with the civil authorities. We are doing so as co-belligerents. The problem comes when the banner reads "Christians United for Life." Under such circumstances, faithful believers begin to have serious reservations. We are not allies.

If the banner reads "Christians United for Life," then of course there may be various churches represented—churches which may differ on numerous things. But they must be Christian churches—allied churches—which agree on the basic truths which the apostles delivered to us. Presbyterians and Baptists differ on whether infants should be baptized. But they agree that the triune God of Scripture, Who is known by grace through faith alone, forbids the dismemberment of infants. It is an abomination. They may therefore come together in the civil realm as Christians to protest such atrocities together in the name of Christ. They are allies, not co-belligerents. At the same time, it is certainly lawful for us to protest such things together with Jews, Orthodox, atheists, Mormons, *et al.*, but not as allies.

The reason we oppose abortion is because it is a violation of God's law. We should not oppose abortion because it violates the sanctity of human life—it is an outrage upon the sanctity of God's law and is consequently an outrage upon the dignity of human life. But if we are opposed to abortion because it violates God's law, it hardly makes sense for us to break the ninth commandment as a means of upholding the sixth.

When a Christian church has apostatized, as both Rome and the East have done, then it is bearing false witness for us to proclaim that they remain Christian churches in order to smooth the way for us politically. The principle applies also to smaller and more recent religious groups. There are more than a few which claim the name Christian, but which deny some of the apostolic teaching which is of "first importance." But at the same time, they still uphold some of the fundamental ethical requirements for the civil realm which are taught in the Bible. Both the LDS church and Unification church fall into this category. For example, there will be many situations in which a Christian and a Mormon vote the same way—but if the Christian has any control over it, he must not do it arm in arm as fellow Christians.

As any politically-active Christian knows, these are not hypothetical questions. How should we handle our work with men and women from religious groups which are not at all faithful to the gospel? Concerned for their souls, we should pray for their repentance and eventual salvation. We must not work with them in the name of Christ, as fellow Christians. But in the civil realm, if they are willing, we should shake hands and ask for a placard.

Moving Beyond Pro-Life

Having said all this, it is important to note how much theology plays a role in the work we do in the civil realm.[8] More than two decades after the abortion carnage began, biblical Christians remain rather confused and battle weary in the pro-life struggle.

The causes of this are many. The first is that the pro-life movement has been often driven by the sorrow of sentimentalism rather than a zeal for biblical righteousness. What follows is an introductory statement that admittedly goes against the grain of much current pro-life thinking. It is a view that requires careful exegesis, thoughtful debate, and extensive qualification. But the discussion really has to start.

We should begin by reviewing what the pro-life struggle has moved us to learn from Scripture. Only then will we be in a position to provide a biblically faithful challenge to our bloodthirsty culture. We should strengthen that which remains before we seek to press on.[9]

First, man is created in the image and likeness of God. Even though the image has been defaced in our rebellion against God and is restored fully only in Christ, still that image is a shield against all lawless bloodshed. In Genesos 9:5–6, the Lord says: "And surely your blood of your lives will I require; at the hand of every beast will I require it, and at the hand of man; at the hand of every man's brother will I require the life of man. Whoso sheddeth man's blood, by man shall his blood be shed: for in the image of God made he man." In this passage, even the animals are held accountable for taking the life of a man. In the abortion holocaust, we have fallen below the level of the beasts. The judgment of God will not be less than the outrage of this guilt.

Second, the image of God is not given at birth or sometime after. John the Baptist leapt for joy while in the womb (Jn. 1:41). The law of God protected the unborn, granting the same rights of protection to them as to anyone else (Exod. 21:22–25). The psalmist marvels at the work of God within the womb (Ps. 139:13–16). According to the Scriptures, the unborn are sons and daughters, not bits of protoplasm.

Third, in a nation which has fallen to killing the unborn, the duty of

---

[8] This section was written together with Douglas Jones and originally appeared in *Credenda/Agenda*.

[9] Christians have been involved in this cause for a long time. Michael J. Gorman, *Abortion and the Early Church* (Downers Grove, IL: InterVarsity Press, 1982).

Christians is plain. The required works of testimony, evangelism, charity, and hospitality are many. Regardless of what happens as our civil realm disintegrates, such works remain a central part of our ongoing duty as God's people, we must testify faithfully against the evil. This testimony takes many forms — marching publicly, picketing the death clinics, distributing literature, and counseling participants. We must continue to show charity to women who for various reasons may contemplate abortion. As the gospel, food, shelter, and clothing are offered to these women, we show that Christ is the Lord of the stranger. By these means, many mothers have been drawn back from the brink of a great and unspeakable horror. We also show a profound hospitality as well, as we open the doors of our covenant communities, welcoming children into our midst by means of adoption. In this respect, the work which has been done has been truly honoring to God and should continue and increase. In none of this should we grow weary in doing good (Heb.12:3–4).

At the same time, all is not positive. Our testimony against the evil, while clear in some respects, has been muddled in others. Christians have wanted to think biblically about opposing abortion, but we appear to have allowed the habits of our times to force us into using secular boxes and humanist absolutes. We proclaim the sanctity of human life in the most general, unqualified terms, such as the refrain from the Republican platform: "The unborn child has a fundamental individual right to life which cannot be infringed."

But the real issue is the sanctity of God's law and the resultant dignity of human life. Because of how He created us, we do have a permanent dignity. This dignity is grossly insulted with the abortionists' weapons, but it cannot be removed. The suction tool does not exist which can remove the image of God.

But still, while having great dignity, human life is not sacred. When we speak as though it is, we leave the distinct impression that the foundation of our humanity is the source of our law, and thus the source of our protest. This is how much of our pro-life involvement has become humanistic instead of biblical. Human life has become a god instead of a gift, an idol instead of a valuable creature.

Such pro-life absolutism would force us to charge God with "anti-life" crimes for His destruction of the children of His enemies. As any Bible reader knows, He gave repeated commands to Israel's armies to utterly destroy various rebellious enemies (Josh. 6:21; 7:25; 8:26; Deut. 20:16). Sometimes God wanted His enemies to perish. Their lives were not sacred. God's law alone has this sanctity, and because He is holy, He visited the dignity of punishment upon rebellious creatures.

We have seen the tragic results of this confusion of sanctity and dignity within the pro-life movement. With those for whom the unborn have become the source of law (instead of victims according to the law), they have bombed clinics and shot abortionists. This is not surprising. But the most troubling thing about this is not the actions of a few fanatics, but rather how many responsible Christians, while knowing that such actions are wrong, have been unable to say why. The reason why many pro-lifers are embarrassed when asked why this sort of "pro-life" lawlessness is wrong is that they share many of the premises held by such fanatics, which gave rise to the reactionary violence. One such foundational premise is the claim that the life of any unborn child places an absolute claim upon us. But only God's law places an absolute claim upon us.

What we need is nothing less than a radical shift in the mentality of those who want to call themselves pro-life. This shift requires that we come to comprehend certain neglected biblical principles. When Christians come to this understanding, they will step beyond the term "pro-life," at least as that term is commonly understood.

First, whenever any descendant of Adam dies, he is receiving nothing less than what he deserves. In Adam we all die. This mortality, this bondage to death, is the result of our collective rebellion as represented in our first father. We are a cursed race, subject to death. The administration of this death, however, is in the hands of the sovereign God alone. The Lord gives life, and consequently the Lord is the only one who can authorize the taking of it.

Second, regardless of our sinfulness, and whether we are Christians or not, God requires that our persons be honored and respected on the civic level. We bear the image of God, and whenever anyone is slain outside of the due process of law, the land is defiled with blood. An individual does not forfeit his civic right to life simply because he is unregenerate. The defilement caused by any such murder occurs whether or not a nation professes to follow the God of the Bible or not. And when the murder is formally approved by that culture, as it has been in ours, the judgment of God is certain and inevitable.

Third, when a culture rebels against this ordinance of God in such a profound way, its days are necessarily numbered. Those followers of God within such a culture must prepare themselves for a deep civic division — a culture war — which will either destroy that nation or rend it to pieces. Wisdom says, "all those who hate me love death" (Prov. 8:36). A culture which loves death cannot stand. If any of the godly are present within a culture possessed with such a death wish, the presence of two separate cultural orders will become increasingly obvious over time. At some point, two nations will emerge. Our fellow Americans will become to us Amalekites.

Fourth, when God judges a nation, His judgment does not fall only upon those who are eighteen and over. When God judges America for her contempt for her children, the judgment will fall not only on the adults, but also on the children—children considered so contemptible that even their own parents slaughtered them.

In the hard providence of God, He sometimes allows His enemies to destroy themselves. When the pagan nations outside Israel sent their children into the fires of Molech, Israel wasn't called to blockade the fire and rescue the babies. And when Israelite kings followed Molech, the people were not commanded to revolt. Israelites were to make sure they didn't kill their own children (Lev. 20), but God-haters were left to destroy themselves (Is. 57:13; Jer. 5:19; 6:19, 21).

God does not delight in the death of the wicked (Ezek.18:23), and neither should we. But if they persist in loving death after hearing the truth over the course of decades, then we ought not force this emergent alien nation into external righteousness. Let them kill themselves, for "God gave them over to a debased mind, to do those things which are not fitting" (Rom. 1:28), even "murder" (Rom. 1:29). This is the wrath of God.

Fifth, when God judges a nation, He spares those who provided a faithful and consistent testimony within that nation. We can and will face the anger of the humanist state—that tinpot deity!—but we will never have to face the wrath of God. Lot's duty was not to save Sodom, but rather to save himself and his house.

Our duty in providing a faithful testimony has three parts. First, we must continue to preach the holy law of God and the gospel of forgiveness. We provide faithful testimony as we preach the gospel to every creature (Mk. 16:15). Part of this testimony includes the insistence that abortion is murder. In this respect, every Christian must be constantly pro-life. Second, we must flee when we are persecuted, if flight is possible (Mt. 10:23). Third, we must take up arms to defend God's covenant children (Neh. 4:14). But we may not use violence until they come after our children. We ought not take up arms to overthrow the established authorities or to defend the lives of Molech worshippers and their children. This is far more secular than biblical.

We must remember the antithesis. Scripture always remembers that deep chasm between those seeking to honor God and those who hate him. But this has not been a part of contemporary pro-life rhetoric.

The unbelievers are destroying themselves in a frenzy of child-murder and fruitless sodomy. Let them go. These are hard words. But Christians must learn to say them. Paul taught us that the children of God-haters are "foul" or "unclean"(1 Cor. 7:14). We must come to the day when the Christian can truly rebuke those who are "without natural affection" and say—"The ancient psalmist blessed the one who would take little ones of those who hate God and dash them against the rock (Ps. 137:9). We see by your pro-abortion position that you clearly agree with this kind of treatment. And we in the Church, in a way you cannot truly comprehend, are now prepared to say *amen*."

Marriage Licenses

Another common area where the minister bumps into the civil authority is the realm of the wedding.

"Do you have the marriage license?" "Do you have a preacher lined up?" Such questions are common as a wedding is planned, and they each reveal how we have not thought carefully or biblically about the role of civil and church authorities in a Christian wedding. Some have simply gone along with the prevailing assumptions, while others have reacted to this and have maintained that neither the Church nor the state have any lawful role to play in a wedding. Both acquiescence and reaction are errors.

In our culture, church weddings are standard, and it is often assumed that without a preacher to tie the knot, the knot will not be tied. Further it is assumed that weddings are gifts of the state to be bestowed on good boys and girls who come in to get their license. We somehow, unbelievably, have come to think that in ordinary cases, we are dependent upon the good pleasure of the Church and the state. Not surprisingly, when many have assumed the Church and state to have this power, others have denied it, claiming that weddings fall under the government of the family only.

According to Scripture, what role may the Church play in the formation of families? The government of the home and the government of the Church are quite distinct. When the minister pronounces a man and woman husband and wife, is he a usurper? Is this a vestige of some medieval priestcraft? When properly understood, the answer is *no*. The church has an authoritative voice in teaching and defending the scriptural boundaries of marriage. Herod was not lawfully married, and John the Baptist said so. A man may not marry his sister, and he may not marry his boyfriend. When dealing with members of the church, the church may authoritatively respond to all attempted marital disobedience. For example, if a young woman in the church determined that she was going to marry a non-Christian, she should come under the discipline of the church. This would mean that the church would be absent from the wedding, refusing to give her blessing.

In a biblical wedding an oath is being taken which directly affects the constitution and membership of the church. In the New Testament, members of the church are frequently brought in by household. In any moral culture, formal recognition of lawful sexual relationships is absolutely necessary. The society of the Church is such a moral culture, so in the interests of propriety and good government, our practice of having an officer of the church administer and witness the vows is clearly acceptable. But in this, the officer of the church is acting as a witness and minister — and not as a priest. Marriage is not an ordinance of the Church; it is a creation ordinance in which the Church has some interest. A minister must never reckon that the authority to "solemnize weddings" is included in the "power of the keys." His presence helps to solemnize the vows, but vows could be exchanged without him.

The case is similar with civil authorities. The fact that our modern statist masters want to license everything from barbering to interior design has led some Christians to say that these overweening authorities have no lawful role at a wedding. But this is also false and an overreaction. The civil magistrate has authority under God to say that a marriage between Billy and Bobby is an abomination and should be attended with civil penalties. In the book of Ezra we see a lawful use of civil authority to enforce the teaching of the Church on marriage and divorce.

> Then arose Ezra, and made the chief priests, the Levites, and all Israel, to swear that they should do according to this word. And they sware . . . And they made proclamation throughout Judah and Jerusalem unto all the children of the captivity, that they should gather themselves together unto Jerusalem; And that whosoever would not come within three days, according to the counsel of the princes and the elders, *all his substance should be forfeited, and himself separated from the congregation of those that had been carried away.* And Ezra the priest stood up, and said unto them, Ye have transgressed, and have taken strange wives, to increase the trespass of Israel. Now therefore make confession unto the LORD God of your fathers. (Ezra 10:5-11; emphasis mine)

Disobedience on this question of marriage was attended by two sets of penalties — civil and ecclesiastical. Those who did not come to Jerusalem would have all their property confiscated (civil) and would be excommunicated (ecclesiastical).

On the face of it, the practice of having weddings registered in such a way that makes prudent adjudication by the state a possibility makes good biblical sense. Weddings result in joint property and children, and in a fallen world this means disputes over property and disputes over children. Solomon had to determine one child custody dispute (1 Kgs 3). Such disputes are within the sphere of the civil magistrate. The statists should stop issuing licenses, as though they were the lords of marriage, but there would be no impropriety for the state to pass a law requiring proper registration for any lawful marriage. Further, there would be no impropriety in the state's refusing to acknowledge the registrations of biblically unlawful weddings.

A wedding is a covenantal act involving two families, resulting in the formation of a third family. At such a wedding, the state and Church have a strong interest and should have their ministers and witnesses present. But such ministers and witnesses must remember their place; they have authority as far as the Word gives them, and no farther.

✣ CHAPTER XI ✣

OUTREACH

Reformed Missions and Evangelism

A common charge against Reformed churches is that they are uninterested in evangelism. As with many such charges against the Reformed faith, there is an element of truth here, and an element of slander.

The truth to the charge is the result of Reformed churches being comprised, unfortunately, entirely of sinners. There are two basic ways in which a gross lack of evangelistic zeal can develop. The first would be the result of natural human laziness or complacency. There is no explanation for why the task of evangelism is not addressed other than the obvious reason that the task was difficult and hence readily shoved off to the side. Satan fell, Chesterton once said, through the force of gravity.

The second way in which neglect of evangelism happens in Reformed circles *is* the result of a doctrinal problem. From the outside it is easy to say that belief in election is the culprit, but this is far too simplistic. There is a doctrinal problem but it is a problem caused by a combination of the doctrine of election and the doctrines surrounding a pessimistic view of the future. In short, Calvinism and a pessimistic eschatology *are* a bad combination for evangelism. If we believe that the number of the elect is fixed, as all Calvinists do, and if we combine this with an eschatology that says, on the basis of infallible prophecy, that the number of the elect was fixed *small*, then it would be easy to see how this would dampen a zeal for evangelism. The soldiers are being commanded to capture a hill that they all believe, on prophetic grounds, to be untakeable. When Saul found out night before how the battle would go, the information affected his attitude about the fight. The principle problem here is not the fact that evangelicals adopted Calvinism and consequently lost their zeal for evangelism, but rather that postmillennial Calvinists abandoned their postmillennialism and consequently lost their conviction that the gospel would go forth into the world, conquering and to conquer.

And this, in part, addresses the slander concerning the Reformed faith. There have been many periods in history when the Reformed have been in the forefront of evangelistic preaching and various kinds of mission work. It would be difficult to maintain that William Carey, George Whitefield, or Charles Spurgeon had a lackluster approach to evangelism.[1]

But *current* evangelistic efforts by Reformed believers are commonly not recognized from outside as such. This is the result of the fact that a consistently Reformed view of evangelism is hard for non-Reformed evangelicals even to recognize as evangelism. The assumption with modern evangelical circles is that the definition of evangelism is self-evident, and when that definition is not apparent in the Reformed world, then the whole enterprise is dismissed as nonevangelistic.

The Reformed believe that the gospel encompasses the world, while evangelicals tend to think of the gospel in terms of bare minimums. The gospel was preached to Abraham when he was promised that the world would be blessed through him (Gal. 3:8). The gospel was preached to the Israelites in the wilderness (Heb. 4:2). The book of Matthew *is* a gospel. But none of these things can be neatly worked into a four spiritual laws approach. The modern evangelical tendency is to *distill* the gospel, getting it down to its saving essence. The Reformed approach is to declare as much of the whole counsel of God to as much of the world as we can. The lordship of Christ over all things is a *gospel* issue, and so this includes economics, the environment, war and peace, worship, and of course, personal salvation at the heart of it. As a result, when modern evangelicals look at the Reformed doing what is called worldview evangelism, it might not look like evangelism at all because there was no point where the three or four point gospel presentation was introduced.

Doctrinal debates over the nature of the gospel within the context of the church are even evangelisitic. The Reformed believe that the gospel is offensive to the natural man, and so it must be preached in the power of the Holy Spirit in order to be effective at all. Modern evangelicalism has stated the gospel in such a way as to be flattering to the natural man. Thus, it need only be presented in a winsome fashion, because the nonbeliever has the full ability to respond to the gospel if he chooses. The Reformed evangelist believes that he is preaching the good news to dry bones in a valley of dry bones. He may preach as he pleases, but unless the resurrecting power of God is evident, nothing whatever can happen. The modern evangelical sees himself as trying to give medicine away in a hospital ward. He may succeed or fail, depending on what *he* does.

---

[1] For more than a little edification on this, see Dallimore, *George Whitefield Vols. 1 and 2* (Westchester, IL: Cornerstone Books, 1979), George William Pilcher, *Samuel Davies* (Knoxville, TN: The University of Tennessee Press, 1971), and Iain Murray, *Jonathan Edwards* (Edinburgh: The Banner of Truth Trust, 1987).

How we define the gospel as a result of our debates in church has a direct impact on the evangelistic endeavor outside the Church. Monumental issues ride on the results of this debate: will our evangelism rest upon the power of God or the persuasiveness of man? But regardless, the debate over the gospel is, at the base, a debate over evangelism.

Differences over methodology are also in evidence. The Reformed believe that evangelism is an assigned task to the Church and tend to put effort into the training of evangelists and apologists. Modern evangelicals tend to emphasize the fact that it is the duty of every Christian to share the gospel every day. Because of this we see the Reformed conviction that the principle engine of evangelism in the world is to be preaching. Modern evangelicals have gravitated to other methods like one-on-one sharing, small-group Bible studies, radio programs, and so on.

This understanding also should direct a Reformed understanding of missions. The missionary should be sent out by the church and not by a parachurch sending agency. The Church is responsible for the evangelization of the world, not *ad hoc* agencies. The Church is the pillar and ground of the truth, and thus responsible for the content of the gospel and not voluntary agencies, assembled for this particular purpose.

On a related matter, our common system of having missionaries gather support from fifty different churches, at fifty dollars a church per month, if they are lucky, does not provide the accountability that is necessary. The goal should be to have one church sponsor one missionary and provide close prayer support and accountability for that missionary. This has the added benefit of making the missionary furlough an actual furlough, instead of a time when the missionary has to scramble around to all fifty churches to keep his financial base intact.

All this is to say that the Great Commission was a commission to the Church. It is time the Church returned to that commission, recovers a sound understanding of the gospel, and picks that commission up.[2]

The Beauty of Apologetics

When we consider the disarray of the unbelieving culture around us, it should help us come to the realization that biblical Christianity makes good sense. There is no need to "apologize" for the faith. It is the truth of God. We should therefore find no basis for thinking that apologists should go around with a hangdog expression, hoping to find someone gullible enough to listen to them.

When the Christian evangelist or apologist presents the gospel to an unbelieving world, he is presenting a message which, when properly

---

[2] A good strategic understanding is also necessary. Jim Wilson, *Principles of War* (Moscow, ID: Community Christian Ministries, 1964, 1983).

understood, is true, good, and beautiful. A full-orbed presentation of the
Christian faith will always do justice to all three aspects of the good life,
a life which is offered to us only in Christ. This is made relatively easy by
the fact that we live in a time when the alternatives to the Christian faith
are manifestly the antithesis of all three. We have the great opportunity
of preaching and presenting the Gospel to a world which is obviously
ensnared by the false, the evil, and the ugly.

So as the Christian apologist takes up his position, and presents the
message of Christ to the unbelieving world, the antithesis between faith
and unbelief should be sharp and defined at all three points. The message of the Cross is true, and all the other modes and ways of salvation
are false. The standards of God's Word are righteous altogether; the
standards of those without faith are just like the men who invent them —
both fickle and wrong. And last, the Gospel of Christ is beautiful. We are
told to worship the Lord in the beauty of holiness. The alternative to this
is a slow and inexorable descent into the realm and domain of the ugly.

With regard to the first two aspects of this — the true and the good —
contemporary Christians have done a good job with their apologetical
spadework. We have developed sound arguments for dealing with the
epistemological and ethical relativists. When someone maintains that
there is no truth, C. S. Lewis, in his fine book *Miracles,* teaches us simply
to ask if that claim is true. If it is, then he has contradicted himself. If it is
not, then why are we listening to him?

If someone says that no ethical standards are fixed, and so we ought
not to apply our standards to anybody else, we now know what to ask.
What does the good gentleman mean, "we *ought* not?" If ethical standards are not fixed, then the conclusion could just as easily be that we
ought to apply the first whimsical standard that comes into our head to
everybody and his dog. If there is no absolute standard of morality, then
anything goes, including the worst forms of absolutism. If biblical absolutes are figments of our own minds, then the first thing we could do, if
we wanted to be consistent, would be to hang all the relativists and burn
all their houses. Of course, trying to be consistent like this is inconsistent, which, in an odd sort of way, makes it consistent again. It is kind of
like looking at that endless series of the back of your head in the opposing mirrors at the barber shop. Ethical relativism is not just wrong, it is
incoherent.

Sadly, the aesthetic sense of the modern Church is greatly lacking
and is making a balanced apologetic difficult. We know what is true,
and we know what is good. We have trouble with the beautiful. What we
as evangelicals produce in the realm of the arts is frequently just as ugly
as what the world cranks out. They produce what is self-consciously
ugly — deliberately — trying to make the point about the
meaninglessness of everything. We produce *kitsch* by the ton that

pretends to look good and so trebles the offense.

But the Christian faith really is beautiful. Therefore the worship of God should be beautiful. And the task of the evangelist and apologist is to present that worship as the present duty of all men. Thus the "call to worship" should be as lovely as the worship itself should be. The words we use to present the faith to nonbelievers should be lovely, well crafted. The books we write defending the faith should not look as though they were written by a computer programmed to write like a committee. One of the central reasons C. S. Lewis is such an effective apologist for the faith was just this: He was able to make righteousness readable. He knew how to craft a sentence.

It is not enough to be a theology wonk, able to define all the ins and outs of epistemology. It is not enough to be able to blow the arguments for ethical relativism out of the water. An apologist is one who dresses out the gospel according to its nature. And that gospel is as lovely as it is true. It is as beautiful as it is good. We must repent of our tendency to dress the loveliness of wisdom in rags.

When we forget this balance, we cannot be surprised that the world uses our inconsistency as an excuse to continue to ignore what we say. So the task we have in winning those without faith requires that we understand the full nature of what we present. An apologist, rightly understood, is a missionary of the lovely.

Twice the Children of Hell

In discussions of evangelism and missions, we too often assume that everything goes under these names and off we charge.

Of course, nothing is wrong with missions, considered in itself. "Missions" is not to be thought of as something the Church does, but rather as a central part of what the Church *is*. This is why Christianity is necessarily a missionary faith. A professing Christian's rejection of the idea of converting members of non-Christian faiths is really just part of his own fundamental rejection of the Christian faith. So not surprisingly, the faithful church has always been characterized by an intense interest in missions.

Jesus left us no option on this. In the Great Commission, He tells us to evangelize the world. And the book of Acts presents an interesting table of contents early in the text when it says that the gospel will go from Jerusalem, to Judea, to Samaria, to the uttermost part of the earth. As the book of Acts progresses, these concentric circles move steadily and remarkably outward. That is the hallmark of a thriving Church — it constantly spreads out.

But this is a fallen world, and no situation is automatically rosy. Consider that Jesus, when he commented on the missionary zeal of the Pharisees, taught a principle that is too infrequently considered in discussions of the modern missions movement. He said that they would cross the sea to make a single convert, and, when they had him, they would make him twice as much a son of hell as themselves. This should be reckoned among those things that make one go *hmmm*.

The principle here is that you cannot export what you do not have, and, if you try, you will only wind up exporting what you *do have*. Whenever Pharisees go on a mission, the result is Pharisaism overseas. When scriptural ignorance goes on a crusade, the result is crusading ignorance.

The applications to our situation should be obvious. The evangelical world in North America is doctrinally confused, morally compromised, liturgically anemic, and culturally superficial. So what happens when we take the show on the road?

Either we succeed or we don't. If we succeed, then what have we done but make a bad thing go international? If we do not succeed, then what was the point? Further, if we do not succeed, it might be worthwhile to ask why our particular brand of happy-clappy Christianity did not appeal to those third-world residents who do not share our peculiar American quirks and enthusiasms.[3]

The point is not to put missions on hold, nor is it that we have to evangelize all the nonbelievers here before we turn our attention to foreign missions. As the church grows, the scriptural expectation is that borders and oceans will be crossed long before the work is completed in any given place. A healthy church should be sending out missionaries long before the local work is completed.

But it does mean that there is an important precondition for successful missions, biblically defined. The church which sends out missionaries must be reforming itself according to Scripture. The region of the church which sends out missionaries does not have to be evangelized before that church can turn its attention to the foreign field. But the *church* should be evangelized before they try it. The beam should be out of our eye before eye surgery is attempted across the world.

Missionaries are sent to preach the gospel. But today most evangelical churches on our continent do not have a clear understanding of what the gospel is. Missionaries are sent to teach men how to establish godly leadership in their churches. But do we have godly leadership in *our* churches?

Why do we assume that we have something to share with the world? One possibility might be simple American hubris. We think we have something of spiritual value for them for the same reason that our State Department thinks it knows what is good for Bosnia. We are Americans, and we are used to being bossy.

[3] George M. Marsden, *Understanding Fundamentalism and Evangelicalism* (Grand Rapids, MI: Eerdmans, 1991).

Paul once commented that the assemblies of the Corinthians did more harm than good. It is possible to meet in the name of Jesus Christ, he argued, and then do a lot of damage to the kingdom. As long as we are in that condition, and we are, the call should be for reformation *here*, and not for more volunteers to export whatever our liturgical and doctrinal wrecking crews are doing to doctrine and worship in our own churches.

None of this is said to discourage missions, rightly understood. It is simply the recognition that, when God is pleased to grant reformation to us, much of what will have to be reformed will be that which we have been laboring industrously to accomplish, both here and abroad.

In other words, when God grants reformation here, it will begin to dawn on us that we have been making a mess — all over the world. Now, this is no argument for delaying the sending of missionaries. It is a plea to redouble our efforts for reformation here, a plea to learn that we can't give what we don't have.

A Literature Ministry

Another important tactic in outreach is that of printed literature.[4] But this leads to yet another problem.

Many of us have sympathized with a poor classmate — perhaps in a speech class somewhere — who had been called upon to give an extemporaneous speech. After several painful minutes of foot-shuffling, throat-clearing, and so forth, it became apparent to all that this hapless individual had — nothing to say.

But perhaps the classmate was the garrulous sort, concerning whom it took a few minutes longer for all to realize that he had — nothing to say. The modern evangelical church has this very affliction — nothing to say — and this affliction manifests itself in just the ways described above. We live in a time when the invention and development of desktop publishing has thrust the church to the front of the class, and there we stand, slightly red, doing our best to mutter indistinctly through.

But our ranks contain the garrulous as well. From our publishing houses and evangelical magazines pours forth a veritable torrent of fluff. That which is not heretical is simply trite, and even the heretical stuff is pretty lightweight — gone are the days of the magisterial heretics! The most we can produce is heretical treacle. And all this stuff, this Jesus junk, is hawked through a vast network of Christian bookstores, dominated by the Christian Booksellers Association (CBA). If the Lord were to attend one of their conventions, it would take Him all day to overturn the tables and the display booths.

---

[4] Klaus Blockmuel, *Books: God's Tools in the History of Salvation* (Vancouver, BC: Regent College, 1986).

This is our problem. We live in a time of unprecedented opportunity; it is an opportunity which dwarfs the significance of the invention of the printing press. But the modern Church, unlike the Church at the time of the Reformation, has thus far exhibited a very lackluster response to that opportunity. That we, as Christians, people of the Book, have responded in this way should horrify us.

Where do we start? First, and primarily, the Church must recover the content of the central doctrines entrusted to her in the Scriptures. The main reason we say so little in print is that we have so little to say. The truth of God has been entrusted to the Church, and the doctrinal neglect exhibited by professing evangelicals over the last one hundred years is a shabby story of abdicated responsibility. "But if I tarry long, that thou mayest know how thou oughtest to behave thyself in the house of God, which is the church of the living God, the pillar and ground of the truth" (1 Tim. 3:15).

By the "truth of God," I am referring to the mind of God as revealed throughout Scripture, and only in Scripture. For those who are interested in a summary of what the central doctrines of Scripture are, I would refer them to the very able abstracts of scriptural teaching found in the great confessional statements of the Reformation — the Belgic Confession, the Heidelburg Catechism, the Canons of Dordt, the Westminster Confession, etc.

The reader will have perhaps noticed that I did not include the stripped down, Lowest Common Denominator statement of the National Association of Evangelicals — a statement which is quite good and useful up to a point, but as our current theological poverty illustrates, it is a point which we are long past.

Some readers may also have seized upon the fact that I have pointed to uninspired creedal statements. "Didn't the Reformation also give the principle of Scripture alone?" Such an objection demonstrates a frightening ignorance of the content of both the confessions and the Scriptures and is a prime example of the appalling "nothing to say" ignorance which afflicts the modern Church.

In order to teach, the Church must first be taught. Writers must be readers. "A fool hath no delight in understanding, but that his heart may discover itself" (Prov. 18:2). The Church will never have a shortage of people who want to "say a few words." But mere talk, or writing, or publishing, is worthless. Teachers must be teachable themselves, and should have demonstrated that teachable spirit in their willingness to sit at the feet of others — older teachers, both deceased and living. As they study, they should be seeking to understand their teachers and to compare what they are saying to the Scripture. If the student has chosen his teachers wisely, he will acquire much that is precious and will be equipped to remove what is dross. And even where he differs with his teachers, he will be humbled through his contact with them. "The way of a fool is right in his own eyes: but he that hearkeneth unto counsel is wise" (Prov. 12:15).

But a warning is in order here. There is an optical illusion created when the elders of a church begin manifesting this teachable spirit. Many Christians may know someone like this — someone whom they believe to be very learned and godly. When they are in his study and see the mountains of books ("Have you *read* all these?"), they perceive him as being very scholarly and so on. But if the man is in fact seeking to be godly, his books strike him as being nothing more than monuments to his ignorance. Why? Our business as Christians is to know the Lord. How many volumes does it take to exhaust a study of His attributes? The more we study, the more we realize how little we know. The more books we buy and study, the more we realize that we all are doing theology among the Dufflepuds.

Far from producing a prideful dogmatism, sanctified study produces humble certainty. The truth is ours because it was given to us and not because we earned it. Consequently, in order to recover true literature ministry, our first order of business is serious and humble *study*.

In what follows below, I will be arguing that the Church needs to recover a sense of her mission with regard to literature, and needs to resume the task of flooding our communities with the doctrine of Christ. Because the task is immense (and dangerous), we will be preserved from horrible calamity only if we begin with utter humility before the Lord. "Seest thou a man that is hasty in his words? there is more hope of a fool than of him" (Prov. 29:20). If there is no hope for someone who is hasty in his speech, how much worse will it be for those who are hasty in publishing?

So, what is the great business of the Church? "And Jesus came and spake unto them, saying, All power is given unto me in heaven and in earth. Go ye therefore, and teach all nations, baptizing them in the name of the Father, and of the Son, and of the Holy Ghost: Teaching them to observe all things whatsoever I have commanded you: and, lo, I am with you alway, even unto the end of the world. Amen" (Mt. 28:18–20).

One of the central tasks given to the Church in the Great Commission is that of teaching the disciples of Christ everything that He commanded. This is to be done with words. From the beginning, obedient Christians have been people of the Book, and consequently people of books.

Jesus here commands, *inter alia*, a preaching and teaching ministry. But this involves more than simply having a sermon delivered on the Lord's Day. While preaching is the principal means of evangelism and discipleship the Lord has given to the Church, it is not the only means at our disposal. With regard to our concern for literature ministry, there are several interesting features in this command.

One is that the command is self-perpetuating. If we are to teach disciples to obey everything He commanded, then we are certainly to include instruction on obedience to this last command. But if we do this, then we find that the Great Commission is handed, like a baton in a relay race, from one generation to the next. We see the same kind of generational thinking in Paul's writing. "And the things that thou hast heard of me among many witnesses, the same commit thou to faithful men, who shall be able to teach others also" (2 Tim. 2:2).

Now if the task of the Church is handed across generations (and it is), one of the best ways to aid in doing this is through books. This does not preclude or replace the teaching of younger men by older men. It is one of the best ways to reinforce such teaching. For example, Peter said that he wanted to remind his students (in writing) of what he had taught them orally, so that when he was gone, they would have a good reminder. "Moreover I will endeavour that ye may be able after my decease to have these things always in remembrance" (2 Pet. 1:15). This is why diligent students in classes take notes. Even though they have heard the teacher in person, writing is a natural and scriptural way to help retain what was heard.

Second, the Lord uses the word teaching in His Commission to the Church. Now what is the instrument by which teaching is done? When we baptize, the instrument used is water. What instrument do we use when we teach? The answer (quite obviously) is words.

What kind of words? The Bible uses the word *teaching* both for words that are spoken and words that are written. For example, it is used very frequently in Scripture for oral instruction: "And Jesus, when He came out, saw a great multitude and was moved with compassion for them, because they were like sheep not having a shepherd. So He began to teach them many things" (Mk. 6:34). Jesus was speaking to the multitude, instructing or teaching them.

But Jesus has taught many more than just those who heard Him. This is because His teaching was recorded and preserved. "The former treatise have I made, O Theophilus, of all that Jesus began both to do and teach" (Acts 1:1). Jesus pronounced a blessing upon those who heard Him and believed. But He also went out of His way to bless those of us who have *read* His words. "Neither pray I for these alone, but for them also which shall believe on me through their word" (Jn. 17:20). How did all of us come to believe in the Lord Jesus? It was because of the words and deeds of Christ, recorded for us in Scripture. In short, Christianity exists at this day because of literature ministry. Christ condemned the Jewish leaders of His day for their neglect of this truth. "But if ye believe not his writings, how shall ye believe my words?" (Jn. 5:47).

The Bible refers to the spoken exposition of God's truth as teaching.

It also does the same for written exposition of truth. "For when for the time ye ought to be teachers, ye have need that one teach you again which be the first principles of the oracles of God; and are become such as have need of milk, and not of strong meat" (Heb. 5:12). The author of Hebrews was explaining here why he was unable to proceed immediately to his more difficult teaching concerning Melchizedek.

There is therefore no ground scripturally for making a fundamental distinction between written teaching and spoken teaching. (This, incidentally, is not the same for preaching, which does not transfer to the page in the same way.) This is especially the case when we consider that the foundation of all modern oral teaching is to be the written Word of God. Both are teaching, and both are to be held up to the standard of God's Word. Our first question of all teaching, of whatever form, should be, "Is it true?" If it is biblical, then how the truth was delivered to us is of secondary importance. If it is not true, then the means of delivery is also of secondary importance. It is true that the form of teaching does affect our ability to know the qualifications of the teacher. This will be addressed below.

Because the business of the Church is to multiply sound teaching, this means that we should be about our business — utilizing all available means. The early Christians were accused of filling Jerusalem with their doctrine (Acts 5:28). Isn't it about time we were accused of doing something similar? In ordinary circumstances, the Church should utilize all available means to multiply sound teaching. This means ongoing personal, verbal teaching of the truth — sermons, Bible studies, web pages, one-on-one biblical counseling. It means electronic duplication of sermons, Bible studies, etc. Some may object, and say that the sermons they hear are not good enough to tape and distribute. But if they are not good enough to tape, they are not good enough to preach in the first place.

It also means that the modern Church must seriously undertake literature ministry. It is our job to fill the earth with our doctrine. At least with regard to literature, the Church has abdicated in this. The parachurch publishing industry exists because the Church has abdicated her teaching role in literature. It is little wonder that there are no doctrinal or moral constraints in Christian publishing anymore. This is because there is no church discipline in the area at all. The Church, entrusted with the job of maintaining doctrinal and moral discipline in these areas, no longer publishes anything significant. That is done by major publishers of literature for Christians, which in some cases is controlled completely by non-Christian corporations. The Christian literature business is exactly that, a business. It is therefore immaterial whether or not a Christian publishing house is owned by Christians. Whether it is or is not does not affect how the business is done.

The result is that Christian publishing is no longer driven by the truth. The Christian book industry and most Christian bookstores are market-driven. Because most bookstores simply stock that which the public is currently demanding, a sort of literary Gresham's Law takes over on their shelves—bad books drive out the good. But because the Church is the pillar and ground of the truth, the literature ministry of the Church should be truth-driven. The people should be supplied with sound literature, which they need to be reading. This is not the same thing as supplying them with what they would have requested had it been left up to them. This task belongs to the elders of their church.

Churches of any size at all should consequently be points of literature distribution, and those with the resources should be publishing houses. And given the task assigned to the Church, and given the monetary and technological resources we have, there is no reason why each church could not eventually be printing large amounts of tracts, booklets, and books. This must not be done for the sake of vanity ("Our pastor wrote a book!"). May God grant that this soon becomes an unremarkable commonplace—if we are blessed, such words will sound just like, "Our pastor preached a sermon!"

Consider again the commission given the Church by our Lord. The gospel is to be presented to every creature. The saints are to be taught and edified and equipped, so that they grow up into their Head, the Lord Jesus Christ. For those who understand the magnitude of this task, any attempt to do it apart from immense amounts of printed literature is simply quixotic.

There may still be some concern about the nuts and bolts. Given this teaching responsibility which has been given to every church, each church should therefore be a literature ministry of *some* magnitude. This is not to be done as a replacement for verbal teaching and preaching, but as a preparation for it, a supplement to it, an extension of it. Preaching is at the center, supplemented by teaching, which is then extended by means of print.

By literature ministry, I mean that every church should distribute Bibles and doctrinally-sound tracts, pamphlets, booklets and books. The goal should be to do this by the ton. The mission should be to distribute as much of God's undiluted truth as we possibly can. Because there is so much to do, it is important that we start immediately. At the same time, we should wade in from the shallow end of the pool. It *is* important to start well. But it is more important to start at all than to avoid starting at all in the name of "starting well." Chesterton once said that anything worth doing was worth doing badly.

A good place for many churches to start would be with a booklet table at church. At the beginning, the congregation should be given sound literature in small doses. A church should start with a booklet table, and with an occasional book. I suggest a good starting point would be the various booklets put out by Banner of Truth. If the church starts a book table with the collected works of John Owen, then a handful of theology wonks in the church will be very happy indeed. But the goal is the reformation of the whole congregation, not just part of it. Another way of stating this is that the literature put out for the congregation should be good, and it should be readable.

When a church turns to the work of publication, there are certain tasks that need to be done within the church. The literature ministry of the church should have specific marching orders from the elders of the church. The elders are responsible for the content of what is published, and they should exercise that oversight. In our church, the publication of books is overseen by one of the elders, and the publication of our magazine is overseen by another elder. Both publication ministries answer to the elders as they exercise their collective authority in session. This does not mean that the elders of the church should be merely tolerant of the literature ministry. They should be committed to it, understanding the importance of it.

It should be obvious, but in order to publish, there must be writers with something to say. The church needs writers. And if no one in the church has anything edifying to say, then it is time for that church to shut down. The content of what is published can come in different ways. The first is if in the preparation of sermons, lectures, and so forth, the ministers commit what they are learning to print. There can also be younger men who may be aspiring to church office who can have a significant part of their training be given to them in the discipline of writing.

The second way is to have sermons and lectures transcribed and edited. This involves a little more work for additional people but it is still relatively simple to do. (It can also be beneficial in other ways. I can still remember how horrified I was the first time I saw a written transcript of what I had said.) One time we had a taped message which my father had presented on bitterness transcribed to computer disk. There it was edited and formatted for publication. A cover was designed, and it was sent off to the printer. When the shipment arrived, I had the great pleasure of showing my father a booklet he had written without knowing it. Again, if it isn't worth saying in print, it isn't worth saying in the pulpit. Sermons should not be preached because tradition requires that it be done. They should be preached because we want to get the Word out. Do we want to get the word out, or not? If we believe the word is good, then we should act like it.

There is another important point that needs to be made with regard to writers. The Bible says that the lives of elders should adorn their teaching. There are stringent moral qualifications placed upon those who would lead in the church (1 Tim. 3:1–7; Tit. 1:5–9), and those who are influenced by their leaders are told to consider the outcome of their way of life (Heb. 13:7, 17). This was addressed at length earlier in this book. Because the Christian book industry is now a parachurch business, with no accountability apart from market forces, we have seen in recent years a radical divorce between what a man may say in his books and what he can get away with in his life. The immorality of Christian writers has reached scandalous proportions. Space limitations prevent me from launching into a list of well-known Christian authors who have shipwrecked their families, and who continue to write and publish.

The answer to this is to have Christian authors who are accountable to a biblical church (i.e., one that disciplines in accordance with Scripture). What happens now if a well-known pastor/author runs off with the choir director? He (sometimes) is asked to step down from the pulpit. But in order for his book deal to fall through, the sin would have to be pretty rank. And even then, the publisher may allow the rank sin to become the topic of the next book — *Recovering from Ministerial Promiscuity/How to Regain Your Flock After Sleeping Around in It.*

The solution is to have writing and publishing done under the discipline of the church. One of the best ways to maintain this is through the accountability provided through personal acquaintance. If a man preaches a sermon on how to love your wife when it is very clear within the church that he doesn't love his wife, there is accountability. But if he does the same thing in a book, under our current system, there is no accountability. The church should insure that they do not publish material written by someone whose personal life is not in order.

The church also needs editors. One of the advantages of word processing is that it makes editing relatively painless. In a previous era, editing, corrections, revision, etc., were a major production. It astonishes me that our generation is so ill-equipped to produce good, solid literature when our equipment is so good. And it is an even greater astonishment to consider what Richard Baxter was able to do (to pick a Puritan out at random) with a quill pen.

There are two kinds of editing. One is technical or copy editing. This is a task for which many women are superbly qualified (since many of them actually paid attention back in English class). Everything that is published should be proofed, and proofed again. The magazine our church produces has numerous technical editors, all of whom go over the whole magazine before it goes to press. It is important that they be given a free hand. No one should hold back a comment for fear of damaging egos. Our publications should be done for the glory of God; this means we must strive for excellence. Excellence means encouraging and accepting correction. For example, when my dear wife is given a red pen and some hard copy, she can really make it bleed. This is a ministry.

The other kind of editing is content editing. This should be principally done by the editor responsible for the publication. At the same
time, he needs wisdom and input from others. Again, to use our magazine as an example, after the columns are written, the contributing editors have a meeting and go over each column, offering comments and
criticism. "Iron sharpeneth iron; so a man sharpeneth the countenance
of his friend" (Prov. 27:17). Almost every Puritan could have used a
good editor.

The church needs computer experts. There are exceptions, but many
of those who are able to teach and expound the Word of God are help-
less when it comes to the interpretation of a software manual (and the
present writer is not one of the exceptions). Consequently, many teaching writers are in desperate need of software support. Those who are
teaching through the printed word can have access to many programs
which will make their work much simpler. Without some sort of competent computer support, there will be many hours squandered in doing
things the hard way. In addition, there is the problem of hardware maintenance and upgrades.

One of our church's deacons has, as part of his responsibility, the
computers and software within the church. When there are hardware
problems, he serves as the exorcist, and when we are confronted by a
computer manual written in tongues, he provides the interpretation.

The church also needs graphic artists. It is unfortunate, but many of
those who reprint great literature also subscribe to the "ugly cover"
school of thought. Oftentimes the soundness of teaching in a reprint is
in inverse proportion to the hideousness of the cover. The author of
Proverbs tells us that a beautiful woman without discretion is like a
gold ring in a pig's snout. In the same way, glorious truth encased in
some monstrosity of a cover should be equally objectionable.

The church needs a printer. There are various options here. Desktop
publishing produces something that is "camera-ready." From this point,
there are a number of different choices — but I will just mention one. The
best option is to find a short-run printer. Because most literature produced by a church in this fashion is not likely to become a best-seller, it
is wise to print limited amounts of your first title (one thousand to five
thousand copies). For most print shops, short-runs like this are expensive. This is because most of the costs are "set-up" costs, and once the
"set-up" is complete, it doesn't cost that much more (per copy) to keep
the press running for a while. Nevertheless, it is unlikely that a church
just starting to publish will have the capital necessary to underwrite a
large press run. Fortunately, there are a number of printers who specialize in short-runs.

A church which decides that literature ministry should be important to their work as a church should seek to go up the following stairs one at a time.

The leaders in the church should be diligent readers. They should seek out books from other eras, particularly the great body of literature produced by the Puritans. The best means at our disposal for recovering these precious truths concerning the gospel is the reading and study of old books—books that were written at a time when the Church had something significant to say. Smaller publishers that reprint this material are springing up now, like reformational mushrooms, with some regularity.

The church should then become a point of distribution of such good literature. Particular emphasis must be placed on distributing booklets and pamphlets. There should be a booklet/book table at church. If there is a particularly good title, it should be recommended to the congregation.

The church should then undertake the job of reprinting good Christian literature that is already written but currently out of print and unavailable. Again, particular attention should be paid to the publication of booklets. It makes good teaching accessible to more believers, it is relatively inexpensive, and it is a good training ground in the area of getting something into print. The printing of larger books will come soon enough.

The text of older books can be scanned onto a computer disk, although some of the older font styles may provide some difficulty. But if the church is reprinting *booklets*, there is little difficulty in retyping it. If the book is so old that the style, spelling, etc., make it difficult for a modern reader to handle, then it can be edited for the modern reader.

The church should begin to print and publish the teaching of the elders and teachers of the church. After short exposure to the Christian literature of a previous era, the reader should be left wondering what hinders the modern Church from producing such material. What would the Puritans have done with word processors? And what hinders us from the doing the same? We have already addressed the "nothing to say" problem. This is not the same as asserting that there is nothing to be said. The Church in every generation is responsible before God to teach and preach the whole counsel of God. We will know that God has answered our prayers for reformation when we see modern Christian churches testifying in their own words to the same truths held forth in previous generations.

We do not at all disparage the literary contributions of the church in previous eras. At the same time, if we content ourselves with reprinting the insights of others, then that shows that we have not really been taught by them. Another way of stating this is that we will know that we have recovered the basic doctrines of Scripture in a living way when we are not limited to reprints, and we start publishing great literature produced by a reformed modern Church.

A good outlet for such teaching and writing, at least at the beginning, is the church newsletter. Everything should be done with edification in mind — including the church newsletter. This does not exclude information, news, and potluck information, but it most certainly should include some ministry from the Word. It is a tragedy that among those churches which have published anything, boring newsletters and cookbooks top the list.

✝ EPILOGUE ✝

Having written this book, I must now apologize, at least in part, for how the book came to be written by someone like, as the Victorians used to say, the present writer. At the time of writing, I have been a minister of the Word for twenty-three years. But how *that* came about contains more than a few ecclesiastical irregularities.

I came to the University of Idaho in the fall of 1975, fresh out of the Navy, and ready to study philosophy. My intention was to study various unbelieving philosophies and to then get involved in some kind of evangelistic literature ministry in a university town somewhere. Right around the same time, a church was being planted in our town by an Evangelical Free Church in a nearby community. The fellowship was successfully planted, but this new church never affiliated with the Free Church. This was not due to any doctrinal or personal differences; it was due mostly to the fact that it was the seventies. I was at the organizing meeting for this church and wound up as one of the guitar-playing songleaders. The best way to describe this would be to say that it was some kind of "Jesus people" operation.

After about a year and a half of meeting, the man who had been doing the preaching (ordained by a Baptist denomination) announced that he had gotten a job elsewhere and that he was moving. We were on our own the following Sunday. As I said, it was the seventies. The idea of going into pastoral ministry had not occured to me, but when it did, I didn't like it very much. Nevertheless, as things turned out, I was up in front with the guitar. That was my call to the ministry; I knew all the chords. I began to preach.

Our church had been planted by an established denomination, but we had no constitution, no doctrinal standards, no established leadership. I started what we called a "responsible brothers" meeting to fill the void of leadership—*ad hoc* elders. We knew from the Scriptures that we needed to be governed by elders, but we didn't have any. We received some teaching on elder qualifications from the pastor of the Evangelical

Free church that had established our church, and as a result different men among the responsible brothers removed themselves from consideration. In this situation, I presented myself to the congregation and asked them to bring forward any objections to my holding the office of elder within the next few weeks. If no one did, then I would assume the office. As it turned out, no one did, and I have been working with this congregation of faithful and longsuffering saints ever since.

All this, as I said earlier, was highly irregular, and I would rather be dead in a ditch than to go back to that way of doing ecclesiastical business. But God repeatedly showed His kindness to us, and the church survived, grew, and matured in the Word. An irregular ordination is not a nonordination, and a church with questionable origins can reveal through subsequent faithfulness to the Word that Christ is indeed her head.

In the time of the Reformation, such confused situations were not at all uncommon. The reasons for the confusion varied, but the turmoil was a regular feature nonetheless. In this setting, the Reformers had to answer Roman Catholic challenges based on historical continuity and claims of apostolic succession. By what authority are you doing this? The answer of the Reformers was that the marks of a church are not rightly-ordered government, or established constitutional procedures, or historical, "apostolic" succession, but rather the presence of Word and sacrament, protected by godly discipline. The Word calls forth the Church, not the other way around.

The father of presbyterianism, John Knox, was ordained in even more irregular circumstances than our seventies weirdness. He was a renegade priest, a wanted man making a living as a schoolteacher, who took refuge in a castle where some assassins were holed up in a hostage situation. The existing minister, an uneducated man named John Rough, preached a sermon to the tiny band there, saying that any assembly of saints (numbering even two or three) had the authority to establish someone in the ministry if they saw the calling of God upon that person's life. This they did, and the reluctant Knox began his world transforming ministry.

But the lure of "historical" authentication and respectability is a strong one. It is so strong that people will often accept any set of historical credentials, as long they are not grounded in the *immediate* present. The situation is like those evolutionists who try to solve the problem of life on earth by saying that it all started from spores that came from outer space. But of course, this just pushes the question back a step. Where and how did *they* originate?

In a similar way, many will readily accept Lutheran, or Reformed, or Presbyterian, or Methodist legitimacy because the tradition originated somewhere back "in history." But of course, when they originated, back in the day, they were all hotly challenged. To all this the Roman Catholic nods assent and wonders when we will recognize the obvious and return to the true *apostolic* church. But of course, the same scenario was played out back then, when the training of the apostles had been that of fishermen and car mechanics. When Christ and the apostles preached, the established religious authorities were on the scene asking what appears to be their favorite question: "By what authority?" John the Baptist was an eccentric hill preacher, Caiaphas had better establishment credentials than Jesus, and the Sanhedrin was amazed that men so obviously uneducated as the apostles could say anything intelligent. Following a wonder worker over hill and dale hardly counts for seminary credit.

We should care very much for orderly government of the church, and we should labor and strive for those coming days when everything *will* be done decently and in order, and in all faithfulness. But we are not there yet, and we should not undertake the task as perfectionists. This book was written in the conviction that the modern evangelical Church must return to her first love, and to a reformational spirit. When this happens, and as it happens, many irregularities will occur. But as we return to a right understanding of word and sacrament, and as we show our love for the gospel preached and the gospel displayed through discipline, we will see that under God's pleasure order arises out of the turmoil. We will see beauty for ashes, the oil of joy for mourning. We will see the name Ichabod erased forever.[1]

---

[1] David Bruce Hegeman, *Plowing in Hope* (Moscow, ID: Canon Press, 1999).

✝ APPENDIX ✝

QUESTIONS FOR ELDERS
AND THEIR WIVES

In wooden, legalistic hands, the following questions could easily be abused. We use them among elders who already share many qualified assumptions about community and marriage. We publish these hesitantly in the hope that folks with some level of maturity might benefit from them but not for those who might use as them to strangle their elders.

The purpose of these questions is to provide true and ongoing account-ability within the families of our elders, while at the same time preserving our privacy. The elders of Christ Church are adopting these questions with the understanding that each elder will go through these questions with his wife annually at a time to be assigned by the elders. Our expectation is that these questions will be a tool for the couple to determine whether anything has arisen within the home which would disqualify the husband as an elder, or which threatens to. If either of these two conditions pertain, then the husband is charged by the elders to take appropriate action, whether that action is simple repentance or arranging for pastoral counsel.

For Wives of Elders

Above reproach

1. Is your husband guilty of any offense over the past year that would cause a serious reproach to Christ, His Church, or the gospel if that offense were to come to light (1 Tim. 3:2)?

2. Does your husband hold to any distinctive view which might bring you, or your houshold, or Christ Church under reproach?

One-woman man

3. Is any person or thing (e.g., work or hobby) causing you to compete for the time and affection of your husband so that it has aroused a godly jealousy? Has your husband developed any unhealthy emotional/

relational attachments to any other women that cause you jealousy (1 Tim. 3:2)?

4. Is your husband still pursuing you (1 Tim. 3:2; Eph. 5:25–27)? Does he render to you the honor and love you should have as his wife? Does he demonstrate tenderness to you (Eph. 5:29)?

5. Is your husband sexually pure (1 Tim. 3:2)? Does he use pornography? Is he given to ungodly lust or fantasy (Mt. 5:28)?

6. Has your husband met your sexual needs (1 Cor. 7:1–4)? Does he consider *your* desires in lovemaking and giving *you* pleasure (Phil. 2:3)?

7. Does your husband pursue you in nonsexual ways? Does your husband understand you (1 Pet. 3:7)? What is he doing lately to know you better?

Temperate

8. Is your husband given to any excess (1 Tim. 3:2)? Is there any area in which he substantively lacks self-control? Is he given to great highs or lows emotionally? Is he judicious or given to extremes in the counsel he gives?

Prudent

9. Does your husband manage your household finances with prudence (1 Tim. 3:2)? Does he allocate to you enough resources to feed, clothe, and otherwise provide for the needs of the family (1 Tim. 5:8)? In comparison to spending for the family at large, does his spending on himself appear selfish? Is your husband planning for the family's long run needs?

Respectable

10. Do you find rendering respect to your husband something you must strain to do (Eph. 5:33)?

11. Do others respect your husband (1 Tim. 3:2)? Why or why not?

Hospitable

12. Is your husband ready to show hospitality to others (1 Tim. 3:2)? Do guests enjoy visiting your home? Does your husband bear with unexpected inconveniences graciously?

Sound in doctrine, able to teach

13. Is your husband well-equipped to encourage saints of differing maturity levels in the truths of Scripture (1 Tim. 3:2; Tit. 1:9)? Can he discern and refute error readily (Tit. 1:9)? Is he vigilant in his care of those allotted to his charge (Acts 20:28; 1 Pet. 5:2)? Is he taking any steps to study and equip himself to discharge his responsibilities to the flock more faithfully?

14. Does your husband have a solid grasp of the church's doctrinal statement and general Bible content (Tit. 1:9)? If called upon, could he defend and explain these doctrines from the Word?

Judicious use of alcohol, food, and other substances

15. Has your husband been drunk in the last year? Does he "need" an alcoholic beverage after work to unwind? If your neighbors knew the frequency and volume of alcohol he drinks, would they say he is enslaved to wine (1 Tim. 3:3)?

16. Periodic feasting aside, would others consider your husband a glutton?

Not pugnacious or contentious, gentle

17. Is your husband ever given to violent outbursts (1 Tim. 3:3)? Has he struck you or any member of your family in a fit of anger? Is he harsh with the children or with you? Is he argumentative or ready to find fault?

18. Would you be satisfied if your sons were to treat their families as your husband treats you and the children? Does your husband honor his parents and yours in tangible ways (1 Tim. 5:8)?

Free from love of money / A good steward

19. Is your husband greedy? Does your family's spending reflect biblical priorities? Does your husband's job in any way conflict with his God-given responsibilities to your family? To the Church?

20. Would you trust your husband to manage someone else's money?

Household management / Leadership

21. When your husband arrives home from work, does he positively or negatively influence the spiritual and relational climate of the home?

22. How would you characterize your husband's relationship with *each* child? Does each child love and respect your husband, and do they feel they can approach him with any problems? Would your children say their father loves them, enjoys their company, and is really interested in what is going on in their lives? Does he do anything that causes the children exasperation (Col. 3:21)?

23. How healthy is each child spiritually? What steps is your husband taking to shepherd them and help them to develop into fruitful adults? Do either of you ever find yourself having to raise your voice or repeat commands before your children obey? Does your husband back you up and support you in your discipline of the kids? Are any of your children beginning to manifest attitudes that trouble you?

24. Do you believe your husband has given thought to your spiritual state and is actively nourishing and cherishing you? Has he had a purifying influence on you as his wife (Eph. 5:26–27)?

Leadership

25. Do you feel your husband's personal conduct and care for your family is worthy of emulation by other husbands in the church (1 Pet. 5:3)? Why or why not?

26. Is your husband bossy (1 Peter 5:3)?

27. How would you characterize your husband's leadership style (1 Tim. 3:4)? Are there any areas of responsibility at home where your husband is not taking leadership?

28. In what ways does your husband practically serve you (Mt. 20:25–28; 1 Pet. 5:3; Jn. 13)? Do others characterize him as a servant? How can he improve?

Not self-willed

29. Does your husband demand to get his own way in nonessentials (Tit. 1:7)? Would you say he is submissive to legitimate authority and willing to defer to others?

Good reputation

30. Does your husband have a reputation for hard work, honesty, and integrity amongst others (1 Tim. 3:7)?

General spiritual health

31. If you were to identify your husband's greatest weakness, what would you say it is (1 Cor. 10:12)? Is *he* aware of it? Have you seen any improvement in this area over the last year?

Serving willingly

32. Does your husband think of the eldership as a burden he must reluctantly carry (1 Tim. 3:1; 1 Pet. 5:2)?

For Elders

Above reproach

1. Are you guilty of any offense over the past year that would cause a serious reproach to Christ, His church, or the gospel, if that offense were to come to light (1 Tim. 3:2)?

2. Do you hold to any distinctive views which might bring you, or your household, or Christ Church under reproach?

One-woman man

3. Is any person or thing (e.g., work or hobby) competing for the time and affection you owe your wife so that it has aroused a godly jealousy

in her? Have you developed any emotional/relational attachments to other women that provoke her jealousy (1 Tim. 3:2)?

4. Are you still aggressively pursuing your wife (1 Tim. 3:2; Eph. 5:25–27)? Do you render to her the honor and love she should have as your wife? Do you demonstrate tenderness to her (Eph. 5:29)? With what frequency do you see that your wife gets a sabbath rest from her work with the household and children?

5. Are you sexually pure (1 Tim. 3:2)? Have you used pornography in the last year? Do you ever allow yourself to fantasize about sex with another partner (Mt. 5:28)?

6. Would your wife say she is sexually satisfied (1 Cor. 7:1–4)? Do you consider *her* desires in lovemaking and giving *her* pleasure (Phil. 2:3)? Do you pressure your wife to perform any sexual favors that violate her conscience? Are your relations frequent enough?

7. Do you pursue your wife in nonsexual ways? Do you understand your wife yet (1 Peter 3:7)? Are you still trying to learn more about her?

Temperate

8. Are there any areas of behavior that are normally lawful in which someone could rightly accuse you of excess (1 Tim. 3:2)? In what areas do you most lack self-control? Are you given to great highs and lows emotionally? Would others say you are judicious in your counsel, or given to extreme and overreaction?

Prudent

9. Do you manage your household finances with prudence (1 Tim. 3:2)? Do you allocate enough resources to your wife to feed, clothe, and otherwise provide for the needs of the family (1 Tim. 5:8)? In comparison to spending for the family at large, does your spending on yourself seem selfish? In what ways are you planning for the family's long run needs (old age, inheritance, higher education for the kids)?

Respectable

10. Does your wife respect you (Eph. 5:33)? Does she lead the family in respecting you? In what ways do you cause her to stumble in this duty by being difficult to respect?

11. Do others respect you (1 Tim. 3:2)? Why or why not?

Hospitable

12. Are you ready to share with strangers (1 Tim. 3:2)? Do guests enjoy visiting your home? When an unexpected inconvenience arises, do you lead the family in responding to it with grace?

Sound in doctrine; able to teach

13. Are you skilled in encouraging saints of differing maturity levels in the truths of Scripture (1 Tim. 3:2; Tit. 1:9)? Can you discern and refute error readily (Tit. 1:9)? Are you vigilant in the care of those allotted to your charge (Acts 20:28; 1 Pet. 5:2)? Are you taking any steps to study and equip yourself to discharge your responsibilities to the flock more faithfully?

14. Do you have a solid grasp of the church's doctrinal statement and general Bible content (Tit. 1:9)? If called upon, could you defend and explain these doctrines from the Word?

Judicious use of alcohol, food, and other substances

15. Have you been drunk in the last year? Do you "need" an alcoholic beverage after work to unwind? If your neighbors knew the frequency and volume of alcohol you drink, would they say you are enslaved to wine (1 Tim. 3:3)?

16. Periodic feasting aside, would others consider you a glutton?

Not pugnacious or contentious, gentle

17. Are you ever given to violent outbursts (1 Tim. 3:2)? Have you ever struck your wife or a member of your family in a fit of anger? Are you harsh with the children or your wife? Would your children and wife say that you are never satisfied with anything they do?

18. Would your wife be satisfied if your sons turned out just like you? Do you honor your parents and your wife's parents in tangible ways?

Free from the love of money / A good steward

19. Do you often think of how you can acquire more money? Does your family's spending reflect biblical priorities? Does your job in any way conflict with your God-given responsibilities to your family? To the Church?

20. Based on how you exercise stewardship of your own resources, would others trust you to manage theirs?

Household management / Leadership

21. When you return home from work, do you positively or negatively influence the spiritual and relational climate of the home?

22. How would you characterize your relationship with *each* child? Is there any distance or feeling of alienation with any of them? Does each child feel they can approach you with their problems? Would your children say their father loves them, enjoys their company, and is really interested in what is going on in their lives? Do you do anything that causes the children exasperation (Col. 3:21)?

23. How healthy is each child spiritually? What steps are you taking to shepherd them and help them to develop into fruitful adults? Do either of you ever find yourself having to raise your voice or repeat commands before your children obey? Do you back up and support your wife in her discipline of the kids. Are any of your children beginning to manifest attitudes that trouble you?

24. Have you given thought to your wife's spiritual state, and are you actively nourishing and cherishing her? Have you had a purifying or putrefying influence on your wife (Eph. 5:26–27)?

Leadership

25. Do you feel your personal conduct and care for your family is worthy of emulating by other husbands (1 Pet. 5:3)? Why or why not?

26. Are you bossy (1 Peter 5:3)?

27. How would you characterize your leadership style (1 Tim. 3:4)? Are there any areas of responsibility at home where you are not taking leadership?

28. In what ways do you practically serve your family (Mt. 20:25–28; 1 Pet. 5:3; Jn. 13)? Do others characterize you as a servant? How can you improve?

Not self-willed

29. Do you demand to get your own way in nonessentials (Tit. 1:7)? Would others say you are submissive to authority and willing to defer to others?

Good reputation

30. Do you have a reputation for hard work, honesty, and integrity amongst others (1 Tim. 3:7)?

General spiritual health

31. If you were to identify your greatest weakness, what would you say it is (1 Cor. 10:12)? Have you seen any improvement in this area over the last year?

Serving willingly

32. Do you think of the eldership as a burden you must reluctantly carry (1 Tim. 3:1; 1 Pet. 5:2)?

For Husband and Wife Together

Action items

1. Have any of the answers to these questions provoked a discussion between the two of you that should have been discussed long before?

2. Have any of the answers to these questions revealed a problem that reflects on the eldership of the church?

3. Have any of the answers to these questions revealed the need for outside counsel or accountability?

4. Have you taken the necessary steps to address these problems?

———————

SCRIPTURE INDEX